A NEW DEAL FOR THE HUMANITIES

THE AMERICAN CAMPUS

Harold S. Wechsler, Series Editor

The books in the American Campus series explore recent developments and public policy issues in higher education in the United States. Topics of interest include access to college, and college affordability; college retention, tenure and academic freedom; campus labor; the expansion and evolution of administrative posts and salaries; the crisis in the humanities and the arts; the corporate university and for-profit colleges; online education; controversy in sport programs; and gender, ethnic, racial, religious, and class dynamics and diversity. Books feature scholarship from a variety of disciplines in the humanities and social sciences.

A NEW DEAL FOR THE HUMANITIES

Liberal Arts and the Future of
Public Higher Education

EDITED BY

GORDON HUTNER AND
FEISAL G. MOHAMED

RUTGERS UNIVERSITY PRESS
New Brunswick, New Jersey, and London

This publication was supported in part by
the Eleanor J. and Jason F. Dreibelbis Fund.

Library of Congress Cataloging-in-Publication Data
A new deal for the humanities : liberal arts and the future of public higher education /
edited by Gordon Hutner and Feisal G. Mohamed.
    pages cm. — (American campus series)
    Includes bibliographical references and index.
    ISBN 978-0-8135-7324-3 (hardcover : alk. paper) — ISBN 978-0-8135-7323-6
(pbk. : alk. paper) — ISBN 978-0-8135-7325-0 (e-book (epub) —
ISBN 978-0-8135-7326-7 (e-book (web pdf)
    1. Humanities—Study and teaching (Higher)—United States. 2. Education,
Humanistic—United States. 3. Public universities and colleges—Curricula—United
States. I. Hutner, Gordon. II. Mohamed, Feisal G. (Feisal Gharib), 1974–
    AZ183.U5N49 2016
    001.3071'073—dc23

                                                                    2015011170

A British Cataloging-in-Publication record for this book is available from the British
Library.

Visit our website: http://rutgerspress.rutgers.edu

Manufactured in the United States of America

To our children

CONTENTS

ACKNOWLEDGMENTS

This volume was conceived in the summer of 2012, when we were first struck by the nearly complete absence of professors from public institutions in the Academy of Arts and Sciences' committee charged by Congress with developing a vision for the humanities. As professors trained at public institutions and who had worked in such universities for their entire professional careers (more than forty years combined), we held out no great hope that the committee would have much to say about the issues confronting the humanities at schools like ours. That summer, some ten months after the Occupy movement, we were also cognizant of how the growing aggravations of income disparity were affecting the cultural climate in ways that, for us, would yield most rewarding possibilities for debates about the humanities.

We resolved then to convene a forum for September of 2013, drawn up mostly from the voices excluded from the conversations that the Academy report, *The Heart of the Matter*, and a similar Harvard report, "The Teaching of the Arts and Sciences at Harvard College: Mapping the Future," later generated in the interim. We were aware that many fine professors, from many distinguished private universities, had important things to say, but we wanted to shape a different conversation, one that we immediately understood as a communal meditation on the public investment in humanities instruction and research. That led us to remember that we were astride two great commemorations: the 2012 sesquicentennial of the Morrill Land-Grand Act and the seventieth-year anniversary of the GI Bill. It seemed to us a propitious opportunity to hear what public-university professors and administrators had to say about our past, present, and future.

In creating a collection of this kind, the coeditors have accumulated a great many debts, first and foremost to the Trowbridge Initiative in American Cultures at the University of Illinois. Its support has been indispensable for the furthering of this project. We are also grateful both to the dean of the College of Liberal Arts and Sciences and to the Office of the Provost for their enthusiastic help in sponsoring the all-day symposium out of which the current volume has emerged. The Illinois Program for Research in the Humanities and the Unit for Criticism and Interpretive Theory enhanced the funding and also helped to publicize the event.

Along the way, a dizzying number of Illinois departments and programs also made contributions to our forum, including African-American Studies, American Indian Studies, Anthropology, the Center of Latin American and Caribbean

Studies, the Cline Center for Democracy, Communication, Comparative Literature, East Asian Languages and Cultures, English, the Forum on the Future of Public Education, French, Gender and Women's Studies, Germanic Languages and Literatures, the Higher Education Collaborative, History, Linguistics, Medieval Studies, the Program in Jewish Culture and Society, Religion, and Sociology. On a campus with the kind of vibrant intellectual atmosphere such as we enjoy in Urbana–Champaign, where there is always so much going on, it is truly gratifying to find so many dedicated partners.

We are also extremely grateful to the several University of Illinois faculty who collaborated with us by serving as respondents to papers that day, especially because their poised and cogent critiques of our symposiasts' presentations helped to bring out the true potential of the arguments. Our Illinois colleagues gave generously of their time and expertise, so we are happy to thank Bruce Michelson (English), Jennifer Delany (Educational Policy, Organization, and Leadership), Dianne Harris (Illinois Program for Research in the Humanities), Richard Rodriguez (Latina and Latino Studies), Debasish Dutta (Dean, Graduate College), Anke Pinkert (Germanic Languages and Literatures), Michael Simeone (Institute for Computing in the Humanities, Arts, and Social Sciences), Colleen Murphy (Philosophy), and Lauren Goodlad (English).

At Rutgers University Press, we are grateful to its director, Marlie Wasserman, to editors Katie Keeran and Kimberly Guinta, copyeditor Robert Brown, and series editor Harold S. Wechsler, for their continuing interest in our project and for the chance to work with such accomplished professionals.

Finally, we would like to thank our families for their willingness to take up yet another obligation and to defer our fulfilling still another promise while we worked, first, on the planning of the symposium, and then bringing the essays into print. To Dale and to Sally, we say, once again, thank you. And we dedicate this book to our children. To Jacob and Daniel, now embarking on their undergraduate careers. And to Chloe and Kate, just embarking on lives that, one hopes, will include the option of world-class public higher education.

A NEW DEAL FOR THE HUMANITIES

INTRODUCTION

GORDON HUTNER AND FEISAL G. MOHAMED

The humanities are either in a crisis threatening their very existence on college campuses or they are in no crisis at all. It depends on whom you ask. And a major impetus for this collection is that those of us who teach and study at public institutions are asked all too seldom. Our view seems relegated to an afterthought, as if the implications of what happens at elite private universities merely ripple out to the rest of us to encounter as we may. The obdurate fact remains that we in public institutions confront such issues in even more exacting, potentially farther-reaching ways, and we do so on a much greater scale, with even more resounding repercussions for society. That this needs to be asserted suggests the very problem: what is the perceived social function of the humanities if so many would comfortably relegate them to small private colleges and elite private universities? The committee authoring the congressionally mandated report titled *The Heart of the Matter* is so overwhelmingly drawn from such schools it is a wonder that public universities are even acknowledged.[1] The severe, at times toxic, challenges we face ought not to be forgotten or made negligible. How we who teach in public institutions deal and should deal with the position of the humanities needs a new, collective voice, as the various perspectives assembled here try to model. Out of that discussion lies the hope of a new deal for the humanities. And it can't come soon enough.

Those who do see the humanities suffering a crisis point to a decline in enrollments, especially pronounced since the financial collapse of 2008. Facing more-uncertain futures and ever-rising tuition, students and their families are supposedly opting for four-year degrees perceived to be immediately marketable. A decline in enrollments also reflects, for this argument, an increasing detachment of academic humanities departments from the culture at large. The recent Harvard report on the humanities suggests that faculty and graduate

students teach their abstruse research interests, isolating a student body puta-
tively inclined to value great texts and grand histories.[2] Implied is a revival of
the late-century canard that Francophile intellectual predilections and so-called
political correctness constitute a closing of the American mind: "the most serious cause of decline in the number of humanities students," William Chace
declares, is the substitution of "good books" with a scattered array of "secondary
considerations (identity studies, abstruse theory, sexuality, film and popular culture)."[3] Had defenders of tradition been given fuller audience in the culture wars
of the 1980s and 1990s, this D'Souza band blares, we would not be in this mess.

[handwritten margin note: Do we have to embrace a narrow definition of humanities?]

"What mess?" replies the opposing camp. For these observers, students are
not fleeing the humanities, despite economic conditions; the perceived decline
in humanities enrollments misreads the data. As Anthony Grafton and James
Grossman point out, the Harvard report relies on a document created by the
American Academy of Arts and Sciences' Humanities Indicators Project, which
takes 1967 as a baseline, since that is the earliest date for which online records of
enrollment are available.[4] Yes, the numbers are markedly lower now than they
were nearly a half-century ago, but that particular decade had seen an anomalous
uptick in humanities degrees, led largely by women of the Baby Boom generation entering college but not yet welcomed in many preprofessional programs,
especially in the sciences. Male graduates of humanities programs accounted for
13 percent of degrees awarded in 1970 and roughly 7 percent today; their female
counterparts accounted for more than 20 percent in 1970, though that number
has now also dropped to approximately 7 percent.[5] If we disregard that bubble,
the decrease in the number of humanities degrees has steadily fallen about three-
quarters of a single percent each decade, which is not quite so alarmingly precipitous: from 14 percent in 1966 to 8 percent or so today. The only period of steep
decline was from the mid-1970s to mid-1980s, but even then, as Michael Bérubé
has shown, the humanities fared much better than did other disciplines:

> Between 1974 and 1985, humanities enrollments did, in fact, decrease by 18.2 per-
> cent. But enrollments in the social sciences fell much further, by 33.7 percent, and
> even in the physical sciences the drop was a considerable 19.4 percent. Where
> did those students go? To business (a 65.3 percent increase), engineering (up by
> 92.2 percent), and computer science (a staggering, but altogether historically
> appropriate, increase of 627.3 percent). Interestingly, between 1986 and 1997 busi-
> ness majors underwent a dramatic decline: in 1986 they accounted for 24 per-
> cent of all degrees awarded . . . whereas in 1997 they had slipped to 19.3 percent of
> all degrees.[6]

The most recent and comprehensive data available, those generated by the
Humanities Indicators project, do not show sweeping declines in enrollments

in humanities programs from 2007 to 2012: English shows a decline of 0.9 percent in degrees awarded in 2011–2012; art history and religion show declines of 4.6 percent and 4 percent, respectively, in juniors and seniors in the major at the start of fall 2012. These figures are partly offset by increases in linguistics, both in degrees awarded (2.5%) and in juniors and seniors in the major (5.3%), and by new degree programs for which the *Survey of Humanities Departments* does not account. All other humanities departments included in the 2008 and 2013 surveys show no statistically significant change.[7] From this point of view, much of the talk about the collapse of enrollments is overblown. We've taken a hit, but overall we're holding on.

This camp tends to be populated by faculty in English and history—those who don't have everything their hearts desire but whose programs generally are not threatened with closure. Departments of classics or German may not enjoy the luxury of such contentment. As Charlotte Melin observes in her contribution to this volume, thinning tenure-stream job postings in MLA's *Job Information List* and cuts to foreign-language instruction in Title VI and Title VIII programs bode ill for the future of foreign languages and literatures.[8] The problem can be exacerbated, she continues, by the proliferation of "Global Studies" programs having no language requirements—these tacitly endorse a troubling view of the ideal international citizen, to say the least. Data from the Humanities Indicators project also raise concerns: more than other humanities disciplines, language departments are likely to lose degree-granting status, with 12 percent having done so between 2007 and 2012, and this is more than twice as likely to occur in public universities than in their private counterparts. Reductions in languages also disproportionately impact women, who comprise almost two-thirds of the faculty in literatures and languages other than English.[9] In a way that is quite typical, our own campus houses dozens of experts on British and American literature and history, but only two or three faculty whose work is devoted primarily to any aspect of Iranian culture: ancient or modern history, art history, literature, or religion. The attention paid to Far Eastern nations other than China and Japan is thinner still. We are not alone in worrying that instead of an informed citizenry, we are training tomorrow's consumers of Fox News, who will not swerve far from know-nothing nationalism and fearful incomprehension of foreign nations and cultures. Current trends toward shrinking or eliminating departments of foreign languages and literatures mean that intellectual contraction and cultural isolationism will only worsen in the years to come. Now *that* is a closing of the American mind worth worrying about, one that many programs in women's studies, which have adopted an increasingly international focus, currently strive to remedy. We are running directly opposite to the estimable goal of humanities education that Helen Vendler espouses in the Harvard report: to turn the undergraduate into an "internationally competent mediator of cultural history."[10] To paraphrase Ed Tom Bell in *No Country for Old Men*, if that ain't a crisis, it'll do until a crisis gets here.

At the same time we would emphasize that the term "crisis" is worth rejecting for more powerful reasons. We sympathize with the need to direct national attention to the beleaguered situation of the humanities on college campuses everywhere and in the culture at large, and we understand that there must be an italicizing of our predicament so that it can compete for attention. We also appreciate that public interest will ultimately raise the stakes for university administrators to move to ameliorate our circumstances. But the concept of "crisis" is self-defeating. If in executive-speak crisis is "opportunity," it is not hard to divine the ends to which a perception of falling enrollments might be put: broadly conceived austerity measures designed to eliminate programs deemed to be a drag on institutional resources—which is to say programs that hold limited potential of generating conspicuous alumni donations and large external grants. "Crisis" can thus lend cover to program closure, receivership, and "restructuring"—often the byword for terminating or conflating programs; for freezes in tenure-stream hiring that inevitably aggravate inequalities of academic labor and that choke off at the source new possibilities of scholarly research and pedagogic innovation; and for a reactionary assault on programs in critical studies of race, gender, and sexuality. Our project strains against all of these trends.

The debasing term "crisis" is a distraction, and the debate over its applicability largely unproductive, a sideshow that wholly misses the predicament of the humanities in public higher education. We face not only a steady deprivation of state support, but also destructive, now firmly entrenched, orthodoxies on the way universities ought to direct the resources they do have: the "seed-money" model where expenditure is an investment toward generating revenue. A new deal must entail an administrative recommitment to the principle of the comprehensive public research university. As Roger Geiger points out in this volume, a more technically oriented approach to the public university has been tried before. It failed.

Suffice it to say that the humanities find themselves at a moment pregnant with import and portent. Maybe survival is not at stake, and we can continue to teach many humanities subjects as we currently do. Can does not imply ought. We hope that the essays in this volume will stimulate humanists and administrators to concentrate on avenues we *should* pursue. We are not powerless to imagine and to design ways of enlivening the humanities so that even in troubled economic times they will flourish. What a new deal entails is reintegrating our purpose and the rationales for reinvigorating the study of the humanities today. For there is a great deal of potential for growth, for conceiving new ways of teaching the humanities and of restructuring the dissemination of newly arrived at understanding. Such claims are augmented, on the one hand, by the ever-increasing welcome that fields like the digital and medical humanities are meeting in the academy and beyond, but just as salient and perhaps even more determining, is the reconceiving of what we have always thought we've known but can now refocus by our ever-expanding global lens. It is one thing to teach Shakespeare as Matthew Arnold's still, smiling bard out-topping all knowledge, but it is something else to explore the complex web of cultural expression arising from his works, from Dryden's *All for Love* to Brecht's *Round Heads and Pointed Heads,* to Robeson's performance of *Othello,* to Kurosawa's *Throne of Blood,* to Vishal Bhardwaj's *Omkara,* to name but a few ways that the ever-expanding legacy of this traditional curricular cornerstone inherently demands a constant restructuring of our pedagogy and scholarship.

Even if enrollments in the humanities remain normal, witnessing barely visible daily decreases, punctuated with periodic rises followed by sharper declines, we are dubious that they will be sustained by the purest intellectual motives. It seems increasingly likely that current enrollments are buoyed as much by affection for books and ideas as they are by students merely ticking off degree requirements and forum-shopping for the path of least resistance to a GPA with the appearance of achievement, an entirely natural instinct of late adolescence that perhaps some faculty indulge all too willingly. Many of our undergraduate programs have changed their particulars only superficially in the past quarter century, and our graduate studies even less so. Perhaps the most dismal feature that we observe in the current debates is the *institutional* conservatism that has settled into discussion of the future of the humanities, both at the departmental level and in the upper reaches: either cut and combine or, in response to the threatening axe, ossify what currently exists. We need compelling models of reorganizing humanistic learning to meet the needs of twenty-first-century publics, and these are either in very short supply or taking place in disparate, diffuse ways. What is a constructive balance between such emerging, often well-funded fields as digital humanities, and traditional, rather poorly funded fields like philosophy and classics? How can we devise an intellectually robust, coherent humanities core curriculum for every undergraduate, while placing diversity at the center of our attention, as Yolanda Moses urges in this volume, and heeding the pragmatic challenge of transferability, to which Sheldon Rothblatt draws our attention? Our contributors address many challenges and directions in imagining a new deal; they also model the energetic, practical-minded qualities required to put it in place.

The new deal for the humanities that we advocate seeks a concerted re-envisioning of institutional structures on three fronts: (1) providing stable sources of funding; (2) allowing humanities programs to generate their own means of evaluating learning outcomes and program viability, not necessarily based on generating grants (which they cannot do) or watering down curriculum to fill undergraduate seats (which they ought not do); and (3) marshaling resources to develop new models of academic departments, or even dispensing entirely with this limiting habitus that was scarcely conceived with the humanities in mind. That we call this a 'new deal' implies major reinvestment by government. While we certainly hope that state and federal support might be restored in higher education, we emphasize that none of our proposals is contingent upon that admittedly unlikely prospect: for the immediate aim must be that universities themselves recommit to liberal education even as they seek to re-create it for the future.

1. STABLE FUNDING

For years, the thinking goes, the humanities flourished, in part with the revenue generated by the science grants. Cogent challenges to this vision, such as Chris Newfield's, have not yet done enough to sway this underexamined conventional wisdom. It remains nonetheless clear that despite the hubbub of the decline of the humanities major, seats in humanities classrooms are still regularly filled by undergraduates across the campus, including the sciences, just as it remains clear that science and technology faculty are often glad to help fund humanities research. The idea of sweating the humanities for the money they cost has a tantalizing charm to university-budget overseers, yet we wonder if that appeal is more symbolic than anything else. Reducing humanities funding below the poverty level is on par with politicians alacritously attacking NEH or public TV as proof of their stout resolve to lighten the nation's economic deficit. Defunding the humanities will not mend unsustainable twenty-first-century university budgets, which often seem concentrated on funding increasingly byzantine administrative apparatuses and engaging in speculative investment in STEM research and online education. The last of these is only the latest symptom of an administrative *mentalité* that has dealt especially acute harm to the humanities, though also affects disciplines campuswide: that instruction is the last thing in which a university ought to invest, the chief aim of catalog offerings being to generate maximum tuition dollars at minimum possible cost.

2. GENERATING MEANS OF EVALUATING OUTCOMES AND PROGRAM VIABILITY

The rationale for increasing cuts to the humanities often evolves out of flawed metrics. The measuring of the humanities will never be acceptably nuanced, much less accurate or fair, if conducted on schemas developed to assess the viability of scientific and technical curricula and instruction. Humanistic study

Yes

inherently refuses to elide skill acquisition with learning; the current mania for quantifiable learning outcomes necessarily marginalizes such a style of thought.

One of us (Mohamed) was an assistant professor at Texas Tech when its accrediting agency, the Southern Association of Colleges and Schools (SACS), ordered the university to create measurable skills-based learning outcomes for its degree programs. In a series of particularly tiresome departmental meetings, English faculty set themselves to the task of compliance, developing language on program deliverables that was only mildly odious. The best proposal by far came from the poet William Wenthe, who suggested that as a testable outcome all graduating students be asked to write a critical essay on William Carlos Williams's "The Poem" ("It's all in / the sound").[11] Although it arose from sardonic frustration, Wenthe's proposal was partly delivered in earnest. Why shouldn't this be an acceptable way of testing learning outcomes for a program in literature? Do we not teach the analysis of poetry? Is this oft-anthologized poem so esoteric that we can't expect students to interpret it intelligibly? The answer, we all know, is that none of that matters: the prevailing regimes of evaluating outcomes are aimed squarely at marginalizing learning that cannot be circumscribed within the bubbles of Scantron sheets. Texas Tech learned just how activist SACS was in promoting such quantification when its first efforts in providing learning outcomes were rejected and the entire university placed on probation, under threat of a loss of accreditation that would lead to every student on campus being denied access to federal financial support.[12] Needless to say, all programs fell into line, though, for some, with a deep sense of foreboding: the battle seemed a prelude to a coming war over standardized testing at the college level.

problem w/ assessment in humanities

The episode was an extreme case, but the urge to squeeze learning into quantifiable outcomes is by now commonplace, especially at the kind of institutions this volume addresses. In some ways SACS was responding dutifully to federal directives stated in the 2006 report of the Commission on the Future of Higher Education, which chastised accrediting bodies for their laxity in encouraging universities to establish mechanisms of gauging student achievement.[13] Also responding to that federal directive was another accrediting body, the Middle States Commission on Higher Education, which in 2007 released revised accreditation guidelines with "greater emphasis on institutional assessment and the assessment of student learning."[14] Recent legislation in Iowa requires all courses—not sections, but courses—with 300 students or more to "collect and use the results of formative and summative assessments in its continuous improvement plan."[15] As it is rolled into effect, the legislation will eventually cover all courses with 100 students or more, which imposes a significant bureaucratic burden on instructors. The phrase "continuous improvement" sounds much too ominously like the central imperative of No Child Left Behind.

> yes

its our job to be reflexive & improve — the problem is external imposition of assessments that aren't functional or useful.

None of these regimes of assessment seems reconcilable with something as sensible as the Wenthe approach. The materials of study and objects of inquiry demand radically opposed forms of investigation, but little work has been done to account for such considerations. We find ourselves largely sympathetic, for example, with the critique of measuring "seat time" in the 2012 report of the New America Foundation, *Cracking the Credit Hour*. As that report shows, the credit hour has been destructively transformed from a convenient accounting device designed to track faculty labor to the fundamental currency of undergraduate education. Combined with a national trend toward grade inflation, it creates a system insufficiently attentive to tracking student learning and overly concerned with measuring the accumulation of credits, a simulacrum of education.[16]

But we stress that if reforms are to be pursued, the humanities must shape their own plan of making sense of their effectiveness. The reason we have not yet been so charged perhaps speaks to a basic, even seminal prejudice infecting the whole discussion: there are too many in command of constructing these assessments who fundamentally distrust how the humanities are practiced *at all*. Because our vision can't be quantified, one might suppose, through this logic, its verification does not or cannot even exist. Such prejudice may present itself as umbrage against the politicizing of the humanities, but, for us, it's a rejection based on a much more basic, even epistemological premise. From the point of view of questionnaires, it's just too supposable that we do not know what we are talking about; and because we are thus understood as not knowing what we are talking about, we presumably cannot know how effectively we transmit the knowledge we impart. Or worse, the knowledge we impart, when all is said and measured, is not worth knowing, if it is knowledge at all. Yet how can we ever make our case if the evidence for our success is tampered with from the beginning?

3. THE ORGANIZATION OF KNOWLEDGE

Knowledge is always revising its organization, and we have held too long to the single-subject major that inadvertently but ineluctably renders so many undergraduate curricula stale and limited. Such an artificially defined specialization of programs has more than ever seemed to have outlived its original purpose and now serves all too little a function—pedagogical or otherwise, as Kathleen Woodward so helpfully elucidates. The sciences are always refurbishing the late nineteenth-century concept of the major as a unilateral category of investigation by cultivating evermore venturesome cross-disciplinary paradigms, but we cling to this vestige of late nineteenth-century emphases on philology and single-language or national traditions, categories that cannot be expected to act as the most viable way of organizing inquiry. "Are . . . our undergraduates best served," asks the Harvard report, "by studying one discipline (literature) within a series of linguistically self-enclosed, competing units?" The answer seems obvious, and we might extend it even further: one would search in vain for any moment in cultural history best studied at any level, undergraduate or graduate, by confining one's attention to a single nation or language or by isolating literature from art history and philosophy, whether the Middle Ages, or Renaissance, or the age of the Romantics or Moderns.

If some colleagues resist our claim on the intellectual debility of the current system, consider at least the urgency of how economic factors also militate against the single-subject major. That employers see humanities education as important does not mean that they are necessarily eager to hire majors in philosophy or anthropology. We need to be responsive to the fact that the cost of higher education makes it exceedingly difficult for many students to focus on one humanities subject to the exclusion of all else: idealizing that pursuit under the banner of citizenship or critical thinking may be well-intentioned but, at this late date, also seems increasingly a manipulative, even reckless form of advertising for the student-loan industry. Why would we not offer a broader array of options than the major or minor, ones that allow for sustained study of periods or themes without crowding other pursuits, including more instrumental ones, out of a student's degree plan? Or combining a student's professional and intellectual interests, in the ways that medical humanities, for example, is making good its promise of doing? For that matter, why do we not consider programs drawing from the humanities disciplines to give business or engineering students their own acculturating opportunities, to make them more thoroughly integrated business executives and engineers?

A further risk of cleaving to the single-subject major is that it perpetuates potentially disastrous university economics. The single-subject major inevitably favors large departments like political science and psychology and almost as inevitably compromises smaller ones. All of us in the humanities should be anxious about the economic logic of first isolating and then clustering small-enrollment majors, as the University of Kentucky did in collapsing classics with modern languages. To UK's credit, the foreign-language professors seized the opportunity to make themselves less dispensable by envisioning and adopting a successful Foreign Language and International Economics curriculum well in advance of the growing concern about the need to prepare students to compete globally, from preschool to b-school.

However sensible such instrumentality is and however much it can show us further ways to contribute meaningfully to the aspirations of our students, it was born out of the exigency emerging from the precarious academic economy, whether it is real or administratively manufactured or both. Any consideration of instrumentality can perhaps feel like defeat, a compromise of humanist ideals born of financial necessity. It need not be so. Everywhere are the reasons for pursuing broad and rich humanities programs that meet the intellectual needs of students while acknowledging the practical concerns weighing too heavily upon them. No reasonable observer can fail to notice that there are vivid and salient differences between our students and those of wealthy private institutions. And the first difference is how much time ours are out of the classroom holding down a job—and often more than one. The liberal arts ideal was long ago meant to be pursued with a certain element of leisure, and if we have catered to the young, throughout higher education, by building palatial recreation centers and luxurious dorms, a great many students at public institutions are spending their time not at football games and frat parties, but working midnight shifts at convenience stores or delivering pizzas or manning the cash registers at discount department stores or handing out menus at local restaurants. They are also more likely to be living off-campus, often at a significant distance, and more likely to be nontraditional students and parents themselves.

They can often have more to overcome in their preparation, too. Our best students might just as easily have gone to more-prestigious universities, but for one reason or another felt excluded from or indifferent to the possibility. But our larger constituency is formed by students who are not so well prepared and who are less oriented to reading and doing research and critical thinking, the students who will more thoroughly populate the educated citizenry we all hope to shape. We face unique struggles in public institutions, of creating syllabi students can manage, crafting assignments that help students to flourish, sustaining the experience of liberal education. In this regard, the Harvard report, *The Heart of the Matter,* and a dozen similar documents, are like news bulletins from foreign wars. Although well-meaning, they address an educational experience at odds with what we daily encounter.

Many people make eloquent cases for the importance of humanistic learning and argue cogently for its civic imperative. A democracy can only be as energetic as the minds of its citizens, and the questions fundamental to the humanities are also fundamental to a thoughtful life (What is the good? the nature of beauty? Do we need God?). What does it mean, however, for a culture if these ways of grappling with human experience grow too expendable, too superfluous, to pursue at public universities and thus become the purview of private ones? Such a state of affairs will make even more prominent many of the key divisions among our citizens. At stake in the current discussion of the vitality of the humanities as curricula and their place in public institutions of higher education is not merely the civic benefit of the humanities, but also the civic benefit of making noninstrumental learning widely available. Do we really want to become a society where public institutions provide technical training and private schools cater to the wealthy's virtual monopoly on cultivating eloquence and creative thinking?

The current pressure that parents and students feel to gain admission to the Ivies and deutero-Ivies, no matter how exorbitant their cost, exhibits the national anxiety that these schools are already now the best—and increasingly the only—insurance policy against future generations falling out of the middle class and the best bet for the impoverished and working class ever to gain admission to the world of privilege. Do we dare to make public higher education even less appealing by being unable to produce the very entry-level white-collar workforce that employers routinely insist they most favor: students with strong attainments in talents that the humanities most of all encourage?

*Key

no, we don't

The editors have focused the occasion for these essays on the belief that it would violate the definition of the public institution, and betray its important legacy, were we to fall further into that trap. So we have turned to the conjuncture of two very notable anniversaries—the sesquicentennial of the Morrill Act and the seventieth anniversary of the GI Bill—as a double reminder that at key moments in the past, the United States did choose to make the power of the humanities part of every public university student's education and exerted federal influence to that end. The first Morrill Act in 1862 set up this nation's land-grant universities, expressing a national commitment to promote both the "liberal *and* practical education of the industrial classes in the several pursuits and professions in life," a sense of academic purpose crystallized in our own institution's motto, "Learning and Labor." Eighty-two years later, the Servicemen's Readjustment Act of 1944 (the GI Bill) transformed access to higher education and, in the same stroke, expanded entry to the middle class for the veterans of World War II and, later, the Korean and Viet Nam Wars. As Edward Humes describes it, the bill made possible the educations of "fourteen Nobel Prize winners, three Supreme Court justices, three presidents, a dozen senators, two dozen Pulitzer Prize winners, 238,000 teachers, 91,000 scientists, 67,000 doctors, 450,000 engineers, 240,000 accountants, 17,000 journalists, 22,000 dentists," not to mention thousands of writers, musicians, architects, and artists, but, most importantly of all, millions of citizens who brought the benefit of their liberal-arts educations to all their endeavors, however technical or commercial.[17]

Not only does American history teach us that opening the doors of opportunity in all fields of education enriches us as a society, but our new challenges should also remind us to return to the one strength we have always had internationally. From Berkeley to CUNY, the emergence of the US system of public higher education as a world leader derives from the fully integrated intellectual framework we have upheld. Other countries are increasingly able to compete with us in creating technicians, but few have been able so far to create means of unleashing the full power of the human imagination on the problems now confronting the planet. Nowhere does the importance of this become more crucially apparent than in environmental studies: the science is in. We're degrading

and yet the trend is to regularly remove the study & creative thinking & the cultivation of creativity.

the earth to demonstrably intolerable proportions, yet science itself has failed to make its case as cogently as it must to alter behavior or political priorities sufficiently. So perhaps the hope we must have lies with those who study and teach human culture and who can promote effective articulation of how we need to change the practices endangering future generations.

These transformative pieces of legislation, the Morrill Act and the GI Bill, also remind us that the public university professoriate needs always to adapt its practices to evolving social demands, and obviously there will be much disagreement among humanities professors on just how we should adapt to the new landscape of the public university. The present editors themselves often vigorously disagree on how best to do so. Viewing liberal-arts programs in public research universities as especially well poised to forward cooperative projects campus-wide, Hutner finds promise of vivifying interest in the humanities by developing curricula that meet the needs of other faculties, like environmental studies or the medical humanities. For Mohamed, the more imperative concern must be to foster programs less centered on the Anglo-American tradition and instead sponsor a global, multipolar approach to world cultures. In this view, humanities programs of this century should be custodians of several millennia of the world's humanistic thought and offer every college student a rigorous core curriculum of world humanisms rather than a mish-mash of general education requirements—each one designed primarily to bolster a home department's enrollment figures with undemanding gateway courses.

We hope that a new deal for the humanities would propound an idea of the university for our time, one setting itself firmly in favor of the vitalizing features of humanities education and against the current retooling of our public universities as technical colleges. That conversation is going forward, in one domain or another, to one extent or another, in many places, but it will be doomed from the start if it treats public universities as playing an inconsequential part in national debates. We also believe that these conversations will fall short of their desiderata unless they include dialogue on the commonplace, though readily ignored terrain of the functioning of university administration, particularly its bloat. Good administrators, like good trustees, seek from faculty the best ideas, the fullest uses of available resources, and do not themselves try to commandeer a situation with bywords learned at one conference or another. Presidents and chancellors seldom emerge because they are the most forward-thinking or the most imaginative. Executive talents are best suited to execution rather than direction.

At present, university bureaucracies just do not have mechanisms for valuing the contributions of the humanities, from their means of program evaluation to their standards for appointing new faculty, which some administrators concede sooner rather than later and with varying degrees of indifference. Partnering with resourceful provosts and deans to fill those institutional voids must be high on our agenda. A focus on practical proposals might lead to productive ways of building frameworks that secure vibrant and supple humanities offerings for twenty-first-century students. The alternative is effectively to abandon one of this nation's noblest traditions: that of providing educational opportunities at all levels and in all subjects to ever-broadening segments of society. What a shame that would be.

To address the urgencies we describe above, we inaugurated, in September 2013, what we hope will be the first of an ongoing series of symposia about how the humanities can construct a new deal, and invited the kind of professors that the American Academy of Arts and Sciences (AAAS) might have consulted in preparing *The Heart of the Matter*: leading scholars from various disciplines drawn almost exclusively from public institutions. With enthusiastic support from our dean and provost, and from a startlingly wide diversity of departments and units both in our college and beyond, we began our planning, which was well in advance of the summer when talk of the humanities crisis seemed everywhere to be taking place. We followed those discussions closely and saw how the evolving understanding still obscured the role and character of the public university and its place in American life, especially the kind of research institutions where both of us had been teaching throughout our combined careers. That neglect made it more pressing to carry our purposes forward, which we did, first in an opinion piece for the newrepublic.com and now with this collection.

We know that the conversation will take years, and we have been encouraged by so many people from so many corners of the university to keep it going. The essays assembled here articulate the various ramifications we see initially facing the humanities in the public university. First, we turn to the history of the humanities in public universities in papers by two extremely distinguished historians of US academe. Roger Geiger, of Penn State, provides an important overview of how the humanities were shaped from the late nineteenth century onward, exploring the antecedents for our current struggles. Following the suggestions of the Harvard report, he ends by inveighing against "the prevalence of monolithic political correctness in the humanities" and faults especially the "sociologizing" impulse mapping operations of power in critical studies of gender, race, and class. This narrowing, he claims, has isolated undergraduates craving knowledge of "accessible history and great literature."

We are grateful to have this point of view represented in these pages, but respectfully, if also emphatically, disagree. As with all approaches to the archive, smart, creative, and pedagogically effective scholar-teachers will pull theoretically informed considerations of power into the classroom in smart, creative, and pedagogically effective ways. The scholarship of which Geiger is skeptical frequently offers the most inviting path to intellectually sophisticated examination of texts great and small. Many students otherwise uninterested in Milton's *Paradise Lost* become intrigued by the allegorical representation of Sin as a female body in perpetual incestuous sexual violation and monstrous birth, rife with allusion to James 1.15, to Ovid's Scylla, and to Spenser's Errour. What does that representation tell us about a poet deemed by Samuel Johnson to have a Turkish contempt for women? What does it tell us about the epic tradition? Or about the period, or about the theological imaginary? These are not sociologizing lines of inquiry, nor do they seek to impose intellectually thin "political correctness." They arise instead from the insight that if we take seriously humanist claims on the dignity of every mind, we will scrutinize how power has inflected our traditions, thoughts, and actions in ways that inherently marginalize a great many human beings.[18] A twenty-first-century professional ethics cannot ignore the insights of critical studies of race, gender, and class. And even if we were cynically to engage in such willful ignorance, one must wonder if it would offer the promised benefit: turning back the clock fifty years on undergraduate curriculum will certainly not turn back the clock fifty years on undergraduate enrollments. Our conversations with Professor Geiger suggest that he would not entirely disagree with this assessment, so our differences may ultimately be those of emphasis and expression.

Sheldon Rothblatt, from UC-Berkeley, concentrates his historical acumen on the ends of humanities instruction as defined across time and in several contexts. Touching on *The Heart of the Matter* and pointing especially to the dynamics of public and private higher education in California, he shows how American universities developed their particular forms of institutionalization and how these structures might be made to answer to present challenges. His wide-ranging essay further examines the neglected topics of academically oriented student culture and of our quadrangles and low-rise buildings as humanizing physical spaces—a topic well worth exploring in an age when the ubiquitous advertising of for-profit online colleges typically sneers at the "brick-and-mortar" campus as an outmoded superfluity.

Our essays then turn toward the present and the future. Yolanda Moses, at UC-Riverside, explores the humanities as the key to meeting the challenges that the ideal of diversity exacts, thereby confronting public concerns as immersing and as richly promising as any the university has previously met. Her arguments are all the more pressing given that declining commitment to access in public higher education, as Rothblatt, Woodward, and Williams argue in these pages, has meant that student populations are becoming even less diverse while the general population grows more so. Studying how administrators have responded to recent pressures from governors and legislatures, Daniel Kleinman, of University of Wisconsin–Madison, examines how they might defend the humanities even more insistently and persuasively against antagonistic politicians currying

Why can't we leave education to the people who DO it?

so true and sad! and WRONG!

favor with voters rather than looking out for the best interests of higher education. The challenge that emerges in his account is a need to protect against a narrowly instrumental view of public cost and benefit inherently at odds with the idea of a public university. Kathleen Woodward, of the University of Washington, also aims to give the humanities a more forceful public presence in her focus on new terrain where the research university can make a further impact on American life: in working ever more closely with the community-college system, both to expand possibilities for students there as well as to heighten research universities' potential to engage, and to enrich, their immediate communities.

Our authors concentrate even more concretely on the present and especially its implications for the future in essays devoted to the uses of foreign-language training, the aforementioned account by Charlotte Melin of the University of Minnesota, and the medical humanities, in John McGowan's appraisal of its implementation at the University of North Carolina. A polemic by the University of Virginia's Bethany Nowviskie addresses the state of employment in the digital humanities and the need to give practitioners the stature that will help them guide humanities instruction and research. Such measures will equally allow the university to command a research presence in digital environments increasingly dominated by corporate actors. Her argument is part of a broader commitment to "alt-ac," the preparation of doctoral candidates for fields outside of the university that has become a growing movement in graduate education, and that, she shows, has been pursed in Virginia's Praxis Program.[19] Jeffrey Williams analyzes the state of the humanities from the point of view of Critical University Studies, a branch of inquiry scrutinizing the university's part in current economic logics, and illogics, encompassing everything from complicity with the student-debt industry to the corporatization of online education.

In similar spirit, Christopher Newfield shows how the stop-gap and short-term measures undertaken to make up for declines in government support have rapidly eroded the public mission of public universities. Steep rises in tuition and the decision to court out-of-state and foreign students have significantly reduced access for lower-income in-state students. Newfield recommends that administrators acknowledge these errors, break more fully with the state house, refocus on core academic objectives, and appeal strongly and directly to the masses whose education in the liberal arts is being assailed by a neoliberal ideology of disruptive innovation. The humanities are thus central to the public university in providing access to mass *Bildung*, or personal development.

YES!

Such arguments may increasingly find receptive audiences: with the arrogance of the banking-government complex so obscenely displayed in the financial collapse and bailout of 2008–2009, the zeitgeist seems to have shifted in recent years toward a revivification of democracy defined against rapidly

Who is receptive? How do we encourage reception?

steepening inequality. The kleptocracy of the global 1 percent has been rejected from below, whether in the Arab Spring, or the Occupy movement, or demonstrations in Brazil and in Turkey. It has also been rejected from above, as in consistent, and eagerly received, messages of Pope Francis, or, more significantly, in the UN's initiation of an individual petition process for the protection of economic, social, and cultural rights. If we are in a new Gilded Age, we are likewise seeing signs of a parallel to its early twentieth-century successor in the spread of unionization and demands for a living wage for all workers. This rising awareness of the *demos* should be met with a corresponding public-university investment in cultivating the democratic arts of the twenty-first century.

NOTES

1. The American Academy of Arts and Sciences, *The Heart of the Matter: The Humanities and Social Sciences for a Vibrant, Competitive, and Secure Nation* (Cambridge, MA: American Academy of Arts and Sciences, 2013).

2. *The Teaching of the Arts and Humanities at Harvard College: Mapping the Future* [hereafter *Mapping the Future*], 30, http://artsandhumanities.fas.harvard.edu.

3. William M. Chace, "The Decline of the English Department: How It Happened and What Can Be Done to Reverse It," *American Scholar* (Summer 2009), http://theamericanscholar.org.

4. Anthony T. Grafton and James Grossman, "The Humanities in Dubious Battle," *Chronicle of Higher Education*, July 1, 2013, http://chronicle.com; see also Michael Bérubé, "The Humanities, Declining? Not According to the Numbers," *Chronicle of Higher Education*, July 1, 2013, http://chronicle.com.

5. See Colleen Flaherty, "The Gender Lens," *Inside Higher Ed*, July 11, 2013, http://www.insidehighered.com.

6. Michael Bérubé, *Rhetorical Occasions* (Chapel Hill: University North Carolina Press, 2007), 158; see also "Breaking News: Humanities in Decline! Film at 11," *Crooked Timber*, November 16, 2010, available at http://crookedtimber.org.

7. Susan White, Raymond Chu, and Roman Czujko, *The 2012–13 Survey of Humanities Departments at Four-Year Institutions: Full Technical Report* (College Park, MD: Statistical Research Center, American Institute of Physics, 2014; sponsored by the American Academy of Arts and Sciences), 16, available at http://www.humanitiesindicators.org/content/indicatordoc.aspx?i=457. Appendix D shows how the methodology of the report can emphasize decline rather than growth by measuring only a reduction in the number of departments granting degrees in a given discipline and overlooking new degree offerings in the same discipline: the survey indicates that history of science, for example, had nine fewer universities granting at least one PhD in the discipline, but in ways that the survey does not show, this is more than offset by twenty-four new universities granting PhDs in the discipline in the same period.

8. See "Title VIII Alert," Association for Slavic, East European, and Eurasian Studies, updated November 11, 2013, http://aseees.org. For recent statistics on enrolments in foreign-language programs, see David Goldberg, Dennis Looney, and Natalia Lusin, *Enrollments in Languages other than English in United States Institutions of Higher Education* (New York: Modern Language Association of America, February 2015), available at http://www.mla.org/pdf/2013_enrollment_survey.pdf.

9. White et al., *2012–13 Survey of Humanities Departments*, 8, 32. The same set of data show that classics is much more than ten times as likely to lose degree-granting status at a public university as compared to a private one.

10. Qtd. in *Mapping the Future*, 31.

11. William Carlos Williams, "The Poem," in *Selected Poems*, ed. Charles Tomlinson (New York: New Directions, 1985), 151.

12. See "Accrediting Group Puts Texas Tech on Probation," *Houston Chronicle*, December 12, 2007, http://www.chron.com.

13. See Judith S. Eaton, "Accreditation and the Federal Future of Higher Education," *Academe* (September-October 2010), http://aaup.org.

14. Middle States Commission on Higher Education, *Student Learning Assessment: Options and Resources*, 2nd ed. (2007), http://msche.org.

15. Colleen Flaherty, "Assessment: It's the Law," *Inside Higher Ed*, July 19, 2013, http://www.insidehighered.com.

16. See Amy Laitinen, *Cracking the Credit Hour*, New America Foundation (September 2012), http://higheredwatch.newamerica.net.

17. Edward Humes, *Over Here: How the GI Bill Transformed the American Dream* (New York: Harcourt, 2006), 6.

18. Paul Jay comes to similar conclusions in *The Humanities "Crisis" and the Future of Literary Studies* (New York: Palgrave Macmillan, 2014), Introduction and 55–56.

19. On alt-ac, see Donna M. Bickford and Anne Mitchell Whisnant, "A Move to Bring Staff Scholars Out of the Shadows," *Chronicle of Higher Education*, November 25, 2013, http://chronicle.com; Rebecca Tuhus-Dubrow, "The Repurposed Ph.D.: Finding Life after Academia—and Not Felling Bad About It," *New York Times*, November 1, 2013, http://www.nytimes.com; and L. Maren Wood and Robert B. Townsend, *The Many Careers of History PhDs: A Study of Job Outcomes*, A Report to the American Historical Association (2013), http://historians.org.

1 · FROM THE LAND-GRANT TRADITION TO THE CURRENT CRISIS IN THE HUMANITIES

ROGER L. GEIGER

How important are the humanities for public universities? This chapter is intended to provide some historical perspective on this current issue. It proceeds in three parts. First, the land-grant movement provided a natural experiment. It created almost simultaneously two kinds of institutions, ostensibly having the same purpose: universities that included the liberal arts or what were then called literary studies, and colleges that did not. Second, the experience of those universities that did embrace the liberal arts as they emerged in the twentieth century illuminates the conditions that did or did not facilitate the vitality of the liberal arts. Finally, from this perspective, the chapter will review recent interpretations of the "the crisis in the humanities" and consider prospects for a new deal.

THE LAND-GRANT MOVEMENT

As soon as states began to establish land-grant colleges, two divergent interpretations emerged. Daniel Coit Gilman of Yale's Sheffield Scientific School conducted a survey of the emerging institutions and became the spokesman for the university approach. He proposed that the new institutions be called "our National Schools of Science," stressing that the gift of federal lands made them a national project, and that they were dedicated above all to "natural science in its applications to human industry." He objected to the already prevalent term "agricultural colleges," arguing that "the *liberal education* of the industrial classes is as much an object of the grant as their practical training."[1]

He was arguing against proponents of agricultural colleges, or agricultural and mechanic—A&M—schools. These colleges focused, at least in their rhetoric, on educating farmers to farm. They stressed model farms and compulsory manual labor for students. And they tended to be overtly hostile to the liberal arts—considering them useless for the practical arts and emblematic of the elitist classical education they sought to displace.

Elsewhere, I have characterized these A&Ms as premodern institutions.[2] Namely, these institutions operated partially in the educational space between the common schools and degree-granting colleges—what only later became secondary education. Admissions were exceedingly fluid, reflecting the diverse and problematic preparation of students and political pressures for broad access. Their credentials had little value in the labor market. Hence, there was little incentive to complete a full course and graduate, and few students did.

The most effective model for a public university had been shaped by Henry Tappan at the University of Michigan, the largest institution of higher education in the country. This model was developed more fully at Cornell by Andrew Dickson White, who had taught history under Tappan. Devoted to the liberal arts, White structured Cornell in two divisions, one for academic departments and the other for nine applied and professional fields (including history and political science, intended for educating statesmen). Just eight states, including New York, awarded the land grant to institutions that seriously embraced the university model. Rudimentary universities existed in Missouri and Wisconsin; and California, Minnesota, Nebraska, Ohio, and Illinois created new universities inspired more or less by the Michigan/Cornell model. Specifically, they sought to cover all fields of knowledge, including the liberal arts, and they aspired to keep abreast with the advancement of knowledge.

The liberal arts were challenged in all of these universities by Grangers, populist trustees, and legislators who wanted only practical education. But a commitment to university ideals prevailed in the most successful institutions. Illinois Industrial University is a good example. Its first head, Regent John Milton Gregory, upheld the liberal arts—despite the institution's name—against strong crosscurrents during the turbulent founding years, especially through his hiring of faculty. He sought to raise admission standards in order to secure students ready for higher education. His successor, Selim Peabody, resisted the erosion of liberal arts in the 1880s. He stressed that the growing cohorts of engineering students also needed a liberal education and the liberal arts departments should be preserved. In 1885 it officially became the University of Illinois.[3]

The next president, Andrew Sloane Draper (1894–1904), was a schoolman who had not attended college and had no appreciation of the liberal arts. He kept salaries low in the College of Literature and Arts, and referred to its faculty as "a set of 'cheap men.'" But the college was the fastest growing unit in the university, and its dean, David Kinley, tirelessly promoted it. A product of Johns Hopkins and Wisconsin, Kinley did something essential for top universities: he evaluated faculty against the best departments of other research universities and made excellent appointments as the college expanded. The university, however, lagged its peers in library collections, research, and graduate education (awarding its first PhDs in 1903).[4]

Only in 1904 did the university appoint a president committed to making Illinois a great institution and capable of persuading the trustees of this destiny. Edmund James (1904–1920), a German PhD (Halle) and former head of the University of Pennsylvania Wharton School, believed that academic excellence and public service were mutually reinforcing. He sought excellence in all areas, but particularly the liberal arts. This aspiration was symbolized by his commitment to build a great library, the pride of the university to this day. In 1908 Illinois was invited to join the Association of American Universities (AAU), and in 1910 Edwin Slosson named it one of the fourteen "Great American Universities."[5]

And the A&Ms? They were impeded by several factors. Where states supported both a university and an A&M college, resources were divided to the detriment of both. The cultivation of the practical arts was stunted without the presence of basic science. Agricultural science flourished at Cornell, Wisconsin, and California but much less so in the A&Ms. Low admission standards produced a more basic level of instruction, and low graduation rates meant fewer upper-division courses. Graduate education was virtually absent. Probably Iowa State (Iowa Agricultural College) was the most academically advanced of the A&Ms, but it trailed the universities substantially.[6]

As premodern institutions, the A&Ms had great difficulty adjusting to the two great movements of the age. First was the academic revolution of the late nineteenth century, which transformed the university curriculum into one based on the academic disciplines. Here, universities led in hiring disciplinary specialists, expanding subjects, and fostering research and graduate education. A&Ms were skeptical of academic specialization and preoccupied with teaching basic skills to undergraduates. Second was the standardization movement that became a major preoccupation after 1905, led by the new Carnegie Foundation, which sought to set standards that would define true colleges. Most A&Ms did not require the standard fourteen Carnegie Units for admission; and classifications of institutions put them in the lowest class, their graduates lagging two years behind standard college graduates in preparation for further study.[7]

The handicaps affecting A&Ms proved long lasting. Most did not award their first PhD until the 1920s, and then most graduate work was science related. None achieved the status of a research university until the 1950s. Today, only five of the old A&Ms belong to the AAU, the first three being admitted in 1958 (Penn State, Michigan State, and Purdue). The correlation is clear, but how did the absence of the liberal arts affect these schools?

Although research universities are most readily measured by science indicators, the academic revolution was spearheaded by philology, history, and economics, broadly construed. More Americans studied humanities and social sciences at German universities than natural sciences. Thus, the original research universities embraced these fields as *wissenschaftlich* from the outset. These studies operated on a higher intellectual plane for those few institutions able to cultivate them. By neglecting these fields, A&Ms were isolated from a significant body of academic knowledge; more importantly, they were remote from the intellectual sophistication that scholars derived from those fields and the university ideals that accompanied them. Most of the university builders of the era came from the humanities and social sciences—Edmund James, Benjamin Wheeler, William Rainey Harper, A. D. White, James Burrell Angell, Nicholas Murray Butler, Arthur Twining Hadley, George Vincent. Natural-scientist presidents included Charles Eliot, David Starr Jordan, and Charles Van Hise, but applied fields produced none.

NURTURING THE LIBERAL ARTS

The vitality of the liberal arts depended not only on their adequate representation in universities, but also on the academic environment in which they existed. After the heroic age of university building, a long period of stability ensued. The fourteen institutions that Slosson called "Great American Universities" in 1910 were still the only real research universities in 1940—by objective measures such as leading scientists, PhDs awarded, and peer ratings. University leadership in this era was not very impressive, particularly for state universities. However, they had internalized a logic of academic advancement, and progress now depended largely on deans and department heads. But these figures often became the academic barons of the era, resisting change in the interest of maintaining their current advantages. Under these conditions, for a number of reasons, the former academic ideals were sometimes compromised. This apparently happened at Illinois.

David Kinley, who practically ran the university during James's last years, assumed the presidency in 1920 for the remainder of the decade. One can hardly imagine a more suitable choice; he had been a dean since 1894 and had upheld academic values for the College of Literature and Arts and the Graduate School. But some of that baggage compromised his tenure. As an autocratic dean, he had alienated many faculty. He continued to uphold high standards.

An economist by training, and an econo-chauvinist in temperament, Kinley was openly contemptuous of some other fields, particularly sociology, psychology, education, and agriculture. During World War I, he was also a willing supporter of 100 percent Americanism, a mentality persisting through the postwar Red Scare and afterward. His conservatism was shared and encouraged by the trustees and the business community, ties with whom he cultivated, but not by many of the faculty.

Kinley engaged in practices that today would be clear violations of academic freedom. He forced a historian with socialist leanings to resign. Since he believed, like many others of that era, that students needed to be protected from radical ideas, he routinely vetted the politics of potential hires. He also held a view of the faculty typical of those times—that a few outstanding scholars were desirable, but that most faculty were essentially teachers. Under his watch, there was a notable exodus of some of the university's best scholars, particularly in the humanities. One departing professor decried "the intolerance of independent opinion, the suppression of free speech, the everlasting paternalism . . . the failure to give democratic ideals even a hearing." There was general resentment against the absence of intellectual freedom and excessive, petty regulations (including a ban on faculty smoking, enforced by janitorial spies). Departments like chemistry and engineering operated largely in their own bubble, but disregard for the liberal arts apparently persisted through the next decade, with unfortunate consequences after World War II.[8]

The University of Illinois had an unparalleled opportunity for rejuvenation—literally—after the war. The crush of GI Bill students was accompanied by large appropriations that fueled a rapid expansion of the faculty. The new president, George Stoddard (1946–1953), embarked on a campaign to enhance academic quality and to strengthen the liberal arts in particular. He soon provoked a backlash from the Old Guard, who resented his rejection of the existing utilitarian order and who also, in conjunction with conservative forces in the state, attacked his liberal views. The most notorious casualty of this drama was Howard Bowen, later a university president and influential spokesperson, who had built an extraordinarily good department of young economists. The conservatives in the College of Commerce resented Bowen, and the resulting fracas revealed the deep polarization in that school and the entire university. Trustees ultimately sided with the Old Guard, so Bowen was fired as dean in 1950, and the talented economists he had recruited, including a subsequent Nobel Prize winner, soon departed as well. Stoddard outlasted him by three years before being summarily fired in a trustee coup—done in by the McCarthyite atmosphere and the low politics of the state. The university would eventually reload, but this episode was a great opportunity squandered through the flouting of academic values.[9]

THE "CRISIS IN THE HUMANITIES"

The lessons from these historical sketches should be clear. The humanities and liberal arts have been indispensable components of healthy and vigorous research universities, public or private. The liberal arts cannot flourish without the freedom of investigators to choose their topics and express their findings without intimidation or sanctions. These sentiments are fundamental to US higher education and are shared today by most university leaders in the country. But the humanities at public universities are particularly vulnerable to external pressures, with consequences that can diminish opportunities for a generation of students.

What then accounts for the current perception of a "Crisis of the Humanities"? Through all the rhetoric on this topic, including the 2013 report by the American Academy of Arts and Sciences and the Harvard Faculty report on the teaching of the humanities, four sources of anxiety stand out.[10]

Relative Decline

The immediate stimulus for the report of the Harvard Faculty Working Group was a decline in humanities majors, but looming in the background is the apparent downtrend in liberal arts enrollments over the last half century. However, from a different starting point the trend-line for the last thirty years is up, slightly. But for three recent years (2008–2010), it is down, slightly.[11] Actually, humanists should take heart that since the mid-1980s the proportion of humanities degrees has held steady at around 11 percent. Indeed, there are now more subjects to major in than fifty years ago. For example, if bachelor's degrees in communications and English are combined, the relative level is the same as for English graduates alone in the late 1960s, when there were almost no communications degrees. More important, the recovery in humanities majors since the trough of the early 1980s has been led by the selective universities and liberal arts colleges. These are the intellectual leaders of US higher education, and the most prestigious institutions place the highest value on the humanities. They are also the locus of scholarship in the humanities, which shows no sign of shrinkage.[12]

Relative Deprivation

Yes, but . . . other fields appear to be booming. Universities seem dedicated more than ever to economic development; science and engineering are apparently thriving (even if they do not think so); technological advance, including information science, is transforming society and the university. These trends are particularly conspicuous at public research universities, where contributions to economic development are nurtured and prized. The American Academy, in its recent *Report Card*, complained that federal research support for the humanities was less than one-half of one percent of that for science and engineering.[13] This is a meaningless comparison, an even pathetic appeal to relative deprivation. The Academy wishes to encourage an expansion of specialized research, but the Harvard report fears that the research culture has become too specialized for the needs of undergraduates. This complaint against academic specialization has been around for at least a century, and research in all fields has gone about its specialized course despite such admonitions. And institutionalized research proceeds apace in the humanities. In 2008 the Consortium for Humanities Centers and Institutes listed 121 members; five years later it has 154 members. Institutionalized academic research in the humanities is growing, not shrinking.[14]

The Specter of Vocationalism

Any humanist hearing President Barack Obama speak of higher education could not help being dismayed: the only apparent purpose of college is to train students for well-paying jobs. Conservative governors have been worse, threatening to withdraw funding from the liberal arts because they do not train workers.[15] Data on earnings by majors present a depressing picture (although the humanities are not alone there).[16] The Academy report acknowledges the widespread belief that the liberal arts "do not all contribute visibly and directly to near-term employment." In a rather weak response, the report reproduces results from a tendentious survey to the effect that employers in fact do value the skills resulting from a liberal arts education.[17] Students seem to be most sensitive to near-term employment during economic downturns, as was certainly the case around the 1980 trough and again today. In contrast, Harvard reported its humanities majors to be unconcerned about near-term career prospects, as might be expected. This divergence reflects the realities of American higher education since the 1970s: students at nonselective institutions hope for immediate employment following graduation and they have little interest in the humanities; students in selective institutions have longer-term horizons and are likelier to follow their interests into humanities majors.

The American Public Doesn't Understand Us

Despite an apparently endless succession of eloquent testimonies to the value of the liberal arts, it seems that this message has not reached the American public. It is absent from the public discourse. Hence, the Academy report aspires to (again) "make a clear and compelling case for the liberal arts."[18] It doesn't.[19]

The humanities face two problems in making their case: implausible arguments and a failure to face the realities of humanities disciplines today.[20] For the former, I will simply identify three common claims.

The "Me Too" Argument. Or the contention that liberal arts contribute to virtuous social goals. Thus, the Academy claims: "Humanists and social scientists are critical in providing cultural, historical, and ethical expertise and empirical analysis to efforts that address issues such as the provision of clean air and water, food, health, energy, and universal education." Perhaps, but other fields contribute far more, and the marginal contributions of the liberal arts provide such a weak justification as to make this assertion counterproductive.[21] More fundamentally, Stanley Fish observes, "if liberal arts education is doing *its* job and not the job assigned to some other institution, it will not have as its aim the bringing about of particular effects in the world."[22]

Democracy. "[A] shared knowledge of history, civics, and social studies . . . allows citizens to participate meaningfully in the democratic process." A comforting sentiment, presented most articulately by Martha Nussbaum; but this conventional piety has begun to be questioned.[23] Relating Nussbaum's assertion to the reality of the polarized US democratic process today cries out for critical thinking. Derek Bok (in *Higher Education in America*) rejects the "dubious assumption . . . that one can prepare students adequately as citizens without requiring any specific course for doing so." Or, more sweepingly, Geoffrey Harpham writes, "no responsible scholar believes that humanistic study directly fosters private virtue and responsible citizenship."[24]

Critical Thinking. Much the same is true for critical thinking. An astonishing 99.6 percent of surveyed faculty reported that fostering critical thinking is an essential or very important goal of college.[25] However, few engage in specific practices to bring this about. Fish, perhaps among the 0.4 percent of skeptics, calls critical thinking "a phrase without content." Evidence fails to support the notion that studying a liberal major enhances presumed measures of critical thinking, and the results for general education courses are even more problematic. In other words, staking the claims for the humanities on the quicksand of critical thinking comforts the faithful, but will never convince the skeptics.[26]

The Realities. And what of the realities? Here the Harvard report has value precisely because it addressed a real problem that no amount of rhetoric can obscure. It recognizes, sometimes obliquely and euphemistically, that the intellectual content and practice of the humanities are at least partly responsible for the apparent diminished student interest. Putting the best face on this, it explains that the humanist tradition of *critique* transcended attention to texts in order to impose "scholarly skepticism and distrust" on the "operations of power."[27] The tradition of romantic "engaged enthusiasm" has embraced "liberating, transformative social movements," namely gender and race. The combination has produced "tribalist exclusions of those not regarded as part of the transhistorical identity." Behind these circumlocutions is the real problem—a completely polarized view of the world. This development has three unfortunate consequences.[28]

First, the prevalence of monolithic political correctness in the humanities. The Harvard report admits that students get the impression "that some ideas are unspeakable in our classrooms." It then offers a politically correct excuse by suggesting that these are probably bad ideas anyway, notions that may have been picked up from "parents . . . houses of worship . . . or from the media"! Derek Bok offers a more general criticism, that the uniformity of political orientation deprives these disciplines of the challenge of diverse ideas and views. But further, unlike the past when academic freedom was threatened by presidents, trustees, or legislators, "today, the principal threats are subtler and come primarily from within. . . . from students and faculty with strong personal views on subjects ranging from women's rights, sexual orientation, and race . . . or from . . . marked political imbalances or from methodological orthodoxies within entire departments."[29] "Tribalist exclusions" and "unspeakable" ideas certainly represent internal threats; they belie conditions that are the antithesis of humanistic inquiry and ideals.

These conditions are difficult to address without falling into the polarized dialogue of the culture wars. A neutral perspective might be found by adapting the insights gleaned from research on "cultural cognition." The basic mechanism, validated by experimentation, is that cultural identity operates "as a kind of heuristic in the rational processing of information." When faced with contentious social issues, individuals tend to assimilate "factual beliefs consistent with their cultural orientation" and "to dismiss the persuasiveness of evidence proffered by their adversaries."[30] These effects were found to increase with greater education and intelligence, since such persons were more adept at culling congenial material. The overall impact of cultural cognition is to promote erroneous beliefs, since comforting notions from trusted sources will be privileged over empirically accurate facts. From the perspective of cultural cognition, then, the commitments of humanists to "liberating, transformative social movements" are perhaps no different from the commitments of Tea Party followers to small government: both draw their facts and beliefs from sources congenial to their affinity-group identities, a process, in both cases, fraught with unfortunate consequences.

In the most thorough examination of faculty political orientation, Neal Gross emphasized self-selection as the source of liberal bias. As an example he uses the strongly leftist feminist movement in sociology. Since it is "important to the discipline's current intellectual content. . . . it would be foolish for anyone with truly antifeminist sensibilities to become a sociologist; such a person would be destined to spend his career bashing his head against the wall."[31] Cultural cognition would predict further difficulties. Although there are critiques of feminism, they originate from sources that are beyond the pale—that have no credibility among sociologists (or for that matter humanists: *vide* Harvard's negative typing of the "unspeakable" ideas, above). In the absence of critique, increasingly radical or exaggerated expressions of favored doctrines are accepted, if not applauded, further defining cultural identity and polarization.[32] Thus, political correctness in the humanities is pervasive, although not necessarily perverse: it stems from the same process of cultural cognition that has produced polarization throughout American society, rather than an inherent leftism of the humanities. Nonetheless, by precluding subjects and ideas, let alone critique of its own biases, the intellectual purview of the humanities has been diminished.

Second, Geoffrey Harpham makes the case that by indulging first in high theory in the 1980s and then in race, class, and gender, the humanities have abandoned their core *raison d'être*—the individual and what is human. Louis Menand has similarly condemned "aimless eclecticism" as humanists deserted their disciplinary moorings to dabble in other subjects.[33] I consider this the sociologizing of the humanities—focusing in an ahistorical manner on social causes rather than individuals and literary texts. When I was a graduate student in literature, I considered sociologists to be class enemies; they reduced human experience to bloodless abstractions and meaningless truisms. Now humanists claim to expose "operations of power," not in the abundant and rich literary representations of human relations, but in crude generalizations (embellished with recondite language) about class, race, and gender. Michael Bérubé categorically rejects criticism of such approaches, maintaining "that the study of the humanities is more vibrant, more exciting, and (dare I say it) more important than it was a generation ago." But then he complains: "we can't avoid the conclusion that the value of the work we do, and the way we theorize value, simply isn't valued by very many people, on campus or off."[34]

And so, thirdly, this dovetails with the conclusion of the Harvard report. While acting as "warriors of the theory and culture wars of the 1980s and 1990s," faculty failed to consider "what our undergraduates needed in the here and now." Harvard undergraduates, it seems, arrive with great interest in the humanities and were untroubled by careerist anxieties, but their curiosity, it would seem, has not been met by faculty interests and scholarship. The report gently suggests a "reaffirmation of the generalist tradition of undergraduate teaching," ensuring that great "books are placed in the hands of each incoming wave of students."[35] Perhaps a reformation in both teaching and content is the path away from the crisis in the humanities.

SOME MODEST PROPOSALS

In this light, what is needed for a "New Deal for the Humanities"? I offer the following modest suggestions.

Avoid claims of instrumental usefulness. Helen Small warns that "any defence that gives primary place to the instrumental value of a humanities education will quickly disfigure the broader kinds of good it nurtures."[36] Of Derek Bok's three fundamental aims of a college education, the third is "to help students live a full and satisfying life by cultivating a wide range of interests and a capacity for reflection and self-knowledge."[37] This is a time-honored mission of the humanities, as Sheldon Rothblatt explains elsewhere in this volume, and one that the humanities are uniquely capable of fulfilling. Indeed, it is difficult to imagine an education that would widen and deepen intellectual horizons and feelings without a substantial contribution from the humanities.

Student engagement with the humanities and the liberal arts generally cultivates a more profound facility for dealing with theoretical ideas and, concomitantly, improved skills in reading, writing, and comprehending abstract concepts. These same qualities have been found to be deficient in vocational majors. A positive case can and should be made, and documented, for the cognitive enhancement that these studies produce, without making exaggerated claims for critical thinking or citizenship.

Furthermore, the Harvard challenge needs to be addressed: how can teaching and content be altered in ways that would better engage students intellectually? This constitutes a huge challenge, but no progress is possible unless humanities professors seriously question existing practice. They need to ask *why* their studies are not valued. Humanities faculty should ask why students are uninterested in their scholarship, and think about how that might be rectified—not by pandering to student culture, but by enticing them to a higher common ground. Inspired teaching has traditionally been a hallmark of humanistic studies, and this is certainly an aspect of tradition that merits reemphasis.

Finally, a large demand exists in American society for accessible history and great literature. Humanistic studies ought to contemplate how this incredibly rich material might be presented in new and creative ways, while incorporating the critical lens of humanistic scholarship. Of course, a few scholars do bring their work to broad audiences and do it quite well. Reducing the distance between the academic humanities and the educated public's interest in the larger body of humanistic material might reenergize appreciation of and involvement in the multiple realms of humanistic studies.

NOTES

1. Daniel Coit Gilman, "Our National Schools of Science," *North American Review* (October 1867): 495–520.

2. Roger L. Geiger, "Land-Grant Colleges and the Pre-Modern Era of American Higher Education, 1850–1890," Paper presented to the Morrill Land-Grant Conference, October 3–6, 2012, Mississippi State University.

3. Winton U. Solberg, *The University of Illinois, 1867–1894: An Intellectual and Cultural History* (Urbana: University of Illinois Press, 1968).

4. Winton U. Solberg, *The University of Illinois, 1894–1904: The Shaping of the University* (Urbana: University of Illinois Press, 2000).

5. Winton U. Solberg, "President Edmund J. James and the University of Illinois, 1904–1920," in *The Land-Grant Colleges and the Reshaping of American Higher Education*, ed. Roger L. Geiger and Nathan M. Sorber (New Brunswick, NJ: Transaction, 2013), 225–246; Edwin E. Slosson, *Great American Universities* (New York: 1910).

6. Geiger, "Land-Grant Colleges."

7. Roger L. Geiger, *The History of American Higher Education: Learning and Culture from the Founding to World War II* (Princeton: Princeton University Press, 2015).

8. Karl M. Grisso, "David Kinley, 1861–1944: The Career of the Fifth President of the University of Illinois" (PhD Diss., University of Illinois, 1980), quote p. 571.

9. Howard R. Bowen, *Academic Recollections* (New York: Macmillan, 1988), 25–36; George D. Stoddard, *The Pursuit of Education: An Autobiography* (New York: Vantage, 1981), 104–178. Doctoral education at Illinois in the social sciences was decimated in the 1950s: Roger L. Geiger, *Research and Relevant Knowledge: American Research Universities since World War II* (New Brunswick, NJ: Transaction, 2004 [1993]), 106.

10. Commission on the Humanities and Social Sciences, *The Heart of the Matter* (Cambridge, MA: American Academy of Arts and Sciences, 2013); [Harvard Faculty Working Group], "The Teaching of the Arts and Humanities at Harvard College: Mapping the Future" (Harvard University, 2013).

11. "Mapping the Future," figure 1. Cf. Roger L. Geiger, "Demography and Curriculum: The Humanities in American Higher Education from the 1950s through the 1980s" in *The Humanities and the Dynamics of Inclusion Since World War II*, ed. David A. Hollinger (Baltimore: Johns Hopkins University Press, 2006), 50–72; Michael Bérubé, "The Humanities, Declining? Not According to the Numbers," *Chronicle Review*, July 1, 2013.

12. Humanities faculty do not appear to be declining, although recent data are lacking: *Humanities Indicators* shows humanities faculty registering the second-largest relative increase, 1999–2006 (figure III-9a); and the percentage of full-time faculty holding constant, 1993–2004 (figure III-11a). See http://humanitiesindicators.org.

13. The American Academy of Arts and Sciences, *Humanities Report Card* (Cambridge, MA: American Academy of Arts and Sciences, 2013), 5, available at https://www.amacad.org/binaries/hum_report_card.pdf.

14. Consortium for Humanities Centers and Institutes. Cf. Roger L. Geiger, "Optimizing Research and Teaching: The Bifurcation of Faculty Roles at Research Universities" in *The American Academic Profession: Transformation in Contemporary Higher Education*, ed. Joseph C. Hermanowicz (Baltimore: Johns Hopkins University Press, 2011), 21–43.

15. See *infra*. Daniel Kleinman, Chapter 5, "Sticking Up for Liberal Arts and Humanities Education."

16. Humanists are near the bottom of the earnings scale, but they have considerable company (majors in fine arts, sociology, biology): Anthony P. Carnevale, Ban Cheah, and Jeff Strohl, "Not All College Degrees Are Created Equal," Georgetown University, Center on Education and the Workforce, 2012.

17. *Heart of the Matter*, 32, 33: employer data from a survey commissioned by the American Association of Colleges and Universities.

18. *Heart of the Matter*, 31. Cf. Andrew Delbanco, "College at Risk," *Chronicle Review*, February 26, 2012.

19. See *infra*. Sheldon Rothblatt, Chapter 2, "Old Wine in New Bottles, or New Wine in Old Bottles?"

20. Helen Small, in contrast, provides a rigorous evaluation of arguments for the humanities, but does not consider American realities: *The Value of the Humanities* (New York: Oxford University Press, 2014).

21. *Heart of the Matter*, 11. In Europe, efforts to justify the humanities by their usefulness have been "humbling" and counterproductive: Geoffrey Galt Harpham, *The Humanities and the Dream of America* (Chicago: University of Chicago Press, 2011), 148–149.

22. Stanley Fish, *Save the World on Your Own Time* (New York: Oxford University Press, 2008), 55.

23. *Heart of the Matter*, 10; This sentiment takes considerable liberty with Nussbaum's "normative"(politically correct) description of the contribution of the humanities, namely "instruction in the arts and humanities . . . that will bring students in contact with issues of gender, race, ethnicity, and cross-cultural experience and understanding"; while warning them against "defective forms of 'literature'": Martha C. Nussbaum, *Not for Profit: Why Democracy Needs the Humanities* (Princeton: Princeton University Press, 2010), 108–109. Nussbaum and the argument that "Democracy Needs Us" is thoroughly critiqued in Helen Small, *The Value of the Humanities*, 125–150.

24. Derek Bok, *Higher Education in America* (Princeton: Princeton University Press, 2013), 181; Harpham, *Humanities*, 27.

25. Cooperative Institutional Research Program, "The American College Teacher: National Norms for the 2007–2008 HERI Faculty Survey" (Higher Education Research Institute, UCLA, 2009).

26. Fish, *Save the World*, 54; Bok, *Higher Education*, 167–175.

27. Helen Small regards such claims as "a questionable assumption of privilege over other fields": *Value of the Humanities*, 27.

28. "Teaching of the Arts," 18–21.

29. Ibid., 42; Bok, *Higher Education*, 376.

30. Dan M Kahan and Donald Braman, "Cultural Cognition and Public Policy," *Yale Law and Policy Review* 24 (2006): 147–170, quotes pp. 149, 163, 164.

31. Neil Gross, *Why Are Professors Liberal and Why Do Conservatives Care?* (Cambridge, MA: Harvard University Press, 2013),149.

32. Something like this occurred with the unrestrained pretensions of postmodern theory in the 1980s, which prompted Roger Kimball's ridicule in *Tenured Radicals* (New York: Harper & Row, 1990).

33. Harpham, *Humanities*, 28–40.

34. Michael Bérubé, "The Humanities, Unraveled," *Chronicle Review*, February 18, 2013.

35. "Teaching the Arts," 30, 32.

36. Small, *Value of the Humanities*, 174–175.

37. Bok, *Higher Education*, 167.

2 · OLD WINE IN NEW BOTTLES, OR NEW WINE IN OLD BOTTLES?

The Humanities and Liberal Education in Today's Universities

SHELDON ROTHBLATT

Liberal education in the United States is more closely associated with private-sector higher education than with public or state-supported institutions, especially the segment often referred to as "selective" or even (sometimes invidiously) "elite." Part of the reason lies with history. The celebrity colleges and universities reach back to the years when liberal education was primary. And part of the reason lies in their relative freedom from political oversight. No institution is ever wholly independent. Media pressures exist, as do alumni interests. Social movements have a bearing on curricula, hiring, and the selection of students, but the relative autonomy of the private sector allows considerable initiative in the setting of academic priorities.

But even stronger reasons for the identification of liberal education with particular American institutions are quality, scale, staffing, a residential mission, and greater resources. These allow for full-time attendance and a total immersion of students in campus life, a capacity to make interesting friends, and readier access to faculty, all of which have long been regarded as the preconditions for a liberal education. Progress to the degree is also steadier. Undergraduates usually complete their first degree in four years, whereas, for example, the aggregated figure for the ten-campus University of California, one of America's leading state systems, indicates a more interrupted campus experience. While improvements have occurred in the last fifteen years, 40 percent of undergraduates take longer than four years to achieve a BA,[1] not impressive when compared to institutions with better-supported undergraduates.

Campus cultures are also factors in predicting student success, and in this respect many private institutions also retain an advantage. Lower achievers improve wherever academic circumstances provide stimulating examples. Conversely, able students do less well in the absence of high standards and intellectual encouragement. This appears obvious, but it is not always noted.[2] In his classic discussion of elite and mass-access higher education, the sociologist Martin Trow mentioned another advantage of select institutions. Their graduates are more confident of landing jobs and are consequently willing to take non-vocational courses, while those attending less-select and more-open admissions programs are more inclined to enter fields where employment opportunities are a major consideration. This pattern is susceptible to finer qualifications, but it does suggest that colleges and universities that carry the burden of mass higher education—mainly the publics—need to be particularly imaginative if they are to offer strong programs in the humanities and liberal arts.[3]

Select private institutions strengthen campus cultures by recruiting a fair number of talented students without means, offering substantial guaranteed scholarships, financial aid, or discounted tuition; but the vast majority of undergraduates—some 70 percent of those in accredited degree programs—enter public institutions. Once famously tuition-free, many, including my own, now charge for course work, and especially for professional-school programs of study, although the university continues to make strenuous efforts to subsidize undergraduates. According to a recent statement by the president of the University of California, Janet Napolitano, 40 percent of the undergraduate student body are from low-income households and just under half of the entering 2013 freshman class are first-generation college students.[4]

Two-year community colleges enroll the largest proportion of undergraduates attending state institutions. Funding problems are greatest in this segment, since the colleges are invariably under local control, and vocational pressures strongest. Overall, most public-sector undergraduates are commuters or work part-time and therefore forgo (depending upon individual circumstances) the advantages aligned with the residential campus experience. The majority, it seems safe to say, are likely to complete a degree program without making the acquaintance of regular faculty.

Given the endless national concern over access to higher education, the percentages provided by President Napolitano are noteworthy. Nevertheless, they are also somewhat misleading. They aggregate numbers in a campus system with centrifugal tendencies and decentralized campus admission practices, so that, in effect, the separate campuses of the University of California are increasingly behaving as autonomous institutions. As in the brand-name colleges and universities, a noticeable correlation exists between high achievers (as measured by high-school grades and standardized tests), family circumstances, and the campuses within the system regarded as more select than the others (Berkeley, Los Angeles, and San Diego—San Francisco is a medical school only). Lower achievers attend the other campuses, and their family income is less. The same correlations hold for underrepresented students, although the state's outstanding African American and Hispanic undergraduates are to be found on the more select campuses.[5]

But for one reason or another—because they have choices or the means or the ability to attract scholarships—a large number of top students are electing to attend private colleges and universities. Admitted to the University of California, they fail to register; and another subset of lower-achieving but eligible undergraduates with little income attend low-cost institutions. The combination of reduced funding, leading campuses such as Berkeley to admit large numbers of high-paying out-of-state students (some 23 percent for 2014–2015), and the loss of exceptional students choosing to go elsewhere has long meant that the national and global reputation of the campuses within the University of California rests on postgraduate research and professional education. Insofar as the very idea of a liberal education has always meant the undergraduate experience, and still does, retaining and strengthening commitment to a liberal education is a formidable undertaking, but, as will be suggested, not impossible.

Underrepresented minorities constitute half of all high school graduates in the state of California, and their college-going rates, especially to the more competitive institutions, lag well behind any desirable outcome.[6] In this respect, the problem of access has worsened. The celebrated State of California Master Plan of 1960 promised entry to one of the state's three public segments for all qualified and willing residents, the segments linked through student transfer. Budget cuts combined with a severe downturn in the quality of California's system of schooling made that historic promise untenable. One consequence is that the university cannot meet its part of the plan's obligation (accepting out-of-state undergraduates hardly mitigates the situation).

A national movement to absorb more undergraduates into underfunded systems has not yet reached the University of California. Two-year lower-division and in some cases four-year colleges are now associated or integrated with large state universities. Ohio State and Penn State have such "branch" campuses, as do institutions in at least sixteen other states.[7] A decline in the number of places threatens the very opportunity structure that has been a hallmark of California's history. It also means that students who do enter higher education have to struggle to meet expenses, and those who lack the confidence gained by growing up in families where education is highly valued will be particularly anxious about their market prospects. This, as has been noted, affects their choices of study.

Yet it must be said that while access is obviously the first step in obtaining a liberal education, and is as much a national as a personal concern, the mere provision for any kind of higher education is not in itself a guarantee that a humanistic outcome will result. Select colleges and universities have particular advantages, but if these advantages are not exploited, they are negligible. Public institutions are currently experiencing serious disadvantages in supporting vigorous programs in the liberal arts, but they are hardly helpless. Furthermore, it is easy enough to exaggerate the differences between public and private colleges and universities. American higher education is highly differentiated. Most private colleges or universities are not in the select category. Many struggle to acquire the necessary funding. Many adopt vocational missions as the simplest way to attract revenue. In some respects the leading private research universities resemble the leading publics, drawing their research funds from the same markets or government sources, and competing for talent and reputation in the national and global academic marketplace. Some private universities have forthrightly embraced a public, urban mission—New York University and the University of San Francisco are examples. Today's colleges and universities are in many respects hybrid institutions, resembling one another in values and course offerings more than they differ.

Consequently, with respect to the teaching of the humanities and providing for the elements of a liberal education, the fundamental issues remain what they long have been: defining the ends of liberal education, identifying the means to those ends, to include academic structures and campus ecologies, and providing the open and enthusiastic commitments to both career and everyday living that comprise the liberal experience at its best.

THE UTILITY CHALLENGES

Ironically, from time to time the argument for practicality has been the target of those who scoffed at "mere" vocationalism. But more typically, especially in modern eras, liberal education is usually on the defensive. A principal charge is that liberal education is useless for employment. In response to the first, defenders argue that any kind of employment needs to be elevated by education that encourages mental agility and large perspectives. Representatives of the business world are sometimes cited for their support of liberal education. A recent survey of business representatives taken on behalf of the Association of American Colleges and Universities states that certain skills—those historically represented in a liberal education—are more important than any actual undergraduate major. Flexibility of mind, independent thinking, some degree of breadth, as well as the ability to engage in collaborative problem-solving and community activities are what today's employers seek. They value communication and signs of personal growth. Internships are advocated as one means to these ends.[8] But those who respond to such surveys are likely to be at the top of particular industries and not directly engaged in the hiring process. Understandably, being in the public eye, they would like to be seen as supporters of practices that appear high-minded. Further down the hierarchy, middle management may be less accommodating.

Judging from scattered media comments and private discussions, it appears that few employers or even academics for that matter are convinced that colleges and universities are educating well-rounded, confident undergraduates who are undismayed by the requirements of today's competitive work environments. The more skeptical among them wonder, and have long wondered, whether in fact mass-access higher education is capable of providing a liberal education to other than an elite of undergraduates. The press continues to report the fears expressed by faculty regarding the command of language, breadth of knowledge, or just intellectual curiosity possessed by the undergraduates whom they teach. Statistics are compiled to prove that student interest in the humanities and the liberal arts is not only waning: it has almost disappeared. Reporting on the numbers of students enrolled in majors described as humanities, the National Center for Education Statistics of the US Department of Education concludes that undergraduates are avoiding disciplines that appear disconnected from labor markets. Some 365,000 bachelor degrees awarded in 2010–2011 were in fields designated as business studies, while only close to 48,000 were in subjects defined broadly (and oddly) as "liberal arts and sciences/general studies/humanities."

But such conclusions rely on questionable taxonomies and are in fact completely misleading, therefore contributing to sloppy and alarming arguments regarding the appeal of nonvocational subjects. For example, second to business is the category of social sciences/history, and further down the Center list we find English language and literature/letters, for a combined total of 229,000. No particular reason exists for separating the social sciences or English from the liberal arts and sciences. And other subject categories in the Center's list that may well be included among the liberal arts and sciences are the visual and performing arts, the biological and biomedical sciences, or even journalism and media studies. When all are added in, the total of bachelor degrees awarded exceeds those in business studies. Clearly the staffs who compiled such data rely on arbitrary and confusing labels. Interestingly, the newspaper article publishing the Department of Education statistics has caveats of its own, notably the dangers of early specialization in rapidly changing labor markets and the value of work experience prior to graduation.[9] This last point is assuming increasing attention by those concerned about the limitations of conventional academic curricula (assuming there is such a thing).

Liberal education is far more than a catalogue listing of academic disciplines and specialties, although that is the form in which it appears to most students. Our universities therefore implicitly encourage the sort of classification schemes erected by staffers in government bureaucracies, and our colleges and universities also group discrete subjects into larger divisions of knowledge, separating the ideas to be gained in one from those in another. Liberal education is indeed nonvocational, but that is hardly a telling accusation. It says little about the role of teachers or the learning environments in which teaching takes place. It overlooks what I believe most people would prefer, careers that provide deeper levels of satisfaction and a richer grasp of life's finer possibilities.[10] How is this to be achieved?

THE PURPOSES OF LIBERAL EDUCATION

Given liberal education's long history, a single overriding statement about its purpose is always difficult. There are numerous versions and variations. Some can be related to one another more easily than others. All, however, unite in a belief in some kind of superior, better, or higher mode of living. One special problem—in some respects a greater challenge than refuting charges that liberal education is impractical—is represented by mass access to higher education. At its best, since it is far more than the inculcation of skills and proficiencies, liberal education requires a demanding and hence expensive educational output.

Hence from its first formulations in Greek antiquity (recent scholars have, however, identified a Hebrew component), those receiving a liberal education were the children, invariably the sons, of social and political elites. A correlation between liberal education and social privilege carried well into the future, strengthened, in fact, by social changes occurring in the early modern period. It was in the academies of the Italian Renaissance and not in the medieval universities where we find the stand-alone liberal education that continued into the modern era. "Ornamental" in many ways and very useful indeed for life in the ducal courts of Renaissance despots, such education emphasized personal style and conduct. This "gentlemanly" tradition entered the English Enlightenment as "taste" and "manners," indispensable for anyone eager to advance socially. Newcomers occasionally found opportunities for upward mobility, but the advantages always lay with those at the top of the social hierarchy.

The gentlemanly version of liberal education was both attractive and superficial: attractive because it stressed getting along with others and living in the public eye; superficial because it led to pretense and affectation in order to gain a personal advantage. An echo of this can be found in Ivy League institutions in the 1920s where style rather than intellect was used to screen out children from poor Jewish immigrant families.

Stated differently, the claim that deportment was the end of a liberal education entered the literature as the argument for education as character development, a step up from the ideal of the gentleman. In the nineteenth century, Noah Porter III, president of Yale, wanted students to be pious, ethical, and informed. He hoped that they would obtain a certain kind of "wholeness" that did not require deep learning.[11] The argument for character formation reappears from time to time, if faintly, whenever universities are accused of educating graduates who are more interested in finding a place within a competitive, capitalist market economy than in serving society. Only a few years ago business schools in American universities, alarmed by accounts of corruption within industry, professed a concern for a more publicly minded graduate, but one may be forgiven a certain skepticism regarding the efficacy of courses in business ethics.

Enlightenment Scottish thinkers added new goals for liberal education, and the various schools of Scottish moral philosophy found their way into the American colleges of the new Republic. Indeed, the Scots of the eighteenth century were an imperial class, and their influence extended beyond North America to Sweden. (Chalmers Technological University in Gothenburg was founded by a Scot named Thomas Chalmers.) Among the Scottish goals was a conception of "civilization" (a word derived from the French) as an advanced level of human development. Scottish "conjectural" historians described stages of social development from primitive economies to the sophisticated (if preindustrial) world of markets, commerce, and banking. While accepting many of the characterological aims of the English version of liberal education, the Scots were particularly preoccupied with transforming a puritanical, feudal, and warrior country into one that was "modern" and indeed "civilized."

Colonial American leaders, not just the political class but also leading members of the professions and business, were well versed in the great literature of the past and well-acquainted with inherited educational models of a good life and particularly models of civic virtue or citizenship drawn from Greek, Italian, and English sources. These have come down to us with various names: republicanism, the "Atlantic Tradition or the Commonwealthman."[12] The historian Joseph Kett has also called civic virtue a "visible Life," or to employ the phrase of Richard Sennett, "public man." The reward for devotion to the public good was honor and merit.[13]

The new Republic formally erased class distinctions and the accidents of birth. How then to design a form of liberal education that made everyone virtuous, that bypassed social class antecedents in order to advance the values of a professedly democratic society? Liberal education had always been for the few with assured places and occupations in the existing social networks. Could liberal education be for the many? And if for the many, what guarantees could be offered to ease entry into suitable labor markets for those without the necessary connections?

This highly abbreviated survey of the varieties of liberal education is not complete without the inclusion of several other inheritances, even departures and contradictions, all of which have echoes in current discussions. First is the influence of the Romantic emphasis on individualism, leading to discussions of liberal education centered on self-realization and moving the argument away from civic virtue and conceptions of deportment, leaving the latter to the writers of etiquette books. Second, reinforcing the first, was liberal individualism, which, however, promoted an aggressive self-interest.

A third and particularly complex inheritance was German. Some 15,000 Americans visited German universities in the nineteenth century, returning home greatly impressed by the intellectual resources and cutting-edge research of the German professoriate. But if there were gains—most notably, a far higher standard of academic teaching and scholarship than obtained in American colleges and universities—there were significant losses. German versions of liberal education could not be easily accommodated to the aims of civic virtue. Quite simply, the "Atlantic tradition" was not suited to authoritarian political systems. Furthermore, the mind was free, but the person was not.[14]

Liberal education in Germany had developed in conjunction with a research ethic and "new knowledge," whereas American versions of liberal education were more or less based on the dissemination of received knowledge, a far less radical conception of knowledge. German views of the importance of research were at first resisted by older generations. Their leadership was threatened, their intellectual qualifications were being questioned, and apart from these were fears that undergraduates, younger and less mature than their European counterparts, would be led astray by unfamiliar or unorthodox ideas. Higher education in the United States was protective. Parents sending their children away from home expected faculty to be *in loco parentis*, an attitude somewhat intact until the 1960s when many institutions eliminated or transformed the office of deans of students responsible for undergraduate discipline.[15]

Two paths lay open to anyone wishing to reconcile the German ideal of knowledge as discovery with American versions of liberal education. One reinforced the individualism attributable to Romanticism and market economics by allowing undergraduates to think, judge, and decide for themselves. The purpose of a liberal education might well be to preserve existing norms and culture but not unless first closely examined by the disciplined and informed intelligence. As Americans moved further away from tradition and came to value personal initiative, the independent questioning of commonly held beliefs was more generally acceptable.

A second path was thornier since it required a grasp of a German idea of self-realization based on conceptions of perfection that could not be aligned with the pragmatism of American culture. *Bildung* is a conception of liberal education that is essentially divorced from the activities of everyday life. The point is made *in extremis* in *The Magic Mountain* by Thomas Mann. His characters engage in convoluted discussions regarding self-understanding in the sickly environment of a mountain sanitarium. An energetic American society could hardly be expected to enthusiastically embrace endless and tiring discussions of high aesthetic and intellectual ideals, but for a few the appeal of *Bildung* lay in its contrast with the faddish, commercially driven culture of the United States. The object was a standard, a norm, a higher culture or indeed "High Culture" itself. Famous writers like T. S. Eliot or Henry Adams went abroad in search of culture that was, as the English poet Matthew Arnold called it, "the best that has been thought and said in the world." (Arnold toured the United States, badly as it turned out, as he was a poor public speaker and required lessons in elocution.)

Small wonder that by the twentieth century, with its numerous legacies, imports, inconsistencies, and contradictions, no consensus on the purpose of a liberal education was possible, and if no consistency existed respecting ends, none could exist regarding means. But each version had and still has its own advocates. Is the essence of a liberal education civic virtue, character, or personal development (and what kind of character?), the forming of the critical intelligence, the pursuit of the best that has been thought and said in the world, the higher culture, the process and act of discovery? Words, words, words, said Hamlet, but behind each of these words lies a long and complex history.

A relatively new entry into the debates involve MOOCs (massive open online courses), although such debates are rarely focused on the ends of liberal education. They are responses to global demands for higher education that cannot be met from existing financial and teaching resources. For-profit Internet courses have been investigated by congressional committees for financial scandals involving federal funds, and their record of degree-granting or academic quality falls far short of the hoopla of supporters. However, universities and colleges are experimenting with online instruction in the hope that certain kinds of in-house teaching may be enhanced, most notably by providing faculty with greater opportunities to interact more personally with undergraduates (more prosaically, to accommodate larger numbers of students, or even to gain outside markets). We are as yet far from knowing whether computer-aided instruction will actually advance the ideals, and I might add, the necessities associated with what we may understand as a humanistic and a humanizing experience.[16]

THE BATTLES OF THE BOOKS

It was probably in the Italian Renaissance that the word "humanities" was connected to liberal education. The point was that certain studies were "humane." They shaped personality, promoted interpersonal behavior, and enhanced the quality of everyday life. Over the centuries the association between the liberal arts and the humanities led to quarrels over the virtues of different bodies of knowledge. Science, that is to say, laboratory or experimental science, posed a threat to the belles-lettres legacies of liberal education. Did science enhance our "human" qualities? In the Ancients versus Moderns debates of the early modern and eighteenth centuries, starting in France and spreading everywhere else, Jonathan Swift excoriated the New Learning (or "modern" learning, his word), scientific discoveries that were to underpin the Age of Reason.[17] Angry and scatological, Swift drew a distinction between conduct that was life-affirming and self-serving using the parable of the bee and the spider. The first symbolized ancient and liberal education, the second, by contrast, the modern and servile. For Swift, the bee was the supreme humanist, flitting about the garden (Eden), leaving the flowers intact but using their nectar to bring forth "sweetness and light." The bee lived comfortably within nature. But (to use the phrase of the experimentalists), the spider "tortured nature." Antisocial and self-congratulatory—the supreme individualist—the spider was the social engineer who wanted to change the world. Out of his inner filthy bile, he spun a web of destruction, killing off life and disturbing the settled habits of mankind. Arnold took over these metaphors and made the bee synonymous with culture. Even an Enlightenment skeptic like David Hume had appreciated the value of tradition in giving comfort to people.

The Ancients and Moderns debate had something of a final fling in Britain in the 1960s in the two-cultures controversies occasioned by the public lectures of C. P. Snow (a chemist who wrote novels) and F. R. Leavis (a Cambridge literary critic with an acid tongue and unforgiving personality, perhaps not the best representative of the humanistic spirit). The lectures started many hares in the United States, making way for an additional entry into the argument with the naming of the social sciences as a third culture. A half century on, the distinction between the humanities and what we now term STEM subjects (science, technology, engineering, and mathematics) remains in use by the National Science Foundation.[18]

Science was of course accommodated into the broad category of the liberal arts, and universities have their colleges of letters and science. American liberal arts colleges are hugely successful in the teaching of science, their undergraduates going on to the leading graduate research universities. *Bildung* made ample room for science and scientific method, but even before, within the Enlightenment, a scientific caste of mind was necessary if the civilizing task of subjecting all values to the test of reason was to prevail. Today, the two-cultures debates appear quaint; and it takes an effort to recall the momentary ferocity of the arguments of yesteryear.

ACADEMIC PROFESSIONALISM

Research requires specialized inquiry; and while the very notion of narrowly directed inquiry might be regarded as antithetical to the goal of broad understanding attached to liberal education, German scholars demonstrated how the two were interrelated. Original inquiry yielded new insights that in turn led to new generalizations, or what Thomas Kuhn taught us to regard as paradigms, broad matrices of understanding.

The building of academic careers, a feature of the nineteenth century, is inconceivable without specialism and research. Specialism led to a new structure within the university, the disciplinary department as a self-governing subdivision, replacing the broader, more inclusive European-style "faculty." Disciplinary departments are guilds. They control budgets and determine the entry and career lines of colleagues. They determine the organization of teaching. Within graduate-degree institutions, they train students and play a part in launching their careers.

The growth of disciplines and subdisciplines characterizes what Clark Kerr, once president of the University of California and a renowned observer of the contemporary university, named the "multiversity," a highly differentiated institution with innumerable subunits pursuing their own ends. The department possesses an extraordinary capacity to generate new knowledge. The drawback for the university is an absence of common purpose, most noticeable to Kerr in the teaching and education of undergraduates, whom he regarded as neglected by faculty in their pursuit of career ambitions.

Disciplinary departments are not equal in their resources, nor, at institutions such as my own, are the hours of teaching and course-loads equivalent. The sciences pure and applied have a greater need for equipment and have a greater obligation to support graduate student research than do departments in the humanities and social sciences. These differences notwithstanding, the distinctions between professional schools and departments are greater yet, with the former now charging tuition at Berkeley comparable to private institutions and paying salaries notably higher than in the departments. Universities are from this perspective a collection of haves and have-nots, a situation, however, that does not necessarily inhibit a strong commitment to liberal education. It does contribute to a feeling, sometimes uttered, that the humanities are in crisis because their position within the campus is materially inferior to those of the grant-fueled science departments and graduate professional schools. A prudent academic administration or academic senate will adopt strategies designed to mitigate grousing, since no institution is well served by a colony of malcontents.

How are the many "ends" of a liberal education to be achieved within complex higher education institutions highly partitioned by disciplines? The question applies to virtually every US college or university since all, whether public or private, are similarly organized with very few exceptions. However much the ends are debated, it is the means that cause the principal difficulties, because the "means" are decided by the specialist guilds. They define the methods of inquiry, organize teaching, assign responsibilities, and distribute rewards. They determine the degree of variation allowed in the performance of duties. But in an important respect the US department is more flexible than, for example, the Oxford and Cambridge single-subject BA, where the subject syllabus guides undergraduate teaching throughout the institution. How that flexibility is best used with respect to liberal education is an open question.

MEANS TO AN END: GREAT BOOKS OR THE CANON

Swift, Arnold, and Leavis ultimately described humanistic outcomes as deriving from studying what was once viewed as the Great Books tradition, or the canon, and of the making of canonical lists there has been no end. Faith in the canon rested on the belief that a carefully selected body of readings—the two Bibles, the outstanding writers of antiquity, Renaissance paragons, great philosophers and poets, certain modern novelists, possibly some writers on politics—contained all the necessary ideas and values of western civilization, the salient knowledge required in order to be considered civilized, "cultivated" or *gebildet*, or to grasp the meaning of being human. The result was supposed to be someone who respected tradition but was not a slave to it and who could claim to have a nodding acquaintance with the best that had been thought and said in the world.

The Great Books tradition, essentially based on literary texts, also incorporated a belief that a liberal education entailed more than a study of the right kind of authors. It was also a study of how they wrote and thought, the language and style of the narratives and discourses. Since realistically the modern reader would not possess the requisite languages needed to read the giants in their original tongues, gifted translators were to be called upon to provide faithful renderings of the canonical intellects.

But already before more recent criticisms of the Great Books tradition as limited, critics were deriding the idea of a canon as snobbish. The criticism drew on the long history of liberal education as the special province of the privileged members of society. Newcomers, in order to gain entry to the stratum of elect, had to demonstrate that they had received the requisite education, could make reference to texts indicating their acquaintance with culture and, if especially clever (or good at rote) could cite the classics in their originals. Here were the echoes of the gentlemanly tradition, and it was the special task of democracies such as the United States to separate the connections that had grown up between particular authors and social class standing.

In response, and to be fair, the canonists tried to update the required lists by adding more texts that could be considered "classics." However, a newer and in many respects unanswerable challenge was that the canon ignored literature or writings that reflected the experiences of ethnic minorities, women, or the working classes, or simply failed to acknowledge the authentic voices of those who did not require intermediaries and spoke for themselves. Marxist critics like Raymond Williams in England tried to bring working-class values into the culture debate. At the same time, anthropologists were exploring cultural relativism, deepening scholarly understanding of other peoples and places, to include urban sociology. Particularly in the last third of the twentieth century, scholars included popular culture and music, newspapers, magazines, comic books, and film as cultural artifacts worthy of exploration. Composers became interested in fusing popular and classical music, much as they had long been interested in folk music.

A liberal education based on classical authorities or representatives of High Culture did not, it was being argued, provide sufficient instruction on how to understand a plural, democratic society in which all kinds and varieties of creative initiatives demanded recognition and utilized new media outlets, eventually digital, to express that demand.

I am sympathetic to the canonical position, but all along it assumed that the reading of the right authors would automatically yield the right outcomes. We may suppose that when the numbers attending university or even secondary school were relatively few and drawn from the more privileged families, a canon might dominate. In the age of mass secondary and higher education, and the proliferation of different kinds of institutions and teaching styles, a canon of sorts might still survive, but today's realities hardly produce uniform analyses (an argument both for and against standard interpretations!). Any author can be read in any number of ways: Jane Austen is a political conservative or she is a closet feminist, and while the two perspectives may be somehow compatible, it takes some ingenuity to cobble them together. Furthermore, as a generation now past of literary critics argued, writers can be deconstructed, shown to be lacking in coherence and unable to control the argument and theme. With such treatment, no authorial standard is likely; no single writer serves as an authority.

BREADTH AND SPECIALIZATION

If there is one feature of the ends of a liberal education upon which virtually all students of the subject agree and to which every commission or committee report returns, it is a plea for breadth, for an education that is "broad" or "general." The phrase "general education" came into use in the United States between the two great wars. Whether "general" carries the same nuances as "broad" is a matter of opinion and use, but the word does not capture the meanings connected to "liberal," with its untidy references to the education of a free person who is a "citizen" (or, in more cerebral versions, to someone whose mind is liberated and independent, unfettered by prejudice).

However appealing, "breadth" is difficult to define. How broad is broad? Even those sympathetic to that understanding have worried that a broad education is likely to be thin, too general and too vague, or so general and so vague that the cognitive ability and knowledge required to undertake a serious analysis is lacking. The report from the American Academy of Arts and Sciences, *The Heart of the Matter*, warns against allowing "students to wander through obscure and irrelevant fields of study in a meaningless quest for breadth."[19] I might agree, if further guidance on this swingeing point were provided. As it stands, nothing can be made of it.

I noted earlier that departmental specialism enhanced the separation of disciplines. Those who advocate breadth as the essence of a liberal education, or cite the capacity of the humanistic subjects to supply the one thing needful, often name departmental specialization as the main difficulty. Yet the same question arises with respect to specialism as arises with regard to breadth. How specialized is a specialty? The disciplines vary dramatically. The opposite of breadth, and presumably the enemy of liberal education, is specialization or the concentration on expert knowledge.

Apart from that, modern society is founded on expert inquiry and on the palpable possibilities of such inquiry: discovery, cutting-edge research, methods of proof, and the necessary and welcome use of systematically developed knowledge to improve our health, communications, food supplies, and standard of living. Adam Smith identified the division of labor or specialization as the necessary basis of the wealth of nations. Specialization is a response to the complexity of life and to the need to uncover the details, the overwhelming and confusing details, inhabiting every corner of existence. If the word "humanities" refers to an understanding of human existence, specialized knowledge is wholly relevant.

The late, distinguished sociologist of higher education Burton Robert Clark, correcting shallow criticisms, made the point that disciplinary specialisms almost automatically branch out into adjacent and cognate fields.[20] The demographer, for example, will eventually need geography, urban planning, some understanding of communications, the sociology of families, the economics of housing. Historians go sideways as a matter of course, biographers certainly, and if I understand postmodern theorists, one of their objectives has been to take literary studies in a great many disciplinary directions, to be "interdisciplinary" or "multidisciplinary."[21]

Here's a fine to-do. Specialization is the foe of liberal education, but specialization is needed because we live in a world built up from highly detailed inquiries. Moreover, the Academy report makes a major point of stating that our world has grown beyond national boundaries, placing an even greater burden on liberal education.[22] Finally, while we are urged to be broad, we are simultaneously warned that some forms of breadth are illegitimate. How do we emerge from all these educational and even moral conundrums?

THE DISTRIBUTION OR "BREADTH" REQUIREMENTS

Not a day goes by when international comparisons of pupil achievement at every grade level locate US schoolchildren well below other countries. Consequently, most American higher education institutions have been unable to unburden themselves from the task of remedial education. The revenues devoted to remedial instruction, even when they are not designated as such, are a particular problem for public and nonselect institutions in general, diverting attention from the main body of the curriculum to address problems that should have been dealt with in earlier grades.

The failure of US secondary education to provide the kind of breadth instruction or quality once and occasionally still found in the top-tier European high school, plus the younger age at which US youth enter higher education, pushes the experience of liberal education into the tertiary sector. But the professionalization of academic careers increases the importance of specialties. The trade-off has been the "breadth requirements" taken at undergraduate levels. Many versions exist, but the working idea is that undergraduates need to acquire an acquaintance with four or five knowledge domains by taking a certain number of courses in each. This exposure is supposed to provide breadth, but it is also justified as allowing students to sample different fields of learning as a guide to later specialization. Except for mathematical or language sequences, the choices are typically disconnected. Students are eager to get past them in order to concentrate on their major field or to enroll in more appealing courses. No one truly regards a collection of disciplinary fragments as tantamount to systematically integrated bodies of learning. Nevertheless, it is not so much the breadth requirements per se that present a difficulty as their embodiment in what Americans understand as "courses of instruction" and "units."

"Courses," and what is elsewhere referred to as "modules," first developed in the United States, although they are now common in other national systems. Their introduction into American higher education allowed for greater concentration in the curriculum in response to the charge that the inherited compulsory curriculum was of school rather than university standard. Discrete modules also made possible the phenomenon of student transfer, essential to a belief in American democracy. But these gains have persistent drawbacks. Quality control cannot be guaranteed across the modules, wherever taken, and professors in a given module must both teach and examine, a combination avoided in other national systems where a student's ability to influence grading through personal intervention is prevented.

BEYOND THE DISTRIBUTION REQUIREMENTS

Numerous experiments have been undertaken in the United States to mitigate the drawbacks of the credit-unit system. Amongst them are team-taught courses where the burden of marking does not fall on one person, or interdisciplinary and multidisciplinary courses combining specialties or viewing problems from multiple subject perspectives. The Berkeley campus rather invidiously calls them "Big Ideas courses" (perhaps implying that ordinary courses never contain big ideas), but the resulting commitments are commendable, even imaginative. Team-taught courses—as many as three instructors—combine integrative biology and history; ethnic studies, law, and architecture; philosophy, law, and physics; molecular and cell biology and East Asian languages and cultures; public health, environmental engineering, statistics, and computer science.

When, decades ago, Clark Kerr dreamed of a curriculum for what he hoped would be the innovative residential colleges of the newly established University of California at Santa Cruz campus, he suggested courses on great themes— world peace, the role of religion, the failure of command economies, the "pathologies of industrial civilization"—to which all disciplines might contribute. He longed for a faculty that had a "genius for integration." Commenting on writings by Ortega y Gasset, Kerr fastened on "general culture" as the goal, downplaying both Great Books and distribution requirements and the tendency of faculty to heavily focus on issues of race, gender, and class, which were then (and still are) favored topics. He called his approach "horizontal" rather than "vertical" teaching.[23] His hope was unrealized, and he died disappointed in the failure of the Santa Cruz campus to develop creative undergraduate programs of study.

But mention should be made of other initiatives strengthening the Berkeley campus's commitment to the humanities. Special short seminars for all incoming freshman (and some sophomores) have been in existence since the 1980s. Taught by senior or emeriti faculty, they ease the new undergraduate's transition to more demanding work. They provide an alternative to larger classes and include a more personal touch, being limited to fifteen students in any one seminar. The seminars also function as an orientation to campus life and expectations but without the usual anxieties that regular courses generate. One might add that such efforts to reduce the impersonality of a large institution also recognize that today's undergraduates are socially and ethnically more highly diverse than ever before, and, often with little family preparation for higher education, can find the environment perplexing.

Another introduction of more recent origin is the integration of regularly taught courses with the enormous variety of performing arts created by the University's Cal Performances program, by any measure one of the finest presenting organizations in the world. Artists of national and global reputation provide some 125 performances on campus each year to audiences of 150,000.

It should be emphasized that these departures from standard modules recognize the imaginative use of teaching based on disciplinary specialization. They are also taking place against a background of continual concern over the funding of higher education. One conclusion must surely be that where faculty are strongly encouraged to provide a richer learning environment for undergraduates, the hurdles presented by budgetary considerations are not altogether insuperable, even within the large public research university.

A LEARNING ENVIRONMENT

A recent poll of 30,000 graduates by Purdue University and the Lumina Foundation concluded that undergraduates who engaged in extracurricular activities or who had ready access to faculty acquired a sense of personal satisfaction and enthusiasm that carried on long after leaving the university. If, as I have been suggesting, all forms of liberal education are in a sense the "arts of living," the former undergraduates responding to the survey have received a successful education. An equally significant finding is that no particular college or university, competitive or less so, private or public, large or small, faith-related or secular, has an inherent advantage over any other in generating a sense of personal worth.[24]

This finding reinforces a perception that the tone, the style, and the arrangements of space within that special American creation of the Romantic period, the "campus," must be included among the principal elements of a liberal education and a humanizing experience.[25] Low-rise structures, lawns, lakes, and historical references in the form of statues, iconography, and architectural follies and styles constitute comfortable allusions on a human scale. The overall effect is of an enchanted world created for the undergraduate, a world intended to stretch the imagination and appeal to the emotions. The feelings carry over into later life, and perhaps are best appreciated by alumni who return for annual festivities. Such inviting spaces and references are to be found in most American higher education institutions, although often competing with the bureaucratic structures more in keeping with an urban and technological civilization. Criticisms have recently emerged that colleges and universities spend more on student amenities than on the classroom itself, or, relatedly, that more resources are being employed to increase administrative and non-academic staff than to strengthen teaching. Nevertheless, the American campus planning tradition keeps alive a belief in the importance of buildings and grounds that are in themselves both humanizing and liberalizing. The idea of a campus is so successful that it has been emulated in all countries.

LIBERAL AND ILLIBERAL

I would like to close with a different point. I have mentioned the various forms of liberal education that have descended from the past, and I have cited some of the structural difficulties in achieving many of their ends. Contradictions abound. I also believe that our current obsession with issues of funding detracts from a consideration of the strengths, the possibilities, and in some cases the vigor of America's search for a liberal experience. Furthermore, too much time is spent on trivial subject classification schemes. The fact is that any subject can be taught as liberal or illiberal. It can be taught from personal or ideological preconceptions or from selfish interests. The history of learning provides many examples of teachers who managed to elevate their subjects and disciplines, gaining enthusiastic responses from their students. Even MOOCs can disseminate values and attitudes, goals, and aspirations that encourage a humanistic outcome. It is not the medium itself, but how that medium is used. As Roger Geiger points out in his contribution to this volume, if there is a crisis in the humanities, the academy itself must bear considerable responsibility. But I am rather of his opinion that students have not abandoned the desire to receive a liberal education; and, I would add, especially when the benefits are made clear.

NOTES

1. University of California Academic Senate, *The Senate Source*, 12 (April 2014), 1.
2. See William G. Bowen, Matthew M. Chingas and Michael S. McPherson, *Crossing the Finish Line: Completing College at America's Public Universities* (Princeton: Princeton University Press, 2010).
3. See the essays in Martin Trow, *Twentieth-Century Higher Education: From Elite to Mass to Universal*, ed. Michael Burrage (Baltimore, MD: Johns Hopkins University Press, 2010).
4. April 21, 2014 newsletter janet@ucop.edu.
5. For the analysis of the University of California student population, I rely on Sol Geiser, "Back to the Future: Freshman Admissions to the University of California, 1944 to the Present and Beyond," Research & Occasional Paper Series, Center for Studies in Higher Education, University of California, Berkeley (April 2014).
6. Ibid., 5–6, 12.
7. Ibid., 21–22.
8. "It Takes More Than a Major: Employer Priorities for College Learning and Student Success," *Association of American Colleges & Universities* 99 (Spring 2013): 22–29.
9. *Wall Street Journal*, November 11, 2013, R1–R2.

10. Hence I have renamed the liberal arts as the "living arts." Sheldon Rothblatt, *The Living Arts: The Academy in Transition: Comparative and Historical Reflections on Liberal Education* (Washington, DC: Association of American Colleges and Universities, 2003).

11. Joseph F. Kett, *Merit: A History of a Founding Ideal from the American Revolution to the 21st Century* (Ithaca, NY: Cornell University Press, 2013), 170.

12. See Caroline Robbins, *The Eighteenth-Century Commonwealthman; Studies in the Transmission, Development, and Circumstance of English Liberal Thought from the Restoration of Charles II until the War with the Thirteen Colonies* (New York: Atheneum, 1959); J.G.A. Pocock, *The Machiavellian Moment: Florentine Political Thought and the Atlantic Republican Tradition* (Princeton: Princeton University Press, 1975); Gladys Bryson, *The Science of Man in the Eighteenth Century as Exemplified in the Scottish Moral Philosophy* (Berkeley: University of California Press, 1930); Gordon S. Wood, *Revolutionary Characters: What Made the Founders Different* (New York: Penguin Press, 2006).

13. Kett, *Merit*; Richard Sennett, *The Fall of Public Man* (New York: Knopf, 1977).

14. It is disturbing to notice such alarming distinctions repeated by US academics and campus leaders today eager to establish overseas programs within the burgeoning universities of Communist China. "We must look at 'liberal' in the sense of broad, rather than free," Kay Kuok, a businesswoman who leads the Yale-N.U.S. governing board, told the government-controlled *Straits Times*. "It's freedom of thought; I'm not necessarily saying freedom of expression." Quoted in Jim Sleeper, "Liberal Education in Authoritarian Places," *New York Times*, September 1, 2013, 4.

15. Willa Cather's 1925 novel, *The Professor's House*, superbly captures the tension between the research mission and the juvenile university culture of the period.

16. Two recent reports discuss the prospects, uses, and some of the successes of online instruction. See Policy and Impact Committee of the Committee for Economic Development, *Boosting Postsecondary Education Performance* (Washington, DC, 2012); and Committee for Economic Development, *Boosting California's Postsecondary Education Performance, a Policy Statement and Call to Action* (Washington, DC, November 2013). But implicit in all such discussions is the sharp distinction between select and mass-access institutions where numbers matter more.

17. According to Joseph R. Levenson, *Confucian China and Its Modern Fate: The Problem of Intellectual Continuity* (Berkeley and Los Angeles: University of California Press, 1966), 170, Swift was preceded by Thomas Shadwell, who wrote the play *The Virtuoso*.

18. American Academy of Arts and Sciences, *The Heart of the Matter: The Humanities and Social Sciences for a Vibrant, Competitive, and Secure Nation* (Washington, DC, 2013).

19. Ibid., 23.

20. Burton Robert Clark, "The Problem of Complexity in Modern Higher Education," in *The European and American University since 1800*, ed. Sheldon Rothblatt and Björn Wittrock (Cambridge: Cambridge University Press, 1997), 263–279.

21. Lawrence Grossberg, "The Formations of Cultural Studies: an American in Birmingham," in *Relocating Cultural Studies, Developments in Theory and Research*, ed. Valda Blundell, John Shepherd, and Ian Taylor (London and New York: Routledge, 1993), 21–66.

22. And also raising the issue about the future of civic virtue, which developed in national contexts.

23. Sheldon Rothblatt, "Clark Kerr, Two Voices," in *Clark Kerr's World of Higher Education Reaches the 21st Century: Chapters in a Special History*, ed. Sheldon Rothblatt (Dordrecht: Springer, 2012), 35.

24. Reported in the Phi Beta Kappa, "State of the Arts & Sciences," e-mail bulletin of May 2014.

25. Sheldon Rothblatt, "Consult the *Genius* of the Place," in *The Modern University and Its Discontents: The Fate of Newman's Legacies in Britain and America* (Cambridge: Cambridge University Press, 1997), 50–105; and idem., "A Note on the 'Integrity' of the University," in *Aurora Torealis*, ed. Marco Beretta, Karl Grandin, and Svante Lindqvist (Sagamore Beach, CA: Science History Publications, 2008), 277–298. See also Stefan Muthesius, *The Postwar University: Utopianist Campus and College* (New Haven and London: Yale University Press, 2000).

3 · WE ARE ALL NONTRADITIONAL LEARNERS NOW

Community Colleges, Long-Life Learning, and Problem-Solving Humanities

KATHLEEN WOODWARD

In US public higher education, the twin values of accessibility and affordability, long prized historically, are today under grievous assault. Of the many dimensions of higher education that demand our consideration, I focus on two decisive demographic trends: 1) forging new relationships between public research universities and community colleges to address the challenge of sharply increasing racial, ethnic, and economic segregation; and 2) creating new opportunities for people who are older than the "traditional student" to participate in purposeful ways in what I call *long-life learning*. At stake are the goals of increasing diversity in, and the sustainability of, higher education, with students—including ourselves—recognized as perpetual nontraditional learners. In pursuing these dimensions of higher education, I am building on the catalyzing report recently issued by the American Academy of Arts and Sciences under the title *The Heart of the Matter*. To that end, I expand on the role of community colleges and the practice of life-long learning, both of which are mentioned in the report but do not receive sustained attention.[1]

How might we imagine "A New Deal for the Humanities" in these domains? I first take a brief step back in the history of public higher education in the United States, a history both inspiring and gravely marred by exclusion. In the conviction that we need a new educational system that is as integrated as undergraduate education should be, I then sketch a broad picture of the place of community colleges in higher education and underscore the need to serve learners beyond the traditional age. Finally, I turn to the role of the humanities in public research universities and suggest that the humanities have fundamental contributions to make to our most pressing public challenges; I offer two examples—the contemporary risk society and climate change. I thus do not begin with the humanities (I confess I find the word provincially academic and, when talking with people outside the academy, refer instead to the study of history, literature, art and media, and language). Nor do I engage what has become a defeating narrative of the decline of the humanities in terms of enrollments and of crisis.[2] The central theme running through my chapter is the power of combining the humanities, as a dimension of the liberal arts, and the practical arts.

KEY MOMENTS AND MOVEMENTS IN US EDUCATION

Congress passed the groundbreaking Morrill Act in 1862 in the midst of the Civil War with the noble vision of establishing public colleges and universities to serve their communities and create opportunities for higher education under the banner of what we now describe as accessibility and affordability.[3] Today one of the fundamental roles of our land-grant colleges and universities is characterized as *engagement* with our communities, with education and research having a civic dimension.[4] I would stress, however, that the distinctive educational mission of our public universities was envisioned *as combining the liberal arts and the practical arts.* As the legislation reads, the purpose of land-grant universities was conceived as promoting "the liberal and practical education of the industrial classes in the several pursuits and professions in life."[5] To this I will return. Eighty-two years later, the Servicemen's Readjustment Act of 1944, popularly known as the GI Bill, established reciprocity as a foundation of the social compact between citizens and the nation with regard to higher education. It was followed two decades later by the Higher Education Act of 1965, which created Pell Grants for undergraduates in financial need. These three moments in the history of US higher education represent high points of the progressive role that the federal government has played in higher education over the past 150 years.

But this history of inclusion is unfortunately notable for also being one of discrimination. There was a second Morrill Act. Passed in 1890, it specifically addressed segregation: states were obliged to demonstrate that race was not a factor in the admission of undergraduates to their land-grant colleges and, if it was, they were required to create separate institutions for students of color. Some historically black colleges and universities emerged from this provision.[6] In *Brown v. Board of Education* (1954), the Supreme Court declared it

unconstitutional for schools to segregate children on the basis of race, conclud-
ing that "separate" in and of itself conferred a stigma and therefore could not provide "equal" education.

Over the past thirty years and more, the progressive impulse of the federal
government with regard to higher education has diminished decisively, beginning with the election of Ronald Reagan as president in 1980. In the same period,
however, the role of the federal government in driving research in the sciences
and in health and medicine at public research universities has thrived. This
development I will not rehearse. Nor will I elaborate on our states' defunding
of our public research universities. This decline in public support accelerated
during the Great Recession that began in 2008, but it had been a long time in
the making; in fiscal year 2012–2013, for example, only 3 percent of the operating
budget of my university—the University of Washington—came from state support. This story of evaporating state support is well known. It is also complicated
by the fact that the federal government today allocates the significant sum of
$130 billion a year in direct grants as well as in subsidized and guaranteed loans
to students and their families.[7]

My basic point is this: if, unlike K–12 education, higher education has not
been conceived historically as a civil right, we have in the past prided ourselves,
and rightfully so, on the strengths of our higher-educational system—in great
part precisely because of its openness to the population at large. Higher education has traditionally been understood as a gateway to social mobility as well
as a necessary if not a sufficient condition for democracy to thrive. Today the
implicit promise of our higher-educational system is at serious risk of ruin,[8]
with many of our institutions effectively closed to poor and working-class
citizens because of prohibitively high tuition and fees. We are living in a risk
society where responsibility for the higher education of the majority of our
undergraduates—for education of the public—has effectively devolved from
the states to individuals and their families. Once a model for higher education in
other countries as well as a magnet for international students, US higher education is now ranked twelfth among developed nations.[9]

At the turn of the twentieth century, William Rainey Harper, the visionary first
president of the University of Chicago, imagined higher education as an ensem-
ble of institutions with pathways among them, including extension courses,
two-year community colleges, four-year regional colleges, and, of course, universities. The goal was to distribute opportunities for education widely and to avoid
exclusively drawing privilege to his university. Indeed, Harper is credited with
helping to found two-year colleges, whose mission mirrors that of the founding
purpose of our land-grant colleges: a combination of the practical or technical
arts and the liberal arts, an honorable conjoining of these two modes of learning. Today there are routes from comprehensive two-year colleges to four-year

colleges, suturing the two kinds of institutions together, at least in theory. But in reality our public research universities devote much more attention to the K–12 schools from which they draw most of their entering first-year students.[10]

DIVERSITY AND COMMUNITY COLLEGES: SEPARATE AND UNEQUAL

One of the clearest signs of the alarming inequities in higher education today is the vast divide between our two-year schools and our public research universities, one even analogous to the enormous economic divide between the 99 percent and the 1 percent. As income inequality has increased steeply over the past years, so too has educational opportunity. Our two-year schools are the canary in the coal mine, alerting us to a growing racial and economic divide. It may soon be a chasm.

Widely acknowledged to be overcrowded and underfunded, community colleges in the United States serve 44 percent of our undergraduates—almost half of all undergraduate college students.[11] They also serve nearly 50 percent of undergraduates of color in the United States. If the student population of community colleges is extremely racially and ethnically diverse, the proportion of low-income and working-class students has been increasing. As Eduardo Padrón, president of Miami Dade College, wrote in August 2013 in a letter to the *New York Times*, "46 percent of our students live beneath the federal poverty standard, and 67 percent are low income."[12] Everyone concerned with higher education should read the Century Foundation's sobering 2013 report on community colleges. Entitled *Bridging the Higher Education Divide*, the report alerts us to the vast disparities in public support of education on both the state and federal levels. Zeroing in on the extreme differences in direct federal support for community colleges, public four-year universities, and K–12 education, the report emphatically echoes *Brown v. Board of Education*: "separate" is not "equal."

Too many of us in public research universities remain unaware of this growing phenomenon. What was the response when President Barack Obama announced proposals in 2009, 2011, and 2012 to fund support for community colleges? No outpouring of enthusiasm that I could see from public research universities and no action by the US Congress. The palpable if inadvertent stigma attached to community colleges by people from different sectors can be seen virtually everywhere. Consider a *New York Times* March 2013 editorial lamenting the decline of the percentage of recent high school graduates who choose to attend California's public universities. Community colleges are mentioned only to be disdained as a bad choice in a throw-away line: "Other students have settled for poorly staffed, overcrowded community colleges and are unlikely to move on to four-year colleges."[13] Surely we should address head-on the worrisome condition of "poorly staffed, overcrowded community colleges" as a crucial component of our higher educational system, one that needs urgent attention, rather than scorn the students who have "settled" for them.

The stigma associated with community colleges can be seen as well in the way those of us in public research universities often frame the issues. It is common for us to measure support for public research universities in relation to private elite universities.[14] Consider, for instance, Wendy Brown's eloquent essay in the 2011 issue of *Representations* devoted to "The Humanities and the Crisis of the Public University."[15] Brown powerfully traces the collapse of public higher education as a foundation for social mobility and egalitarianism. She reminds us of the root meaning of "democracy" and the historical role of higher education to create an educated public, one central to an educated democracy: "Democracy: rule (*cracy*) of the people or poor (*demos*). Democracy is the name of a political form in which the people are sovereign, in which the whole, rather than merely a part, rules the polity and hence itself." Democracy in this sense has come to its end in our neoliberal economy.

Brown underscores the growing gap between "quality public universities" and "private elites." When she does refer to two-year schools, it is mainly to dismiss them, noting that they "largely remain institutions of vocational training for clerical, mechanical, and low-level health and service workers."[16] A similar vision of the community college emerges in *The Heart of the Matter*: "The community colleges that serve almost half of all students in higher education train men and women in job skills; but they also offer broader exposures that develop the talent for a lifetime of career advancement and often a desire for further education."[17] The "but" and the "often" are telling. Community colleges are perceived as predominantly vocational while liberal learning is associated with four-year colleges. In a sense, we have not moved very far from the Greeks in understanding the liberal arts for free citizens and technical arts for the enslaved.

As underfunded as they are, our community colleges are highly adaptable and expansive institutions. Much more is taking place at community colleges than low-level vocational training. Consider the city of Seattle's three community colleges, which enroll, along with an allied vocational institute, more than 50,000 students a year. (In writing this essay I learned that these colleges have excised "community" from their names; they are now North Seattle College, Central Seattle College, and South Seattle College.) Courses of study exist for those who wish to transfer to a four-year college. There is even a special pathway in the associate of arts degree track for Asian studies; also available are certificates of completion in film and video communications, database administration and development, biomedical equipment and technology, sustainable landscape management, and nanotechnology, among many possibilities. Most of these certificate programs offer associate of applied arts degrees that include general education. Quarter-long programs abroad are established in London, South Africa, Spain, Costa Rica, and Florence, Italy. There is in addition an immense array of continuing education courses, including courses in film noir and beginning Mandarin. Available too is worker retraining. Learning outcomes for the associate of arts degree—we would all applaud them—include understanding the "methods and modes of inquiry specific to traditional and contemporary areas of knowledge in the humanities and arts, natural and physical sciences, mathematics, and the social sciences," as well as understanding "the interdisciplinary nature of knowledge" and "the global society and processes of globalization from mostly, but not exclusively, non-Western and indigenous perspectives."[18]

Almost 40 percent of the students at Central Seattle College are enrolled in the college-transfer track. One of those students we hired recently as our administrative coordinator at the Simpson Center for the Humanities, where I serve as director. She had transferred to the University of Washington in her junior year and graduated two years later with a bachelor's degree in the Comparative History of Ideas, our interdisciplinary—and intellectually creative—major in the humanities. When I asked her to characterize the transition to the university, her answer that it was "difficult" did not surprise me. But the reasons did, hitting home my own misguided preconceptions: she found the shift from smaller classes at Central Seattle College to such large classes at the University of Washington daunting, and she missed what was for her easy access to and outstanding guidance from her professors at Central Seattle. I want to add that at the same time she was attending Central Seattle, she also took courses in psychology from North Seattle College as well as from Bellevue College because the three colleges taken together provided a challenging array in her discipline and because it was (bureaucratically) easy to take classes at all three institutions.

What can those of us in public research universities do to create bridges between our institutions and community colleges? To bring our kinds of institutions closer together? The leadership of our public research universities can insist that this is a crucial value and create formal articulation agreements. As faculty we can educate our doctoral students about the rapidly evolving landscape of higher education and call particular attention to community colleges.[19] My hope is that more of our doctoral students will wish to teach in community colleges and ultimately will.

This is an especially propitious time for those of us in public research universities to turn our attention to two-year schools. The mission of two-year schools is expanding to include more purposively the liberal arts; we are also seeing a trend in two-year schools offering four-year degrees in selected fields and dropping the adjective "community" in the process.[20] At the same time, in four-year colleges and in research universities (both public and private), much attention is being devoted to the skills our students need for the workplace, with competency-based education complementing in-class learning.[21] My point is that the educational purposes of these kinds of institutions are not as divergent as they once were perceived to be. Humanistic skills are needed at all levels of higher education as are technological skills of all kinds. And "vocational" needs to be rescued from contempt. The study of the humanities and the development of skills for the workplace should not be understood as being in opposition to each other. That would entail a dubious argument at best. Pragmatically, it is foolish, perhaps even suicidal.

Anecdotally, I can testify that there are doctoral students at my university and elsewhere who are pursuing degrees in the humanities—in history and in the modern languages and literatures—whose ambition is precisely to teach in a two-year school. They typically keep that wish to themselves, fearing a backlash from their advisors (I am not being melodramatic: "fear" is the right word for what many of them experience—and not without justification). Because many doctoral students in the humanities are motivated by matters of social justice, they correctly regard teaching in two-year schools as working in underserved communities. In addition, as we all know, budgetary constraints at public research universities have resulted in the contraction of tenure-track positions. At the same time, demographic predictions reveal that the number of "traditional-age" students seeking four-year schools will decline in the near future while enrollments at two-year schools are growing.

Objections may be raised that a doctorate, with its focus on research, is not required to teach in a two-year college and that the long time to degree militates against envisioning a future at two-year schools (in the humanities the national median time to a doctoral degree is an appalling 9.0 years).[22] To this, I would respond that departments and indeed entire institutions of higher education across the United States are involved today in recalibrating their doctoral programs to offer degrees that can be completed in five years. To this, I would also respond that both the breadth and research focus of a doctoral degree provide invaluable skills for professors who want to inspire students in two-year schools to undertake complex projects in the future.[23] Finally, I would point to one of the recommendations in the new report from the Modern Language Association's Task Force on Doctoral Study in Modern Language and Literature.[24] The report urges doctoral programs to enable their students to gain expertise in different kinds of teaching, with the corollary that doctoral students be introduced to the wide spectrum of institutions across higher education with their different histories, missions, and student demographics. The community college is one of those important institutions.

What can we do to encourage interest in community colleges among our doctoral students? In our departments we can hold mentoring sessions for them with faculty from community colleges.[25] Across our departments we can set up working groups of faculty and graduate students on community colleges, as I hope to do. We can urge our professional associations to create task forces on two-year colleges and to purposively include faculty members from two-year colleges on their executive councils, as the Modern Language Association has done. As the director of a humanities center, I can encourage faculty members and graduate students to develop projects with their counterparts in two-year schools (I'm pleased to report that our Simpson Center for the Humanities recently received a four-year grant from the Mellon Foundation which will provide our doctoral students in the humanities with the opportunity to shadow faculty members at North Seattle College, Seattle Central College, and South Seattle College over the course of an academic year). I want to see strengthened, in both our community colleges *and* our research universities, the model that the founding legislation for land-grant colleges underscored 150 years ago: the need for both the practical arts and the liberal arts in a single institution.

LONG-LIFE LEARNING, SUSTAINING LEARNING

The vision of college as a four-year degree for eighteen- to twenty-one-year-olds on a residential campus remains entrenched in the imagination of many of us in higher education. By and large that is the model of a college education pervading *The Heart of the Matter*. Although lifelong learning is mentioned in the report, it is conceptualized as basically taking place after completing one's education at a four-year college. Learning that comes later is represented as largely untethered to educational institutions and attached instead to cultural institutions—history museums, art galleries, and festivals devoted to the arts and humanities. In this view, postbaccalaureate education and learning are more serendipitous than purposeful, a form of educational tourism or a truncated version of the Grand Tour of Europe undertaken in centuries past.[26] College remains envisioned predominantly for the late adolescent who will become an adult in the course of an education at a residential college. The humanities are defended, often in overblown rhetoric, on the grounds that they provide the strong foundation that will serve people well through all the days of their lives: these young adults, having learned how to learn, having mastered the art of asking the right critical questions, and having become skilled in expressing themselves in writing, will be able to face the future with confidence and aplomb. As we read in *The Heart of the Matter*, although here the language is prosaic rather than soaring, "the liberal arts train people to adapt and change over a lifetime."[27]

At the same time, everywhere we hear that we are living in an innovation economy, one characterized by the rapid coevolution of globalization and communication technologies. We hear that we can expect to change careers at least five times, maybe more, over a lifetime, and, in point of fact, on average people in the United States change jobs every four years. Whole new fields and kinds of jobs—ones we could not have imagined—will be created in the future. It is undeniable that we will *all* have to acquire new skills. We will not be able to rely solely on having learned how to learn. We will all need some systematic way to gain knowledge of new and required competencies. The humanities will have much to contribute: in the process of ongoing and rapid change, new concepts and new histories will be needed. A prime example is the digital humanities: as faculty, we need to learn new skills (including, as an example, multi-modal composition, not just *writing*), so that we can teach with these new tools and deploy them in our research; we also need to understand the historical and epistemological dimensions of the digital revolution in communication, including scholarly communication, to name only two aspects of it. Education guided toward a goal—the liberal arts allied with the practical arts—will become increasingly more common, or at least more necessary, even more urgent, than it is now. Education should not and cannot be limited to one part of the life course. This is what I mean by *sustaining education.* We are all nontraditional students now.

Higher education is no longer confined to campus or to young adults. Today only some 15 percent of undergraduates attend a four-year college or university full-time and live on campus.[28] Higher education is being pursued by people of all ages, a practice that will certainly accelerate in the future, and in a wide variety of institutions, including corporate universities and online learning. Louis Soares, who works with the American Council on Education, calls attention to the fact that there are eighty million people aged twenty-five to sixty-four who lack postsecondary credentials and who want to attain them while balancing family and work with education. Soares calls these students posttraditional learners. (He should not have stopped at the age of sixty-four, however, since many people older than that want and need to work, and many of them need higher education too.)

In 2010, 6.1 million students were enrolled in at least one online course in the United States.[29] That seems an epoch ago, with public universities left and right since then creating more opportunities for online learning. Consider that the Georgia Institute of Technology, a public research university, announced in 2013 the development of an online master's degree in computer science that will be low cost and is expected to attain the scale of a massive open online course. Created in partnership with the for-profit Udacity, this degree launched in 2014. In the state of Washington, there are more than 900,000 adults who have attended college but not attained degrees. My own university is developing a series of online completion degrees for those who have begun college-level work; the first, a BA, is in Early Childhood and Family Studies and launched in the fall of 2013. To those who have not completed their four-year degrees we need to consider those who have already been awarded their BAs and who wish to pursue more education. While interviewing three people recently for a fiscal administrative position at the Simpson Center, I was struck that two candidates were taking courses online; one had a BA, the other, three master's degrees from professional schools.

I've thus shifted the commonly accepted emphasis from *lifelong* learning to *long-life* learning to draw attention to the momentous difference that the increase in life expectancy over the course of the last 150 years has made. When the Morrill Act was passed in 1862, the average life expectancy for both men and women was forty-three years; in 2010, it was seventy-nine."[30] The transformation of higher education is occurring not just because of what we have come to call the digital revolution or because of globalization, but also because of the longevity revolution with the stunning demographic change it entails. The implications of this demographic change for the future of higher education require our close attention just as intently as do other dimensions of diversity, including racial, ethnic, and economic divides in the United States.[31] If the social script for major life events—graduating from high school, getting a college degree, marrying, having children, retiring—had a predictable sequence with chronologically defined points in the past, that is no longer the case. (Indeed, fewer people can afford to retire.) Everyone will need to learn new skills at different points. Mark Huddleston, the president of the University of New Hampshire, put it this way in testimony before the state Finance Committee: the "need for education and skill renewal," he said, is "constant and society-wide."[32] In addition to new skills, we all need to learn new ways of thinking about matters that should matter to us all. For it is certain that participating as world citizens in societies of the future will require more education over our lifetimes as we confront a host of challenges, including climate change, the explosion of new biological knowledge that allows us to manipulate living systems, and social injustice writ large across the continents, to name just three.

Every college and university needs to invent new ways to model education across the life course. How can we in public research universities open our doors to older students both at the level of the bachelor's degree and beyond? Online education is one way. Beyond the BA degree available through online learning in Early Childhood and Family Studies at my university, we are also developing courses in an online completion degree program in the social sciences. I would in addition like to see public research universities develop more flexibility in on-campus programs and in hybrid digital/face-to-face programs at the undergraduate and graduate levels to accommodate people whose work and family lives need more supple educational structures: we need to consider weekend and summer programs as well as an expansion of evening degree programs. I would like to see collaboration between continuing education programs—an

honorable branch of universities that the professoriate often disregards—
and regular degree programs, with more certificates offered. Faculty from the
humanities must play an active role in planning these curricular changes.

If those of us in public research universities don't make these changes, other
institutions will be created and practices invented to offer what is needed.[33] A
case in point is the new initiative entitled Open Badges, underwritten by the
MacArthur Foundation. Its purpose is to spur new ways of accounting for—that
is to say, certifying or credentialing—learning that is both academic and technical, but gained outside of the conventional curricula of higher-educational
institutions. Partnering with the MacArthur Foundation are Mozilla, the free
software community, and HASTAC, the international consortium devoted to
learning in a digital age cofounded by humanities scholars and higher-education
activists Cathy Davidson and David Theo Goldberg. While the label "badges"
has struck some as lacking the gravitas required by higher education, it is a salutary concept. We must find ways to recognize the achievements in learning that
take place outside our difficult-to-change public research universities.[34]

In general, what is needed is more articulation—and more formal articulation agreements—among different kinds of institutions of higher education,
articulation similar to that envisioned by the president of the University of Chicago more than a hundred years ago, with more modular opportunities in addition to distinctly defined pathways (the opportunity to take a minor at a public
research university without having to be enrolled in a major or graduating; the
minor could be conceived as a certificate in such a case). In *College (Un)Bound:
The Future of Higher Education and What It Means for Students*, Jeffrey Selingo
makes a persuasive case for "unbundling" college offerings (as an analogy we
may reference consumers who wish to unbundle the cable channels to which
they subscribe). Just as imperative is more collaboration among similar institutions (joint doctoral programs in the humanities at research universities, for
example). We accept with ease the importance of the interoperability of digital
tools. They need to communicate with each other and work together to create
assemblages that are informational and intellectual ecosystems. Similarly, we need
interoperability in institutions of higher education; we need interfaces that work.
Metropolitan transportation systems—busses and subway systems alike—have
created transfer arrangements. University libraries have formed collaborative networks with regional institutions. We need to imagine what such interlocking and
collaborative systems might look like across the large horizon that is higher education. But at present the relationships among institutions are largely unwork-
able for would-be students who want recombinant higher education. Students
are like Alice in Wonderland attempting to play croquet with a flamingo, trying
to transfer credits between one institution and another, or endeavoring to craft
a major out of courses taken at different kinds of institutions—or even the same

institution. Taken together, our higher-educational institutions should be *mobilizing networks*, not discrete entities.[35] Our public research universities must be accessible and affordable. They must also be adaptable. We have constructed elaborate organizations whose bureaucratic structures are largely byzantine. They must be simplified. And they must build bridges to other institutions.

PUBLIC POLICY, PROBLEM-SOLVING HUMANITIES, AND ZONES OF INQUIRY

I have written elsewhere about the future of the humanities, stressing our need as scholars in the humanities to reimagine our research and to find ways to take our scholarship public.[36] This is crucial: in the humanities, narrow specialization and professionalization are strangling us. Along with Bethany Nowviskie, who has a chapter in this volume, I recently participated in a series of workshops devoted to graduate education in the humanities sponsored by the University of Virginia's Scholarly Communication Institute; one of the capacities we fervently believe needs to be highlighted in doctoral education is collaboration (John McGowan also stresses collaboration in his chapter in this volume on the medical humanities). If I have focused less in the previous pages on a new deal for the humanities than might have been expected, it is because I wanted first to step back and view the transformation of higher education across multiple institutions and in light of economic, demographic, and digital change. In the process, I've come to regard a four-year education at a residential college as a luxury. I've come to appreciate the innovations of community colleges.

Allow me to return again to the Morrill Act of 1862, which promoted, in its words, "the liberal and practical education of the industrial classes in the several pursuits and professions in life." How might we recast this in terms of the humanities for the twenty-first century? First, we must challenge the unbridgeable intellectual divide in the minds of many in public research universities, not only between universities and community colleges, but also *in* the university between the humanities and professional schools—medicine, law, engineering, nursing, social welfare, information, and agriculture, among them. The humanities need to be distributed across the university in terms of research and in terms of teaching. Second, following from the first, we need to embrace the idea of applied humanities. Many who passionately defend the study of the humanities in higher education do so by divorcing what is represented as the learning of lowly skills from an education in the loftier intellectual capacities critical to a flourishing democracy, a divorce I find impoverishing. This is how Geoffrey Harpham puts it in an essay that largely turns on the importance of research in the humanities: "The humanities anchor liberal education, the goal of which is not the acquisition of a skill or a set of facts, but rather the fostering of the

experience of intellectual and evaluative freedom that can support the formation of a democratic citizenry capable of self-directed innovation and adaptation."[37] While I understand the case that Harpham is making, to my mind this
suggests, in practice, a misguided disparagement of professional schools and of
the work that faculty and graduate students in the humanities and professional
schools can do together. The acquisition of skills should be honored. I can still
remember Stanley Chodorow, then provost at the University of Pennsylvania, at
an annual meeting of ACLS some fifteen years ago recommending that people
in the humanities engage the professions, with the potential that such collaboration might "draw us into intellectual work that will have wide influence in society."[38] Some followed his lead; law and literature flourished for some years. But
by and large, his call was ignored. I agreed with him then and I do now.

As I have been stressing, as members of public research universities, we need
to underscore the word *public* in terms of access; that includes people of minimal
economic means, people beyond the age of the "traditional" student, and people
who require flexibility in terms of time (and of course, these can be one and the
same). Another key way of thinking of the humanities in *public* research universities is in terms of *public policy.* We can model the combination of the liberal
and the practical arts that was crucial to the founding of our land-grant universities by creating interdisciplinary *zones of inquiry*—this is Mark Taylor's excellent
term—around issues of *public policy,* broadly construed. These zones of inquiry
would include faculty members from the humanities and across the liberal arts
as well as the professions.[39] I am imagining these zones of inquiry as short-lived
curricula—five to ten years, renewable, with mini-modules open to many; they
would complement rather than substitute for majors at the undergraduate level
(although enrollment in these zones in the humanities and social sciences might
outstrip enrollment in disciplinary majors); certificates could be offered at the
graduate level.[40] Devoted to matters of policy ranging from national security and
human rights to health and illness, and climate change around the globe, to name
a few prominent areas, these zones would be oriented toward change and the
future, meeting students where they are; study—and practice as appropriate—
would be grounded in the present with an inflection toward the future and with
a goal of inspiring a turn to the past, affording historical understanding. These
zones of inquiry would focus on urgent problems and bring faculty together who
do not normally collaborate.

Many of us have refused to embrace the language of problem-solving as one of
the roles of the humanities, declaring, almost self-righteously, that in the humanities we raise questions instead and insisting that many dimensions of the human
condition are not in fact problems that can be solved. We should no longer
shrink from the language of problem-solving. Today's public research university
is characterized by an ethos of interdisciplinarity and a commitment to address

the pressing problems of our world—locally, regionally, nationally, globally—as well as a commitment to undertake basic research. We should embrace the commitment to address the pressing problems of our world. They are urgent and we should not be daunted by the charge of presentism from people in the humanities, especially since providing historical framing would no doubt be one of our essential contributions. For as scholars, thinkers, and teachers in the humanities, our role is to provide telling contexts and illuminating examples, to create large frames and to look closely at individual cases, and to create spaces for thought and occasions for feeling that are intertwined. I offer two examples of potential zones of inquiry.

First and briefly, "risk," which is a mega-keyword in contemporary culture. Imagine a zone of inquiry on the risk society, with modules devoted to the financialization of everyday life and the history of the derivative; the implicit values embedded in statistical thinking and the quantified self; scenarios and accounts of catastrophe, including narratives of illness at the level of the individual and on the scale of global pandemics; comparative histories of accounting and of economic theory about the regulation of markets; affect and risk (I have coined the term "statistical panic"); and, importantly, alternatives to the all-pervasive discourse of risks and benefits.[41]

Second, at more length, consider climate change as a zone of inquiry. Climate change requires decisive, strong, and proactive public policies extending from the microlevel to the global scale. Research universities are uniquely equipped to address climate change and other complex issues of public policy because of the breadth and depth of their faculty, including faculty in the arts and literature, religious studies, philosophy, and geography, as well as economics and the sciences. And history.

In fact it is an historian in the United States—Dipesh Chakrabarty—who has provided the inspiration for many in the academy to turn their attention to climate change.[42] He was well known for his work in postcolonial and subaltern studies; climate change was a new departure for him. Chakrabarty has been in conversation with scientists, policy makers, and engineers. He has read the work of paleontologists and reports issued from the United Nations on development and the planet. He has thought deeply about what is called the "climate justice" position (abbreviated as the West versus the Rest). He understands the terrible irony by which the economic developments of the last two hundred and fifty years, a period that also witnessed the Enlightenment and struggles for democracy around the world, unintentionally caused the phenomenon of global warming. For Chakrabarty, global warming is the shadow that falls on the promise of civilization and its performance over the last two and a half centuries. For him, given human agency at the center of the environmental crisis, the distinction between natural history and human history has collapsed. It is a momentous paradigm change.

As Chakrabarty has argued, making a convincing case for public policy related to climate change is undermined by a failure of the human imagination—both collective and individual—to comprehend simultaneously three vastly different scales of time: geological time on the scale of thousands of years, historical time on the scale of two hundred and fifty years, and the embodied time of the individual, limited as it seems to be to several generations. Thus one of the pressing questions is: how do we bring into the fold of our imagination a future that is so distant with generation upon generation upon generation threatened by our past actions and by what we will do in the near future? How can we imagine what we seem constitutionally as human beings not to be able to envision? How can we come to care, to feel forcefully and not just cognitively, that humans—*we*—are making a decisive, not to say catastrophic, difference of geological proportions—and do something about it? This is work for the humanities: to create occasions for feeling as well as to create spaces for thought.

Many of the humanities centers at colleges and universities around the world are contributing to the study of climate change under the aegis of the Anthropocene. Through groups of fellows, visiting speaker series, conferences, workshops, and websites, they are demonstrating the vital contributions the humanities can make. But generally speaking, such programs of collaboration and creativity last only for a year. A major step would be to create interdisciplinary zones of inquiry that sustain teaching and research over longer periods in areas of public policy. The Consortium of Humanities Centers and Institutes (CHCI), an international organization of some two hundred humanities centers around the world, is experimenting with such a model. Its annual conference in 2012, organized by Debjani Ganguly, director of the Humanities Research Centre at the Australian National University, was on the subject of the Anthropocene. With funding from the Mellon Foundation, the CHCI is supporting a global network of "observatories" (I like this imaginative term)—each of them a zone of inquiry uniting institutions of higher education in a geographical region—with all the participants collaborating under the rubric of Humanities for the Environment. The three observatories are located in Australia, Europe, and North America (the latter is further articulated into three regional clusters—the Southeast, West, and Northeast). To cite an example of the work in progress: the theme of the Observatory in Australia is "Caring for Country," with a focus on the humanistic tradition of an indigenous ethic in relation to the land from 1768 to 2012 and a reimagining of nature in the Australia-Pacific region.

The biologist Rafe Sagarin has written in his remarkable book *Learning from the Octopus* that adaptation emerges from leaving one's comfort zone.[43] Let's create zones of inquiry in our public research universities—they would require us to leave comfort zones that have in fact grown dispiriting—and join others in collaborating on matters of urgent concern: policies for publics. This would be to take up Grand Challenges, as *The Heart of the Matter* explicitly urges to do. In analogy to Big Science, this would be Big Humanities. It would also be Practical Humanities. And Public Humanities. Humanities for the Public.

IN CONCLUSION

We are in the midst of a tectonic upheaval in higher education, facing a future in which the constellation of educational institutions will be radically transformed—online learning is becoming a decisive part of the mix—as well as a profound shift in the populations who will both want and require education.[44] What that future will look like, and who will share in it, depends in great part on what we do. There are encouraging signs—ideas and actions—regarding change. Here are two of them. First, Todd Presner has recently suggested—it is both an inventive and a practical idea—that we expand the time frame for what I have been calling a zone of inquiry. Under the unforgettable term "the twenty-year dissertation," he proposes that universities establish large-scale, multi-, and interdisciplinary research programs in the humanities to which we would commit ourselves for a period of time—say, twenty years.[45] Doctoral students would be admitted into these programs and their doctoral research would constitute a contribution to this area of study; over a period of twenty years would emerge a robust body of interconnected research. One of Presner's prime examples is critical inquiry related to the era of the Anthropocene—in shorthand, climate change. Second, a new alliance in higher education has recently been created to establish pathways for honors students in community colleges—the program is called American Honors—to four-year colleges and universities, both public and private, with twenty-seven colleges and universities across the country participating, including Amherst College, Stanford University, Smith College, Whittier College, George Mason University, and the University of Puget Sound; the program was founded by Quad Learning, a for-profit company. I expect more colleges and universities will join; I hope to see more public research universities in the mix.

Public research universities—these institutions were established for the education of members of the *public* and to undertake research for the *public good*—have a special obligation to serve their communities and to take the lead in higher education. I understand the mission of our public research universities to be the promotion of "the general welfare," to echo the words of the preamble to the US Constitution. I take pride in the mission of public research universities to create social and cultural goods, not just benefits for individuals, and to serve our communities which today stretch from the local and regional to the whole earth. Unfortunately, today a university education is regarded by many Americans predominantly as a private benefit and as an investment on the part of individuals.

We need to reclaim our mission and transform ourselves in the process, embracing the liberal arts *and* the practical arts and creating a true *system* of higher education, with institutions articulated each to the other across scales—local, regional, national, global. We need to foster change that is clear-sighted, deliberative, and progressive. We need a new deal first and foremost for the *idea* of the public good and we need to put it into practice: this would be a public policy *for* the humanities.

NOTES

1. I am grateful to Gordon Hutner and Feisal Mohamed for their invitation to the stimulating September 2013 conference on the liberal arts, the humanities, and the future of public higher education that they organized at the University of Illinois, as well as for their discerning comments on my essay, which emerged from it.

2. Michael Bérubé and James F. English have shown that the narrative is flawed, based on the selection of the years examined and the data available, but the narrative of decline just keeps getting repeated and repeated; see Bérubé, "The Humanities, Declining? Not According to the Numbers," *Chronicle of Higher Education*, July 1, 2013, available at http://chronicle.com; and English, "Who Says English Is a Dying Discipline?," *Chronicle of Higher Education*, September 17, 2012, available at http://chronicle.com.

3. Actually, not all land-grant universities are public, with Cornell University and the Massachusetts Institute of Technology being prime examples. And, surprising to me, one university I assumed was a land-grant university is not: the University of Washington.

4. At the Symposium on the University Presidency held at the Ohio State University on August 30, 2013, the two university presidents who responded to the question of whether the mission of land-grant universities remained relevant today—Elson Floyd (Washington State University) and Teresa Sullivan (University of Virginia)—answered yes, with the language of engagement. Available at http://trustees.osu.edu/presidentialsearch/symposium-on-the-university-presidency.html.

5. A longer excerpt from the Morrill Act of 1862 reads: "the leading object shall be, without excluding other scientific and classical studies, and including military tactics, to teach such branches of learning as are related to agriculture and the mechanic arts, in such manner as the legislatures of the States may respectively prescribe, in order to promote the liberal and practical education of the industrial classes in the several pursuits and professions in life." See a transcript of the law at http://ourdocuments.gov/doc.php?flash=true&doc=33&page=transcript.

6. In 1994 the Equity in Education Land-Grant Status Act was passed, providing thirty-three tribal colleges for Native Americans land-grant status; interestingly, these tribal colleges comprise a mix of higher education institutions, including four-year colleges and community colleges as well as institutions that offer graduate-level programs and courses.

7. This figure is cited in Robert Zemsky, *A Checklist for Change: Making American Higher Education a Sustainable Enterprise* (New Brunswick: Rutgers University Press, 2013), 204. The figure is cited as 45% in an October piece in the *New York Times*, the first in a three-part series on community colleges. See Ginia Bellafante, "Community College Students Face a Very Long Road to Graduation," *New York Times*, October 3, 2014, available at http://www.nytimes.com.

8. I am echoing Bill Readings's influential book *The University in Ruins*, although I confess when I reread it I was surprised by the degree to which he set the humanities, with its traditions of thought, in opposition to and virtually in alienation from other educational pursuits in universities. See Readings, *The University in Ruins* (Cambridge, MA: Harvard University Press, 1996); see also Chris Lorenz, "If You're So Smart, Why Are You under Surveillance? Universities, Neoliberalism, and New Public Management," *Critical Inquiry* 38.3 (Spring 2012): 599–629.

9. This figure is cited in Jeffrey Selingo, *College (Un)Bound: The Future of Higher Education and What It Means for Students* (Boston: Houghton Mifflin Harcourt, 2013), ix.

10. There are welcome efforts to create pathways between two-year institutions and public research universities. Launched in the fall of 2013, the Pathways initiative at the City University of New York is one, notable in addition for the controversy it engendered over faculty governance in relation to curricular matters. The Interstate Passport Initiative, which involves sixteen institutions ranging from two-year colleges to public research universities in four states (Hawaii, North Dakota, Oregon, and Utah) is another, ambitious in its articulation of collaboration among states with students transferring *competencies*, not *credits*.

11. This figure is cited in *Bridging the Higher Education Divide: Strengthening Community Colleges and Restoring the American Dream*, Century Foundation Task Force on Preventing Community Colleges from Becoming Separate and Unequal (Century Foundation, 2013), 3.

12. *New York Times*, August 6, 2013, available at http://www.nytimes.com.

13. "Resurrecting California's Public Universities," Editorial, *New York Times*, March 30, 2013, available at http://www.nytimes.com.

14. Christopher Newfield notes, for example, "The most important trend in the last thirty years has been the growing inequality between private and public universities"; he does, however, mention community colleges as part of the higher educational mix, observing that they "are about basic employability, but not about social mobility"; referencing the knowledge economy, he coins the term "cognitariat" in analogy with the proletariat. See Christopher Newfield, "The Structure and Silence of Cognitariat," *Edufactory WebJournal* (January 2010): 15, available at http://www.edu-factory.org/edu15/webjournal/no/Newfield.pdf.

15. Wendy Brown, "The End of Educated Democracy," special issue on "The Humanities and the Crisis of the Public University," *Representations* 116.1 (Fall 2011): 19–41.

16. See ibid., 23, 26, and 31. The American Association of Community Colleges reported in September 2014 that in 2012 as many associate degrees were awarded in the liberal arts and sciences, with graduates intending to transfer to a four-year college, as in the health professions and business, marketing, and management. See "What Are Students Majoring In?" *DataPoints*, American Association of Community Colleges (September 2014), available at http://www.aacc.nche.edu. Colleen Lye, Christopher Newfield, and James Vernon stress that higher education should be seen as a civil right and that "systemic solutions" need to be found "across all tiers of public higher education" and common cause needs to be made with K–12; see their "Humanists and the Public University," Intr. to special issue on "The Humanities and the Crisis of the Public University," *Representations* 116.1 (Fall 2011): 1–18. For a discussion of community colleges as part of the California Master Plan for Higher Education, see Bob Meister, "Debt and Taxes: Can the Financial Industry Save Public Universities?" *Representations* 116.1 (Fall 2011): 128–155.

17. Commission on the Humanities and Social Sciences, *The Heart of the Matter: The Humanities and Social Sciences for a Vibrant, Competitive, and Secure Nation* (American Academy of Arts and Sciences, 2013), 13, available at https://www.amacad.org/default.aspx.

18. See http://seattlecolleges.com/DISTRICT/catalog/printcatalogs.aspx, 5.

19. For-profit institutions of higher education are also part of the mix, with their enrollments increasing as students transfer down. Meister examines the higher educational system in

California, where an increase in tuition at the University of California campuses results in a relay of transfers, with students ultimately transferring from community colleges to for-profit institutions; students from minority populations are disproportionally part of that relay.

20. See Rob Jenkins, "So Long, 'Community Colleges'?" *Chronicle of Higher Education*, September 29, 2011, available at http://chronicle.com. Located just east of Seattle, Bellevue College, formerly called Bellevue Community College (it changed its name in 2009), offers eight BAs.

21. Consider the example of Stanford University, which recently reconfigured its introductory undergraduate courses in response to the perceived crisis in the humanities and in the conviction that it is crucial to emphasize skills and competencies in the broadest sense, including the appraisal of problems and thus capacities for (re)framing problems and solving problems. In the past, Stanford had general education requirements based on sampling disciplines; the new requirements—Ways of Thinking/Ways of Doing—are based on eight capacities: aesthetic and interpretive inquiry, social inquiry, scientific method and analysis, formal reasoning, applied quantitative reasoning, engaging diversity, ethical reasoning, and creative expression.

22. The Survey of Earned Doctorates, released in 2014 with the figures for 2012, reported the time to degree (from start to completion) for all disciplines in the humanities at 9.0 years. While there are many reasons that can be cited for such a lengthy time to degree (among them, research in archives in other countries, the mastering of uncommonly taught languages, the necessity of working part-time), 9.0 years is simply too long given the many costs (personal, social, economic, institutional) involved. See the *Report of the MLA Task Force on Doctoral Study in Modern Language and Literature* (New York: Modern Language Association, 2014), 3–4, available at http://www.mla.org.

23. Allow me to refer to the experience of Brian Gutierrez, a doctoral candidate in English at the University of Washington who for the past several years has taught courses (predominantly composition courses) at North Seattle College. Recently asked to give a lecture at North Seattle College on how what he teaches is related to his research for his dissertation, he framed his remarks in relation to digital humanities and critical pedagogy. His experience reveals that intensive research is valued at this institution—in great part as a way of showing students the larger horizon of higher education.

24. I was a member of this Task Force, which, in addition to advocating for shortening time to the doctoral degree to five years, also recommends that we identify paths to careers in addition to college and university teaching and develop ways for our students to acquire digital literacies for the twenty-first century. Perhaps the most important recommendation is that our doctoral programs expand the spectrum of possible forms of the culminating research project, commonly called the dissertation, beyond the proto-print book. See *Report of the MLA Task Force on Doctoral Study*.

25. If I were in the Department of History at the University of Washington I would want to introduce our doctoral students to Amy Kinsel, a tenured-faculty member at nearby Shoreline Community College who holds a doctorate in history from Cornell University. I quote from an e-mail she sent to the University of Washington's AAUP listserv on May 8, 2014 on the subject of "College, the Great Unequalizer," referring to a story in the *New York Times*: ". . . teaching at a community college can be extraordinarily rewarding. Students choose to attend community colleges for a number of reasons, but my observation is that the most significant of these are that they are not academically or emotionally prepared to enter a four-year institution, that their personal and work lives are too complicated for them to enroll anywhere as full-time students, or they do not have the financial resources or financial stability to enroll immediately at a four-year institution.

I see my role largely as preparing students who are not yet ready, for whatever reason, to attend a four-year institution to succeed once they get there. My colleagues and I work very hard to maintain academic standards that will allow our transfer students to enroll in upper-division classes at the UW and perform well. Having sent hundreds of students to the UW successfully at this point in my career, I will happily argue that our transfer program provides opportunities for students to earn baccalaureate degrees that would simply have not been possible for them without the access and support provided by community college preparation."

26. This section of *The Heart of the Matter* refers to online learning as well.

27. *The Heart of the Matter*, 32.

28. *The Condition of Education 2010*, U.S. Department of Education, Institute of Education Sciences, National Center for Education Statistics (2010); qtd. in Louis Soares, "Post-traditional Learners and the Transformation of Postsecondary Education: A Manifesto for College Leaders," American Council on Education (January 2013), available at http://louissoares.com.

29. *Going the Distance: Online Education in the United States*, Report of the Sloan Foundation: The Sloan Consortium (2011), available at http://www.onlinelearningsurvey.com/reports/goingthedistance.pdf.

30. I base the figure of forty-three years on my reading of a Life Expectancy Graph 1850–2000 from the University of Oregon (available at http://mappinghistory.uoregon.edu/english/US/US39-01.html).

31. Barbara Vacarr, former president of Goddard College, has called our aging population the new frontier of higher education. See Vacarr, "An Aging America: Higher Education's New Frontier," *The Chronicle of Higher Education*, December 8, 2014, available at http://chronicle.com. In terms of racial demographic change we need to take into account the growth of the Latino population; it is projected that in the 2040s the Latino/a population will pass 30 percent while the non-Hispanic white population will decline, falling below 50 percent. See Matthew Countryman, "Diversity and Democratic Engagement: Civic Education and the Challenge of Inclusivity," in *Civic Provocations*, ed. Donald W. Harward (Washington, DC: American Association of Colleges and Universities, 2012), 47–50, available at http://aacu.org.

32. Mark W. Huddleston, "New Hampshire State Senate Finance Committee," FY 12–13 USNH Operating Budget Hearing (April 18, 2011), available at http://unh.edu/president/concord-testimony.

33. For example, in June 2014, AT&T and Udacity announced a partnership, under the name NanoDegree, to provide education—a credential—for people who are seeking entry-level positions at AT&T.

34. In the fall of 2013 a pilot project was launched at the University of California, Davis, to experiment with badging—and competency-based learning—in relation to a new undergraduate major in sustainable agriculture and food systems.

35. The wonderful notion of *institutions as mobilizing networks* emerged for Cathy Davidson and David Theo Goldberg in the course of their research—much of it with peers online—for their report for the MacArthur Foundation; see their *The Future of Thinking: Learning Institutions in a Digital Age* (Cambridge, MA: MIT Press, 2010), ch. 5 ("Institutions as Mobilizing Networks: [Or, 'I Hate the Institution—But Love What It Did for Me']").

36. See Woodward, "The Future of the Humanities—in the Present & in Public," Daedalus 138 (Winter 2009): 110–123.

37. See also Geoffrey Galt Harpham, "Finding Ourselves: The Humanities as a Discipline," *American Literary History* 25.3 (2013): 509–534. In his effort to characterize the humanities—his essay is masterful—Harpham distinguishes between facts and the general enterprise of the humanities, and in the following formulation I would not want to disagree with him: "it is still

the case that teaching in the humanities aims not at a mere accumulation of facts or information but at a more general sense of illumination that exceeds the subject being taught and outlasts classroom experience" (518). Elsewhere in "Finding Ourselves," he writes that the goal of the single-authored project in the humanities "is not to add to our mass of factual knowledge—a project that humanists treat with occasional disdain—but to persuade readers to accept a different understanding than the one they had" (524). See also "From Eternity to Here: Shrinkage in American Thinking about Higher Education," *Representations* 116.1 (Fall 2011): 42–61.

38. See Stanley Chodorow, "Taking the Humanities Off Life Support," *The Transformation of Humanistic Studies in the Twenty-first Century: Opportunities and Perils*, American Council of Learned Societies Occasional Paper No. 40 (1997), available at http://archives.acls.org/op/op40ch.htm.

39. Mark C. Taylor, *Crisis on Campus: A Bold Plan for Reforming Our Colleges and Universities* (New York: Alfred A. Knopf, 2010). See Taylor's inspiring chapter "Walls to Webs" (139–180). In Taylor's vision, to the traditional divisions of the natural sciences, social sciences, and the humanities and arts would be added a fourth division—"Emerging Zones." These zones of inquiry, in his words, "would be organized around problems and themes that lend themselves to interdisciplinary investigation. They would be designed to maximize the openness and flexibility necessary to adjust to the constantly expanding and evolving intellectual landscape. Whenever possible, these Emerging Zones of Inquiry should focus on questions and problems that have practical relevance and prepare students to become responsible citizens who are capable of pursuing creative and productive careers" (145).

40. A graduate certificate in public policy in the humanities is in development at the University of Michigan under the leadership of Sidonie Smith, the director of its Institute for the Humanities.

41. Regarding risk and the humanities, see, for examples, Randy Martin, "Taking an Administrative Turn: Derivative Logics for a Recharged Humanities," *Representations* 116.1 (Fall 2011): 156–176; on derivatives, risk, and globalization, see Edward LiPuma and Benjamin Lee, *Financial Derivatives and the Globalization of Risk* (Durham: Duke University Press, 2004); and on the history of credit and accounting in the West, see Mary Poovey, *A History of the Modern Fact: Problems of Knowledge in the Sciences of Wealth and Society* (Chicago: University of Chicago Press, 1998) and *Genres of the Credit Economy: Mediating Value in Eighteenth- and Nineteenth-Century Britain* (Chicago: University of Chicago Press, 2008). See also my *Statistical Panic: Cultural Politics and Poetics of the Emotions* (Durham, NC: Duke University Press, 2009).

42. See Dipesh Chakrabarty, "The Climate of History: Four Theses," *Critical Inquiry* 2.35 (Winter 2009): 197–222.

43. Rafe Sagarin, *Learning from the Octopus: How Secrets from Nature Can Help Us Fight Terrorist Attacks, Natural Disasters, and Disease* (New York: Basic Books, 2012).

44. See William Zumeta, David W. Breneman, Patrick M. Callan, and Joni E. Finney, *Financing American Education in the Era of Globalization* (Cambridge, MA: Harvard Education Press, 2012); this book addresses the challenge of financing US higher education in the light of rapid demographic change, focusing on racial and ethnic populations.

45. Todd Presner, "Welcome to the 20-Year Dissertation," *Chronicle of Higher Education*, November 25, 2013, available at http://chronicle.com.

4 · HUMANITIES AND INCLUSION

A Twenty-First-Century Land-Grant University Tradition

YOLANDA T. MOSES

The humanities must be central to a rearticulation of the goals and purposes of public research land-grant universities. The humanities and humanistic fields in higher education in the United States are necessarily tied to key and core institutional values of excellence and access to knowledge. They are fundamental to public education in the broadest, and truest, sense of the term. While these values may not always be visible and transparent, they are there and need to be rearticulated more clearly. In other words, one of the crucial outcomes of the land-grant university mission was, in the nineteenth century and now in the twenty-first, an education that gives students a profound understanding of what it means to be human and to operate within a cultural and social system that is diverse and complex.

The mission of the land-grant university also compels us as educators to examine the human conditions in which our graduates and potential graduates will live and work, conditions continually evolving in social and cultural complexity. Land-grant research institutions were conceived, in part, to be places that combined local, regional, and state contexts of learning; that were charged by the government and (some, not all) citizens to create new knowledge, both basic research as well as practical research; and to make new educational programs available to people in the region and the state. A further mission of the land grant in the mid-nineteenth century was to assist our growing nation in changing the human condition for the betterment of US society. Clearly the humanities were a part of that venture more than 150 years ago, even if the land-grant educational project was not inclusive of all populations at that time.

My chapter argues several things. First, while, at a technical level, Congress established land-grant universities through the Morrill Land-Grant Act of 1862 to help white farmers all across the United States to produce better crops and to understand the latest scientific developments, they also presaged some of the changes we see in public higher education today. Second, I argue that the land-grant mission was broadly defined and was originally designed to be democratic and inclusive while serving the citizens of the local area, the region, and the state. Historically, this meant opening up opportunities for working-class folks, though not necessarily women or men of color. So the inclusion was initially based on status initially, rather than race, ethnicity, or gender. Furthermore, I argue that, in order to fulfill its original charter, the land-grant university of the twenty-first century by definition must embrace diversity and inclusion, not as an add-on but as a core institutional value. Finally, I propose that today we must reclaim the legacy of inclusivity by expanding and reinterpreting it to accommodate new kinds of people with new kinds of local and regional needs. And these people are not only local, regional, and national. They are global citizens as well. The humanities and humanistic sciences are at the heart of this twenty-first-century transformation.

The United States in the twenty-first century sees the presence of a wide array of college and university programs that promote a new humanities agenda on the one hand and diversity programs on the other. But new humanities programs alone, or diversity programs alone, are not enough to guarantee institutional transformation and sustainability of the values of inclusion and excellence. Both topics require a paradigm shift in both society and in higher education. A comprehensive national higher-education institutional strategy of change would involve rethinking what it means to treat the humanities and diversity as an intertwined core institutional commitment. Such a reformulation will involve, among other things, articulating a clear linking of the humanities, diversity, and institutional mission; and building the institutional capacity to do this necessary and important work. I will focus on the intellectual rationale and the processes of capacity building for humanities and diversity leadership at all levels of institutions of higher education, and the leadership strategies and goals necessary to guarantee sustainable institutional change for higher education and for the larger pluralistic nation.

As a professor of anthropology and as a national leader in the field of academic and institutional diversity research and policy, I have followed, through research and praxis, the diversity and educational excellence movement in the United

States and elsewhere for more than twenty-five years. I believe we have reached a crossroads in higher education as it relates to diversity and educational excellence: I see higher-education institutional types and their relationship to diversity and excellence in three different categories. In the first are institutions that talk about diversity and its relationship to excellence and have it as a part of their literature. While the ideas are mentioned in their catalogs and brochures, diversity is not necessarily made operational or linked to institutional practices. The second category includes institutions that have many diversity programs working in isolation from each other. In this second stage, many activities and initiatives are going on, but the overall institutional value of these programs remains unclear; their activities have not been incorporated into the mission or the overall goals of the institution. This chapter will focus on a third level of engagement, which I will call aspirational or "Stage III Diversity and Excellence."[1] These are institutions in the process of making the shift to complete institutional transformation by making diversity central to their mission and core values. And this is where I see liberal arts education and successful diversity missions tied together.

It is important and necessary, then, to make the intellectual and institutional transformation case for diversity and excellence using a humanities foundation. It is the emerging belief of researchers and practitioners, including me, that if the values of diversity are to be sustained in our nation and in our institutions of higher education, it will not be done by individuals working in a piecemeal way. It will be achieved instead when institutions of higher education and their leaders understand the importance of diversity and a humanities framework as fundamental to their missions and their very existence, especially as land-grant institutions.[2] This transformational shift will only happen when institutions share among all their members a deeper and richer understanding of the complexity of diversity through the humanities (for their time and place), and the role they play in all aspects of our institutions' notions of excellence, integrity, democracy, and knowledge production.[3] There are several key components to such an argument, which must overcome cultural barriers mitigating the achievement of this "Stage III Diversity and Excellence" as well as the institutional inertia often resisting this kind of difficult change.

A commitment to a humanistic understanding of diversity in US higher education in the twenty-first century must focus on realigning institutional values. As a nation that has been and continues to be politically committed to serving diverse peoples;[4] implementing the unfinished social justice agenda for its citizens;[5] and providing unprecedented opportunities for post-secondary education for all of its citizens,[6] we need more than ever for colleges and universities (especially those with a public or governmental mandate) to be places where humanistic notions of democracy and inclusive ways of knowing help all our graduates negotiate and thrive in an increasingly diverse society. In the nineteenth and twentieth centuries, higher-education institutions were the engines that drove social, economic, and political change for many citizens.[7] Then as now, these institutions are places where new ideas are conceived and put into practice along the lines of what it means to be "broadly educated," to live in our ever-changing neighborhoods and communities, both locally and globally.[8] These goals continue with even more urgency.

In the twenty-first century, a comprehensive understanding and integration of the realities of humanistic diversity concepts and actions are important for the continued growth and development of our democracy. Getting this right in our colleges and universities is imperative to getting it right for our nation. Our quality of life, which includes our political, social, and economic wellbeing, depends on understanding diversity in all its complexity. Because the humanities remain fundamental to that understanding, we in higher education must address their erosion as a consequence of narrow and siloed thinking about their broad role in the educational process. In order for higher education to continue to play a pivotal role in building and sustaining an educated, inclusive citizenry, we have to create a new diversity and inclusion paradigm to serve all of our diverse populations. While many parts of this paradigm are aspirational, some institutions are further along on this transformation trajectory than others. These will be highlighted where appropriate.

The rest of the chapter will elaborate the theme of making the intellectual case for diversity a national imperative and the part the humanities must play in that endeavor. Throughout the chapter, examples will be used from my own institution, the University of California, Riverside, as well as from others, to illustrate how some institutions are in the first stages of implementing transformative strategies. For the most part, however, we as a nation are only beginning such transformation.

DIVERSITY AND THE NATIONAL INTEREST

Over the past thirty years, I have witnessed an increase in the various ways that the government, higher-education associations, colleges and universities, and NGOs talk about diversity as integral to how we define ourselves as an inclusive and pluralistic nation. In 2001, for example, former Supreme Court Justice Sandra Day O'Connor declared that diversity is in our national interest.[9] What does this mean for our universities and colleges today? I think it means, first, that humanistic diversity is important because it is essential to the practice of democracy in a pluralistic republic. Our understanding of this pluralism is perhaps most effectively communicated through humanistic disciplines: history, literature, communication, anthropology, among others. Changing demographics create an imperative for us to serve the diverse people who need this nation's services (especially a quality higher education). Second, diversity is a national imperative. Our institutions must produce the next generation of citizens and leaders with the ability to function in local communities as well as a global community. Third, humanistic diversity is a national imperative, because there is unfinished business around issues of social justice for all people in this country as events in Ferguson, Missouri, and elsewhere have recently underscored. Again, a set of issues most notably studied in the humanities and the social sciences. And finally, a deep understanding of humanistic diversity is a national educational imperative in this country. Why? Because if institutions of higher education do not provide access and multiple pathways to quality education for diverse students, then we will fall short of our educational-excellence goals. We will look in a bit more detail at how diversity has been framed as a national-interest issue through the following lenses: diversity and democracy; diversity as demographics; diversity as a social-justice issue; diversity and the US competitive global advantage; and finally diversity as an educational-excellence issue in higher education.

DIVERSITY AND DEMOCRACY

While this country has not always accommodated all the different groups who call themselves US citizens today, perhaps most citizens and denizens would say that the key components to a viable, equitable democracy include valuing a diversity of opinions, electoral voices, points of view involving religious, political, racial or ethnic, and class, gender, and sexuality issues.

Indeed, foundations such as Ford, Lilly, MacArthur, and Rockefeller have all agreed over the last twenty years, through the funding of their own special initiatives linking humanistic diversity and notions of democracy, that the two go hand in hand. For example, the 1993 annual report of the Rockefeller Foundation makes the link between equal opportunity and school reform by emphasizing the development of excellent schools for students from the poorest communities as well as from middle-class ones.[10] For over fifty years now the Ford Foundation has funded civil rights, educational access, and diversity programs and initiatives in higher education, both here and abroad, including most recently launching their "Advancing Higher Education Access and Success Program." This program recognizes the success of higher education's ability to reach underserved populations to this point, and is now turning to grant-making that "seeks to generate policy and institutional reforms that improve standards of teaching and learning and that remove structural barriers to successful participation in higher education."[11] In addition, higher-education associations such as the Association of American Colleges and Universities (AAC&U), through their Democracy and Diversity Project and their publications, have reinforced the links among democracy, diversity, and liberal arts undergraduate education. The major publications of this ongoing initiative are *The Drama of Diversity and Democracy, Making a Real Difference with Diversity;* and *Diversity Works: The Emerging Picture of How Students Benefit.*[12]

DIVERSITY AS A DEMOGRAPHIC IMPERATIVE

As our colleges and universities are beginning to articulate, even in a rudimentary way, their commitment to diversity, demographic shifts are taking place across the United States, particularly in the West, on the East Coast, in Florida and the Midwest (Chicago and Minneapolis, for example). What are the causes of these recent demographic shifts and how do they impact universities and colleges? One of the main reasons for demographic shifts is an increase in the number of immigrants. From 1960 to 2000, the foreign-born population of the United States rose from 9.7 million to 36.7 million (12 percent of the total population). What is interesting to note for my purposes is that 29 percent of this population is under twenty-one and 25 percent of that population is under eighteen years old.[13] In addition, there was an increase in minorities as a percentage of the total population: from 10.5 percent in 1960 and 11.1 percent in 1970, the share of the US population counted in a minority group rose to 19.8 percent in 1990, 24.8 percent in 2000, and more than 33 percent in 2010. As the article from the census "Overview of Race and Hispanic Origin" notes, "While non-Hispanic white alone population is still numerically and proportionally the largest majority racial and ethnic group in the U.S., it is also growing at the slowest rate."[14] Data show that from 2000 to 2010, the Hispanic and Asian American populations each increased 43 percent, and the African American population increased 12.3 percent. So, over the past fifty years, the notion of who is an "American" (of the US kind) has changed, and continues to change.

In addition to shifts in race and ethnicity, there has been an increase in the number of people of non-Christian religions.[15] There is also an increase in the growing social, economic, and political rights accorded gay and lesbian citizens, found in laws, policies, social practices, and traditions. We see this in the repeal of the "Don't Ask, Don't Tell" policies in the US military,[16] in thirty-six of the fifty states passing gay marriage legislation, and in the election of the first openly lesbian US senator, from the state of Wisconsin. The United States as a whole is indeed widening and deepening its understanding of diversity. It is against this backdrop that higher education in the United States is also changing.

For example, a national snapshot of who is going to college has changed demographically over the past twenty-five years. Enrollment in degree-granting institutions increased by 11 percent between 1991 and 2001. Between 2001 and 2011, enrollment increased 32 percent, from 15.9 million to 21.0 million. Much of the growth between 2001 and 2011 was in full-time enrollment; the number of full-time students rose 38 percent, while the number of part-time students rose 23 percent. During the same period, the number of female matriculants rose 33 percent, while the number of male matriculants rose 30 percent. Enrollment increases in this case are affected both by population growth and by rising rates of enrollment.[17]

Between 2001 and 2011, the number of eighteen- to twenty-four-year-olds increased from 28.0 million to 31.1 million, an increase of 11 percent, and the percentage of eighteen- to twenty-four-year-olds enrolled in college rose from 36 percent in 2001 to 42 percent in 2011. In addition to enrollment in accredited two-year colleges, four-year colleges, and universities, about 572,000 students attended non-degree-granting, Title IV-eligible, postsecondary institutions in fall 2011. These are postsecondary institutions that do not award associate or higher degrees; they include, for example, institutions that offer only career and technical programs of less than two years' duration. This kind of institution has grown in response to the diverse needs of diverse students.[18]

The biggest news of all is that the percentage of American college students who are Hispanic, Asian/Pacific Islander, Black, and American Indian/Alaska Native has been increasing. From 1976 to 2011, the percentage of Hispanic students rose from 4 percent to 14 percent, the percentage of Asian/Pacific Islander students rose from 2 percent to 6 percent, the percentage of Black students rose from 10 percent to 15 percent, and the percentage of American Indian/Alaska Native students rose from 0.7 to 0.9 percent. During the same period, the percentage of White students fell from 84 percent to 61 percent. This demographic trend is expected to continue.[19]

DIVERSITY AS COMPETITIVE ADVANTAGE

President Barack Obama has called for an increase in the number of students in this country with some higher education training. In an address to the joint Houses of Congress in 2009, President Obama said, "By 2020, America will once again have the highest proportion of college graduates in the world.... So tonight I ask every American to commit to at least one year or more of higher education or career training . . . every American will need to get more than a high school diploma."[20] He sees this drive for higher education for all citizens as a national imperative and has created a national initiative to be run out of the Department of Education, "The 2020 College Completion Plan." This plan is not just designed to prepare students for jobs, or to restore our place as first in the world of commerce, but, according to the president, to prepare Americans "for informed, effective participation in democratic life. We need educated Americans with the capacity to solve the most pressing problems of our time."[21]

Increasing external challenges to the notion of "American exceptionalism" drive this imperative. For example, Thomas Friedman and others write that the United States is no longer the most powerful nation in the world, or the most respected.[22] Our colleges and universities are still world class, but Friedman warns that other countries are catching up. President Obama has issued a challenge to US educators: we as a nation need to graduate more of our students in the sciences and in other fields (including the humanities). The take-away here is that all of our citizens must be engaged in the learning process and must be engaged in discovery and invention and innovation to help keep the United States the global country of opportunity, where only the limits of an individual's determination are the deciding factor in any citizen's success. We know from research that both student access and success are interrelated dimensions of diversity in higher education.[23] We find that today, many of our first-generation students come from communities and from families where higher education has been not only unattainable but also culturally distant. To counterbalance the notion of "American exceptionalism" that is deeply embedded in Americans' psyche, higher education must take responsibility for giving our students/citizens a more nuanced, more balanced understanding of our place in the world. Students should understand that we are part of the world, not the center of it.[24] It is also imperative that our notions of humanistic diversity are both local and global in that we acknowledge and recognize that our students are already enmeshed in a global world through their families, through the media, through immigration and migration patterns.

Our students are funds of knowledge as well. For example, through our Gluck Fellowship of the Arts Program, we provide fellowships to deserving UC Riverside undergraduate and graduate students to conduct arts-related presentations, performances, and workshops in Riverside County schools, residential facilities for elder care, and community centers. Departments participating include art, creative writing, dance, history of art, music, and theater, as well as the Sweeney Art Gallery and the UCR/California Museum of Photography. One of the major goals of this program since 1996 has been to integrate the arts into the broader diverse communities of Southern California, communities from which many of our students come. In this way our students are interpreting the arts of the university through their lived experiences back to their communities.[25]

Why do we, a research land-grant university, promote this kind of engagement with our communities? The Gluck Fellows Program is driven by a core belief here at UC Riverside that open access to the arts is one of the fundamental components of all healthy communities regardless of socioeconomic status and age. The Gluck programs are therefore divided into three different categories, each suited to specific types of learning opportunities within the community, and reflect efforts to reach the largest and most diverse number of participants in the locations where exposure to the arts is most required and appropriate according to the university's and the program's mission.

Gluck Fellow programs are organized into three categories and paired with the best locations: performance ensembles, including the Theatre Improv Troupe, and music ensembles perform in community centers or school assemblies; individual fellow workshops, where fellows develop a hands-on curriculum related to their specialization work designed for a classroom environment; and team-taught camps, where a fellowship team will immerse participants in new arts activities, such as painting with light or making personalized tote bags, as an entry-point into creating ongoing art exhibitions. Gluck fellows also offer team-taught family-learning activities at UCR's ARTSblock in downtown Riverside during the city's monthly Family Funday on First Sunday and First Thursday ARTSwalk events.[26]

In summary, the Gluck Fellows Program of the Arts at UC Riverside brings talented UCR students into the most underserved areas of the Riverside community to provide free performance and arts education experiences. Outreach efforts are concentrated in schools, particularly elementary schools. Visits to elder-care homes bring enjoyment to those who ordinarily would not have access to live art experiences due to limited mobility. Performances and workshops in the community at museums and libraries increase accessibility for a broader diverse audience, especially individuals normally unable to attend performances on the UC Riverside campus. But, lest you think it is a one-way street, Gluck fellows often speak about the life-changing experiences that it provides for them as well.[27]

At the national level, co-sponsored by the arts organization called Imagining America (www.imaginingamerica.org) in partnership with the Kettering Foundation, is a new initiative, "Imagining America: Artists and Scholars in Public Life." This initiative is timed to mark the centennial of the Smith-Lever Act, which established the Cooperative Extension System in May 1914. It is designed to develop and send teams of educators and community members to organize a series of events in Alabama, California, Georgia, Iowa, Kansas, Michigan, Minnesota, Mississippi, New York, Ohio, Oregon, and Wisconsin. State teams are tasked with inviting diverse voices to both plan and participate in the events. These include leaders from community arts organizations, public humanities projects and organizations, and representatives from design fields. The overall goal of this project is to document the events and ideas in these states through video, written stories, and other creative media that can be shared and archived online. The project feeds ideas back to the Federal Cooperative Extension office as it plans its activities for the twenty-first century: "As it enters the second century, the Extension Reconsidered initiative will provide opportunities for people to explore how Extension professionals and volunteers might improve the way they engage people in addressing the new social, technological, and economic conditions of the twenty-first century."[28]

DIVERSITY AS A SOCIAL JUSTICE ISSUE

While the United States has come a long way in using its laws, its courts, and the executive power of the president to create a just society for all its citizens, structural inequalities still abound. The election of Barack H. Obama as the first African American president, both in 2008 and again in 2012, does not mean that racism is eradicated in the United States. As a matter of fact, the Southern Poverty Law Center, a civil rights organization with a long history of fighting racial and other kinds of inequality that tracks hate crimes, reports that since the election of President Obama, racial and other hate crimes have actually increased.[29] This country must continue to find ways to educate citizens and leaders about how to eradicate the many intractable structural issues related to poverty, health disparities, growing wealth disparities, and persistent achievement gaps in education, just to name a few. There is also the unfinished business of the civil rights movement of the 1960s. Who would have thought that the US Department of Justice in 2012 would still be responding to accusations of voting discrimination and voting injustice for minorities in the states of Pennsylvania and Florida during the 2012 presidential election, when voting laws were hastily passed to keep minorities from voting in those states?[30] Unfortunately, the United States of America is still plagued by the scourges of racial, religious, gender, and homophobic bigotry of all kinds.[31] It is therefore a humanistic diversity imperative that higher education continue to play a critical role steering our nation to walk its talk about "justice for all." Our institutions of higher education have the intellectual, moral, and information-age knowledge to create spaces where "difficult dialogues" can take place among our students, faculty, and staff. They have the capacity to help confront these seemingly intractable problems through research, teaching, policies, and practices that will have profound impact in our larger society.

One of the greatest challenges to achieving true social justice in higher education, of course, is skyrocketing tuition in public institutions. The poor are being priced out of the public higher education system. Land-grant universities, with their public mission, must do everything possible to continue providing first-class education at a reasonable cost. Universities like Arizona State University, the City University of New York, and the public higher education system in California are all trying to figure out how to keep education affordable for all students. For example, the University of California sees financing the education of a UC student as a partnership among the students, their parents, and the University of California. Students are expected to cover part of the cost of their education through working (in work-study programs) or borrowing (student loans). In addition, the UC expects parents to contribute based on their financial resources and circumstances. And finally, the University of California covers the remaining costs with gift aid from a variety of sources. Each of the ten UC campuses determines the eligibility of a student at the local level, using state, federal, and local gift-aid programs. So, the University of California, like other public institutions, uses a variety of gift and self-help options for each of their eligible students.[32] These institutions should not be the exception to the rule. It must be the mission of all public institutions to keep higher education affordable for all eligible students. If not, then just as the demographics are shifting to allow more students from diverse backgrounds to go to college, access will be denied to them. We must be vigilant against that happening.

DIVERSITY AS AN EDUCATIONAL EXCELLENCE ISSUE

Given what has just been laid out as the imperatives for diversity, what is the specific role of higher education and the humanities in helping to achieve those lofty goals? The reality is that we are already a nation of diversity on many different dimensions. Our changing demographics make our need for rethinking and reframing the US higher-educational system a national priority. We are not the same institutions that we were just a decade ago. Given such complex demographic changes, understanding how to create equitable spaces for success should be our highest priority. In other words, our institutional structures must also realign themselves with our new commitments and realities. Indeed, our public primary and secondary schools are becoming increasingly diverse in just about every dimension imaginable. We are not just talking about the large urban schools, but schools in small communities are also becoming more diverse (for example, Hmong students in small Midwest communities).[33] Are the schools of education in our universities equipped both administratively and pedagogically to graduate pre-K–12 teachers who know and understand how to engage the many dimensions of diversity in their classrooms? Our nation stands at a critical juncture in its ability to engage both the challenge and the promise of being an inclusive, engaged pluralistic democracy. This means that we need a new way to educate pluralistic and engaged democratic communities across the country. What is the role of higher education to produce new knowledge, new ways of knowing and thinking about, structuring and executing change through the humanistic study of diversity, inclusion, and educational excellence? These are questions we must continue to ask and answer as we transform the land-grant institutions of the nineteenth century into the land-grant universities of the twenty-first.

CONCLUSION

For forty-plus years higher education has grappled with the meanings of diversity, multiculturalism, and equity. The approach to diversity in higher education has been very fragmented and piecemeal.[34] We need a new higher education paradigm that links a deep understanding of the role of the humanities and the value of diversity with national imperatives and with core institutional values and practices. To date, research on this issue is very clear that the kind of institutional change needed to build this new paradigm requires retooling higher education. Daryl Smith and others call it building institutional capacity.[35] While there are many lenses through which we in US higher education look at issues of diversity, it is clearer each year that the solution to building a new transformative and sustainable model for institutional diversity success on our campuses does not rest on the shoulders of the individual underrepresented student, faculty, or staff member. The responsibility to conceptualize, oversee and guide that change is at the institutional level and with institutional leadership. It is the role of institutions and their leaders to build new models to better serve the nation.[36] This calls for increasing the institutional capacity for diversity, and for being clear about mission, institutional structures, policies, goals, decision-making, information, infrastructure (human, physical, technological, financial), and culture.[37] The humanities and the social sciences are critical to this transformation; not just in the curriculum, but in the framing of the whole enterprise.

NOTES

1. See Yolanda T. Moses, "Diversity, Excellence and Inclusion: Leadership for Change in the 21st Century," in *Diversity and Inclusion in Higher Education: Emerging Perspectives on Institutional Transformation*, ed. Daryl G. Smith (London, UK: Routledge, 2014), 68–101.
2. Vartan Gregorian, "Investing in Education Is Key to America's Future Success," *Carnegie Reporter* 7.1 (2012): 1.
3. See ibid.; see also Nicholas A. Bowman, "Promoting Participation in a Diverse Democracy: A Meta-Analysis of College Diversity Experiences and Civic Engagement," *Review of Educational Research* 81.1 (2011): 29–68.
4. Michael J. Bennett, *When Dreams Came True: The GI Bill and the Making of Modern America* (Dulles, VA: Potomac Books, 1999); Charles M. Vest, *The American Research University* (Berkeley: University of California Press, 2007); Abigail Deutsch, "Lincoln's Legacy: Land-Grant Colleges and Universities," *Carnegie Reporter* 7.1 (2012): 3–11.
5. Association of American Colleges and Universities (AAC&U), *The Drama of Diversity and Democracy: Higher Education and American Commitments* (Washington, DC: Association of American Colleges and Universities, 1995); Bowman, "Promoting Participation"; Mitchell J. Chang, Nida Denson, Victor Sáenz, and Kimberly Misa, "The Educational Benefits of Sustaining Cross-Racial Interaction among Undergraduates," *Journal of Higher Education* 77 (2006): 430–455.

6. See Gregorian and the Ford Foundation's *Advancing Higher Education Access and Success: Overview* (2013), available at http://www.fordfoundation.org.

7. See Vest, *The American Research University.*

8. Lori J. Vogelgesang and Alexander W. Astin, "Comparing the Effects of Community Service and Service-Learning," *Michigan Journal of Community Service Learning* 7 (2000): 25–34.

9. See also Patricia Gurin, Eric L. Dey, Sylvia Hurtado, and Gerald Gurin, "Diversity and Higher Education: Theory and Impact on Educational Outcomes," *Harvard Educational Review* 72 (2002): 330–366.

10. The Rockefeller Foundation, *President's Review & Annual Report* (1993), 42–48, available at http://www.rockefellerfoundation.org.

11. See Ford Foundation, *Advancing Higher Education Access and Success*, 2.

12. AAC&U, *The Drama of Diversity and Democracy*; Alma R. Clayton-Pedersen, Sharon Parker, Daryl G. Smith, José F. Moreno, and Daniel Hiroyuki Teraguch, *Making a Real Difference with Diversity* (Washington, DC: Association of American Colleges and Universities, 1997); D. G. Smith et al., *Diversity Works: The Emerging Picture of How Students Benefit* (Washington, DC: Association of American Colleges and Universities, 1997).

13. United States Census Bureau, *Take One: Turnkey Kit* (Washington, DC: U.S. Census Bureau, 2010).

14. Ibid., 22.

15. The Pew Forum on Religion and Public Life, *U.S. Religious Landscape Survey: Religious Affiliation Diverse and Dynamic* (Washington, DC: Pew Forum on Religion and Public Life, 2008), 5.

16. Jesse Lee, "The President Signs Repeal of 'Don't Ask, Don't Tell': 'Out of Many, We are One,'" *The White House Blog*, December 22, 2010, available at http://www.whitehouse.gov/blog.

17. The National Center on Educational Statistics. Fast Facts. Postsecondary Enrollment Rates. Available at http://nces.ed.gov/fastfacts/.

18. Ibid.

19. Ibid.

20. Barack Obama, *Address to Joint Session of Congress* [*State of the Union Address*], Washington, DC, February 24, 2009, available at http://www.whitehouse.gov.

21. Ibid.

22. Thomas L. Friedman, *The World Is Flat* (New York: Farrar, Straus and Giroux, 2005); Thomas Friedman and Michael Mandelbaum, *That Used to Be Us: How America Fell Behind in the World It Invented and How We Can Come Back* (New York: Farrar, Straus and Giroux, 2011).

23. Sylvia Hurtado, "The Next Generation of Diversity and Intergroup Relations Research," *Journal of Social Issues* 61 (2005): 595–610; Hurtado, Cynthia Alvarez, Chelsea Guillermo-Wann, Marcella Cuellar, and Lucy Avellano, "A Model for Diverse Learning Environments: The Scholarship on Creating and Assessing Conditions for Student Success," in *Higher Education: Handbook of Theory and Research*, vol. 27, ed. J. C. Smart and M. B. Paulsen (New York: Springer, 2012), 41–122; Simon Marginson, "The Rise of the Global University: Five New Tensions," *Chronicle of Higher Education*, May 30, 2010, available at http://chronicle.com/section/Home/5.

24. See Friedman and Mandelbaum, *That Used to Be Us.*

25. See http://gluckprogram.ucr.edu.

26. Ibid.

27. Ibid.

28. "At Centennial: Citizens to Imagine Cooperative Extension's Future," *A Public Voice*, Association of Land Grant and Public Universities. Available at http://aplu.org/page .aspx?pid=183.

29. Mark Potok, "The 'Patriot' Movement Explodes," *Intelligence Report* 145 (Spring 2012), available at http://www.splcenter.org.

30. Steve Bousquet, "Feds: Florida's Voter Purge Violates Federal Law," *Miami Herald*, July 31, 2012, available at http://www.miamiherald.com.

31. See Moses, "Diversity, Excellence, and Inclusion."

32. University of California, "Financing Your UC Education Is a Partnership between You, Your Parents, and the UC," available at http://admission.universityofcalifornia.edu.

33. Alan H. Goodman, Yolanda T. Moses, and Joseph L. Jones, *Race: Are We So Different* (New York: Wiley Blackwell and the American Anthropological Association, 2012).

34. Clifford Adelman, *Answers in the Toolbox: Academic Integrity, Attendance Patterns and Bachelor's Degree Attainment* (Washington, DC: U.S Government Printing Office, 1991); Smith et al., *Diversity Works*; James A. Anderson, *Driving Change Through Diversity and Globalization: Transformative Leadership in the Academy* (Sterling, VA: Stylus Press, 2008); Estella M. Bensimon, "The Diversity Scorecard: A Learning Approach to Institutional Change," *Change* 36.1 (2004): 45–52.

35. Daryl G. Smith, *Diversity's Promise for Higher Education: Making It Work* (Baltimore: Johns Hopkins University Press, 2009); Susan Rankin and Robert Reason, "Transformational Tapestry Model: A Comprehensive Approach to Transforming Campus Climate," *Journal of Diversity in Higher Education* 1 (2008): 262–274; Adrianna Kezar, "Tools For a Time and Place: Phased Leadership Strategies for Advancing Campus Diversity," *Review of Higher Education* 30 (2007): 413–439.

36. Daryl G. Smith, "Building Institutional Capacity for Diversity and Inclusion in Academic Medicine," *Academic Medicine* 87 (2012): 1511.

37. Ibid.

5 · STICKING UP FOR LIBERAL ARTS AND HUMANITIES EDUCATION

Governance, Leadership, and Fiscal Crisis

DANIEL LEE KLEINMAN

US public higher education is in crisis. Recent years have witnessed a precipitous decline in state support for public universities and widespread calls for occupationally oriented higher education—a focus on curricula that will provide students with employment-ready skills. In this environment, liberal arts and humanities education have been broadly and regularly attacked as economically irrelevant, unaffordable luxuries. Several Republican governors have been among the loudest voices advocating for employment preparation-focused higher education and disparaging the liberal arts and the humanities.

With the future of liberal arts and humanities education at stake,[1] who is sticking up for this part of the higher-education landscape and how? To what extent are the leaders of our major public universities defending liberal arts and humanities education? When they champion liberal arts and humanities curricula, what arguments are they making?

In this chapter, I look at four of the most prominent states (Florida, North Carolina, Texas, and Wisconsin) where political leaders have proposed policies that would provide budgetary benefits to occupationally oriented higher-education initiatives, while punishing liberal arts or humanities programs and students. I explore the responses of higher-education leaders in those states. While there is variation in the nature of university rejoinders across the four states, I suggest that all public higher-education leaders should be making a specific argument for the employment relevance of liberal arts and humanities education and taking this case directly to the economically concerned and utility-oriented citizens of these states. My aims are strategic and political. I am unabashedly committed to liberal arts education and the value of the humanities, and I am seeking the most-effective ways to defend them.

STATE-BY-STATE

In this section, I briefly consider the positions articulated by governors in Florida, North Carolina, Texas, and Wisconsin and, where available, the reactions of leaders of each of the state's public flagship university and other leaders cited in news coverage. I am interested in how governors frame their criticisms of liberal arts and humanities education, since, as a strategic matter, the nature of their denigrations should condition the responses of liberal arts and humanities advocates. It is in this context that I consider the focus and variety of defenses or reactions provided by university leaders.[2]

I begin with Florida. In 2011, Florida Governor Rick Scott indicated that he did not believe that students in the humanities or liberal arts more broadly contributed significantly to Florida's economy. As a consequence, he suggested that state funding should go to higher-education programs that give students the best job prospects. According to an article in the *Sarasota Herald Tribune*, the big losers in Scott's proposal would be "programs like psychology and anthropology and potentially schools like New College in Sarasota that emphasize a liberal arts curriculum."[3] Said Scott: "If I'm going to take money from a citizen to put into education then I'm going to take that money to create jobs. . . . So I want that money to go to degrees where people can get jobs in this state. . . . Is it a vital interest of the state to have more anthropologists? I don't think so."[4]

Scott wants universities to provide students with data on average salaries for graduates of all degree programs. According to Zac Anderson, "The governor also . . . hopes to come up with other ways to incentivize STEM [science, technology, engineering, and mathematics] programs and discourage liberal arts majors."[5] Scott's position focuses on the direct and immediate effects of college education, or at least the accompanying credentials, on employability and salary.

In response to Scott's public statements and proposals, higher-education leaders in Florida insisted on the value of liberal arts education. In speaking to the media, University of Florida president Bernie Machen bristled at Scott's position: "The totality of higher education includes the sciences and the liberal arts, and you need them both to have a complete educational system. . . . So it should not be either/ or."[6] University of South Florida president Betty Castor said: "We're not a communist country, there's still going to be choice. . . . You can put a lot more money into (STEM) but if you do that at the expense of the liberal arts, I would fear we're not educating students the way they should be educated."[7] In response to Scott's intention to build science and engineering-related programs by cutting liberal arts offerings, a spokesperson for the University of Florida board of governors told the *Sarasota Herald Tribune*: "We . . . don't intend to rob Peter to pay Paul."[8] Not bound by the diplomatic norms of a university presidency, former University of Florida president Charles E. Young described Scott's proposal as "sheer and utter nonsense." Speaking about Scott and his supporters, Young said: "They have a total lack of understanding about what a university is and what universities do."[9]

This pushback didn't stop Scott. In December of 2012, Governor Scott's task force on higher education proposed mechanisms (ultimately not enacted) through which to realize the governor's 2011 proposals. They called for creating a system of tiered tuition, which establishes incentives for students to enter STEM fields by making tuition in these areas lower than in liberal arts fields.[10] Not in direct response, but in a lecture to his campus's undergraduates, University of Florida president Bernie Machen urged students to think not only about jobs, but also about skills, given the rapidly changing economy. He argued that college is about preparing for life in the work world but that it is also about self-discovery and figuring out how to make a contribution to the world. And as for employment, he told the first-year undergraduates in his audience that "Recruiters for companies prefer new employees with the skills of *critical thinking, writing, problem-solving, communication,* and *teamwork.* . . . Ultimately, preparing for your career is about so much more than jobs and income."[11]

In North Carolina, the university's former chancellor, Holden Thorp, blogged about the virtues of the liberal arts before the governor of North Carolina rolled out his anti-liberal-arts proposals. In November 2012, Thorp said that he always talks about "how important a liberal arts education is to the future of N.C. and the U.S." We must, according to Thorp, "teach students to learn and how to understand the world." The job of higher education, according to Thorp, is to prepare students for jobs that haven't been invented yet. "Vocational training can only prepare students for the jobs that exist now. That won't cut it. That's why we have to stay committed to the liberal arts model," said Thorp.[12]

Just a few months later, in early 2013, North Carolina Governor Pat McCrory asserted that universities offer worthless courses that provide "no chances of getting people jobs."[13] According to the *Huffington Post*, the North Carolina governor argued that tax dollars should not be used to pay for degrees and courses in such areas a gender studies and Swahili. McCrory said: "If you want to take gender studies that's fine. Go to a private school, and take it. . . . But I don't want to subsidize that if that's not going to get someone a job."[14] The governor supports legislation that would set the state's funding formula for higher education based on how many students get jobs upon graduation.[15] Like Florida's Rick Scott,

McCrory emphasizes the immediate employment and salary payoffs of a college education.

By the time McCrory outlined his agenda, Thorp had stepped down as UNC's chancellor. Carol Folt was appointed to the position, and while students and professors criticized the governor's remarks, UNC's new chancellor apparently did not. In March 2013, when Governor McGrory proposed substantial cuts to the UNC system, the system president Tom Ross expressed concern about the size of the cuts and committed the university system to operating more efficiently. In public statements, he did not mention the costs to education of these cuts, and he certainly didn't speak about defending liberal arts education.[16] At the same time, in announcing the selection of Folt, Tom Ross indicated that he wanted someone with a commitment to the liberal arts.[17] In her installation speech, while sharing the podium with Governor McCrory, Holt argued that the liberal arts *are* central to the problem-solving mission of UNC. She noted that many see the liberal arts as "the most effective way to increase the creativity and innovation in their business and technology."[18]

In Texas Governor Rick Perry took a position quite similar to the positions of Florida Governor Rick Scott and North Carolina Governor Pat McCrory. Perry argued that: "Our colleges and universities must always strive for more efficiency, including higher graduation rates and better degree programs that will prepare our students for great jobs and provide them with the skills necessary to compete in a global marketplace."[19] Building on a cost-cutting agenda, the basis of which can be found in work by the Texas Public Policy Foundation, Perry did not explicitly challenge the liberal arts or humanities. However, his position parallels Scott's and McCrory's in its emphasis on employment, for Perry also takes an occupational view of education, stressing jobs and skills. Although he did not suggest a need to cut humanities programming, one analysis of his proposals points out that Perry's budget balancing emphasis could put humanities departments in a difficult position, since they "tend to have smaller classes and generate less revenue from research . . . [and are thus] more likely to end up 'in the red.'"[20] That same analyst suggests that Perry's proposals point toward "more vocational degrees at the expense of liberal arts education."[21] This view is echoed by a former UT-Austin president Peter Flawn, who led the institution between 1979 and 1985. He put it this way: "There seems to be a political move, and it's not just in Texas, away from the classical mission of the university—cultivation of the mind and pursuit of knowledge—to a concept of a public university as a sort of a job corps or a trade school."[22]

Tension between Rick Perry and his allies and the current UT-Austin president, William Powers Jr., is long-standing. The friction seems to have three sources: Powers's calls for increasing state funding for UT, his concerns about Perry's reform agenda, and efforts by the Perry-appointed board of regents to micromanage the university. While Powers acknowledged that educational affordability is a crucial issue, he also publicly asserted that universities have "a certain kind of social purpose."[23] Apparently siding with humanities professors concerned that cost efficiencies could threaten their programs, Powers argued that different degree programs will cost different amounts to run. And in a systematic critique of Perry's agenda, a close aide to Powers, UT's dean of the College of Liberal Arts Randy Diehl, argued for the values of the humanities: "Humanities research helps citizens better understand the world in which they live and the overall human condition. It provides the history, cultural contexts, and ethical framework needed to make sense of changes in society."[24]

I turn finally to Wisconsin, where Governor Scott Walker made many of the proposals put forward by the governors in Florida, North Carolina, and Texas. In a speech at the Ronald Reagan Library in the autumn of 2012, Walker indicated that he planned to "tie our funding in our technical colleges and our University of Wisconsin System into performance and say, if you want money, we need you to perform. . . . In higher education, that means not only degrees, but are young people getting degrees in jobs that are open and needed today—not just the jobs that the universities want to give us, or degrees that people want to give us?"[25]

While the words "liberal arts" and "humanities" do not appear in Walker's speech, the idea here is that universities should train students for specific jobs that businesses seek to fill *today* and that academic departments and majors should receive funding in relationship to the jobs graduates receive or data on job availability at the time of graduation. There is little question that this formulation raises the position of occupationally oriented programs, while humanities programs are seen as unaffordable luxuries.

According to a news report at the time, UW System president Kevin Reilly did not respond to the governor's speech.[26] And while the interim chancellor of the University of Wisconsin–Madison, David Ward, did comment favorably about the liberal arts in an "exit interview" with Madison's *Capital Times,*[27] he apparently did not respond to the governor's speech when Walker made it. UW-Madison's previous chancellor, Biddy Martin, undertook several initiatives on the campus to bolster the liberal arts, spiritedly defended the humanities at campus events, and negotiated a major gift for the humanities from the Mellon Foundation, but she apparently did not provide a sustained *public* defense of the liberal arts and the humanities. In 2013, the University of Wisconsin–Madison inaugurated a new chancellor, Rebecca Blank, who, like Carol Folt in North Carolina, initiated a tour across Wisconsin to speak directly to the citizenry. To date, press accounts of that tour have stressed the economic development value of UW-Madison. Blank regularly blogs, and she has not discussed the liberal arts or humanities in her blog entries. At a 2014 talk before the University of Wisconsin's Center for the Humanities, however, Blank sang the praises of the humanities, speaking affirmatively of their economic value.[28]

DEFENSE OR CELEBRATION, INSIDE AND OUTSIDE

One might think about the efforts of public-university leaders to defend liberal arts and humanities education across four distinctions: 1) audience: internal (students, staff, and faculty) versus external (elected officials and citizens); 2) nature of engagement: reactive (responding to criticisms of the liberal arts) or proactive (advancing a discussion and framing position); 3) type of benefits of liberal arts stressed: personal growth and citizenship (traditional) versus career/professional (pragmatic); and 4) educational payoffs: short-term versus long-run. The governors in the states I have discussed have spoken persistently and consistently to elected officials and the general publics of their states (the *external* audience). They have argued for measuring the success of higher education in terms of the *immediate* employment and salary experiences of graduates. At some point, university leaders in all four states have argued *internally—to the populations of their campuses* (i.e., to students)—for the benefit of liberal arts education and humanities. We have some evidence that leaders in Florida, North Carolina, and Texas addressed the general public (focuses *externally*) in their respective states in their advocacy of the liberal arts and humanities. Some *reacted* to gubernatorial criticisms of the humanities and liberal arts, but none engaged in consistent and proactive externally focused argument for the liberal arts and humanities. Among those who spoke about the liberal arts and humanities, leaders in all four states made the *traditional arguments* in favor of the enrichment—learning cultural discernment capabilities—and citizen preparation values of humanities and liberal arts programs. Three of four (Florida, North Carolina, and Wisconsin) also stressed the *economic value* of the liberal arts and humanities. Table 5.1 summarizes the university leaders' defenses of the liberal arts and humanities across these four dimensions.

TABLE 5.1.   University Leaders' Defense of the Liberal Arts and Humanities

	Florida	North Carolina	Texas	Wisconsin
Audience	External and internal	Internal	External	Internal
Nature of engagement	Primarily reactive	Proactive	Reactive	Proactive
Benefits of liberal arts	Discernment and utilitarian	Discernment and utilitarian	Primarily discernment	Discernment and utilitarian
Educational payoffs	Long-term	Long-term	Long-term	

The distinctions I make here are important in the context of thinking about the most effective ways to retain and expand support for liberal arts educational programming in public institutions. The governors in the four states I have discussed have argued to other politicians in their states and to voters that education is primarily of utilitarian value (it is a means to employment and income), and they have focused on the short term (employment and income immediately after graduation). In all four cases, the governors have set policy agendas that pose a serious threat to liberal arts and humanities education in their states. Most importantly, they have defined the terms of discussion.

By contrast, while one finds the occasional op-ed in major newspapers about the virtues of liberal arts and humanities, advocates have not argued for the value of the liberal arts and humanities in a sustained and proactive way to the broad citizenry. Assertions of the value of the liberal arts and humanities have typically been made to and among those who recognize their value. Scholars remind one another of the virtues of the liberal arts and humanities.[29] Brochures and web-sites for elite private colleges tell a self-selected group of liberal arts-inclined prospective students about the value of thinking broadly and deeply. Amherst College's website is typical. The college argues that "education [is] a process or activity rather than a form of production." At Amherst, "students are encouraged to continue to seek diversity and attempt integration."[30] The college's president argues against preparing eighteen- to twenty-two-year-olds for specific jobs. She contends that "We need in this country people who can think broadly, who can think deeply, who can think critically."[31]

Leaders at small liberal arts institutions—especially the high-prestige, selective ones—need not engage in an aggressive, proactive campaign to promote the liberal arts. The bulk of their potential audience already assumes the virtues of the education they offer. This is likely not true for state-based public institutions. The governors in the states on which I focused consistently play on what Richard Hofstadter described as "a national distaste for the intellect."[32] Writing fifty years ago, Hofstadter argued that Americans are resentful and suspicious of "the life of the mind and of those who are considered to represent it."[33]

Hofstadter sees this disposition as rooted in the earliest days of the US republic. Whether anti-intellectualism is as deep and widespread in the United States today as Hofstadter suggests was the case in the middle of the twentieth century, he is almost certainly correct when he contends that US citizens most often see education as a means to solving practical problems. More specifically, Americans seek higher education for greater employment opportunities and an elevated standard of living. According to a 2012 survey of entering college students nationwide conducted by UCLA's Higher Education Research Institute, nearly 90 percent of respondents indicated that "to get a better job" was a very important reason for going to college. Just under three-quarters of the students indicated that "to make more money" was a very important reason to attend college.[34]

In this context, the arguments made by the university leaders in the states I have discussed will not be sufficient to protect liberal arts education and the humanities in public institutions. During an earlier time, public education leaders' limited focus on the virtues of the liberal arts and humanities was probably sufficient to secure the place of this portion of the curricular and academic research landscape. In the mid-twentieth century, the United States had only recently put in place a welfare state (the New Deal), and academic science was widely perceived to have won the war. The country's fiscal house was in reasonable order as well, and that stability deflected the attention of many potential critics of the liberal arts and humanities. Today, we confront a slow-growing economy and serious fiscal challenges at the federal and state levels. We see a long-term downward trend in government support for public higher education and public ambivalence about government programs, and widespread worry about the cost of higher education. In this environment, the liberal arts and humanities are an easy target. Public higher education leaders need to speak directly to voters, and they need to reframe the discussion that the governors of Florida, North Carolina, Texas, and Wisconsin have shaped.

Press accounts make clear that chancellors and presidents are fighting hard to minimize the damage from funding cuts. It may appear as if this leaves little room to maneuver in any effort to promote the value of liberal arts and humanities education. I would suggest, however, that public university officials have more room to act than they realize. These leaders should not stress the enrichment and citizen preparation value of the liberal arts and humanities to voters and elected officials, a position fully fleshed out in the American Academy of Arts and Sciences recent report, *The Heart of the Matter*, and made regularly, consistently, and cogently by advocates of the liberal arts and humanities. Our history and recent polling data suggest that this perspective, while important, is unlikely to resonate with voters and politicians. Instead, I would suggest that an argument for the practical relevance of the humanities and liberal arts made directly to voters is more likely to weaken opposition to the liberal arts and humanities and solidify the place of these fields in public higher education.

Attitude surveys indicate the US public is broadly centrist and pragmatic and thus is likely to be open to a utilitarian argument in favor of the liberal arts and humanities, even if not accepting of a self-discovery and citizenship-preparation justification for such programs. According to one recent survey, Americans believe that higher education is the most important factor in determining a candidate's success on the job market,[35] and while Americans tend to oppose government in the abstract, they support government involvement in enhancing economic security and opportunity. Depending on the survey and the timing, between half and three quarters of Americans believe we are spending too little to improve our education system.[36]

While the views expressed by governors in the states I have considered are consistent with the ideology that Hofstadter suggested was pervasive at the middle of the twentieth century, the attitudes of contemporary business leaders—who one might imagine to be natural allies of Republican governors in the states to which I have pointed—seem to have changed since the nineteenth and early twentieth centuries about which Hofstadter wrote. According to Hofstadter, "During the nineteenth century, when business criteria dominated American culture almost without challenge, and when most business and professional men attained eminence without much formal section, academic schooling was often said to be useless."[37] Today, I would suggest, while many conservatives make a narrowly occupational argument for higher education, business leaders often take a broader view. Public university presidents and chancellors can play on this and enlist business leaders as allies.

In a 2013 article, Steve Strauss, a prominent business writer and entrepreneur, argued in favor of hiring English majors because of "their intellectual curiosity."[38] And, of course, we often hear of the prominent humanities majors who have been successful in business, entertainment, and politics. The field of English alone counts among its graduates Sting, Conan O'Brien, the former Avon CEO Andrea Jung, the former Xerox CEO Anne Mulcahy, and the former CEO of NBC, Grant Tinker.[39]

But this isn't just a matter of one high-profile businessperson's perspective and anecdotal data. A recent study commissioned by the Association of American Colleges and Universities provides evidence of broad support among business leaders for liberal arts education.[40] According to the study, nearly all respondents indicated that a "demonstrated capacity to think critically, communicate clearly, and solve complex problems is *more important* than [a candidate's] undergraduate major." Beyond this, the survey reports that "Eighty percent of employers agree that, regardless of their major, every college student should acquire broad knowledge in the liberal arts and sciences." Finally, "When read a description of a 21st-century liberal education, a large majority of employers recognize its importance; 74 percent would recommend this kind of education to a young person they know as the best way to prepare for success in today's global economy." This view is echoed in recent public polling, which suggests that two of three Americans believe that being well-rounded with a range of abilities (like problem-solving and the ability to communicate) is more important for success in the work world than having industry-specific skills.[41] In sum, the governors whose policies I have discussed are promoting positions explicitly at odds with a significant political constituency, and public university leaders would do well to point to the position of those in the business world, and, indeed, the general public, in arguing for the liberal arts and the humanities.

Public university leaders have additional ammunition. The employment landscape for humanities graduates looks nothing like the image that undergirds the initiatives of a number of state governors. The focused, occupationally oriented education advocated by these elected officials does not lead those with occupation-specific degrees to outperform humanities majors. While new graduates with professional backgrounds do initially make more money than those with humanities degrees, that edge does not seem to last. Drawing from data at payscale.com, Alexander Beecroft concludes that "Undergraduate professional degrees frequently lead to relatively high starting salaries and relatively flat pay scales thereafter."[42] Fifteen years after graduation, classics majors' annual salaries have surpassed accounting majors, English majors are outperforming multimedia and Web design students, and history majors are making as much as nurses. While a sound-bite news environment makes subtle argument challenging to present, public university leaders need to respond to occupationally focused criticisms of liberal arts and humanities education by pointing to the long-term economic value of a liberal arts and humanities education.

Beyond this, there is some evidence of the cognitive and related benefits of a liberal arts education. Sociologists Richard Arum and Josipa Roksa undertook a national test of college student learning. Among other things, they found that liberal arts majors had more substantial gains over time than non-liberal-arts majors in critical thinking, complex reasoning, and writing skills.[43] This is another argument public university leaders should make loudly and clearly.

If we are to believe the Association of American Colleges and Universities survey results and the contentions of those who argue for the cognitive value of liberal arts education, then the governors in the states I have discussed are advocating positions that are not only against the interests of many potentially well-heeled contributors, but also will not help to create the best possible conditions for long-term national economic vitality. What is more, insofar as liberal arts education sets students up for better long-term career advancement than would a narrower, occupationally oriented education, the policies advocated by these governors could ultimately contribute to reinforcing or exacerbating existing patterns of social stratification. This is so because while the economically secure and more well-to-do parents will continue to send their children to private liberal arts colleges, students from lower-income backgrounds will attend our cash-strapped public institutions. The former group of students will get the educations that business leaders advocate and which some suggest produce significant cognitive advance, while the latter will get narrower, occupationally oriented educations offered in public universities. The latter group's upward mobility will be stunted.

One would imagine that the existing state of affairs would position leaders of public universities—especially those under attack by elected officials—to persuade the public that we must preserve liberal arts and humanities education at all costs. While I hope that these leaders would continue to argue for the discernment and citizenship payoffs of a humanities-rich education, public opinion, business leaders' attitudes, and data on the value of a liberal arts education position public university presidents and chancellors (as well as provosts and deans) to reframe the discussion set by the governors from Florida, Texas, North Carolina, and Wisconsin. These university leaders can make a compelling argument for the utilitarian value of a liberal arts education and for the humanities. This should not be an argument that disparages the value of occupationally oriented programs, but it should stress the value of liberal arts and humanities programs for all students, those in STEM fields, those seeking occupationally oriented degrees, and humanities and social science majors.

While some of these university leaders have made muffled sounds in this direction, none has articulated a proactive, externally oriented, comprehensive, pro–liberal-arts and humanities position, and none has voiced his or her position with the persistence necessary to change the terms of the debate. This is the strategy that each should consider in the interest of the economic wellbeing of their respective states and of the liberal arts and humanities.

As I say this, I am quite sure that my analysis and its implications will trouble many of my faculty colleagues—my allies in the fight to solidify and bolster the place of the liberal arts and humanities in higher education curricula. They are advocates of the world-expanding and citizenship value of liberal education. I can imagine their worry that in the age of the audit culture, an essentially metrics-driven political strategy—an argument based on quantitative data on the value of the liberal arts for employment and employability—is vulnerable to new and contradictory data.[44] By justifying the liberal arts and humanities in terms of job market data and cognitive measurement, my colleagues might argue, we subject the education we provide to new assessments and alternative data suggesting that our teaching does not offer the advantages we claim for it. We expose ourselves to the possibility of a war of metrics and measurement. There is certainly a danger here. But a traditional defense of the liberal arts is unlikely to mollify public university leaders seeking fiscal restraint, and it is even more doubtful that such a position will persuade politicians and citizens. Faculty members stand only to lose by turning a cold shoulder to the advance of the audit culture. Measurement of all areas of academic life is not likely to go away anytime soon. We can work to alter the terms of debate by stressing the traditional virtues of the liberal arts and humanities, but this alone will not suffice. Thus, while our public university leaders advance the position I have advocated—a grounded, utilitarian argument in favor of liberal arts and humanities education—faculty should engage in ongoing discussions about how to measure higher education and develop arguments in favor of measurement most likely to capture the values we see at the heart of contemporary higher education. In collaboration, university leaders and the professoriate have a reasonable prospect of preserving and perhaps expanding the place of liberal arts and humanities education in our public universities.

NOTES

An earlier version of this chapter prepared for presentation at "A New Deal for the Humanities: Liberal Arts and the Future of Public Higher Education" symposium, September 18, 2013, University of Illinois at Urbana-Champaign. I benefited from the comments of participants in the symposium and from Susan Bernstein, Flora Berklein, Greg Downey, Steve Hoffman, Gordon Hutner, Feisal G. Mohamed, and Robert Osley-Thomas (who also assisted with the research on which this chapter is based). My research is supported by the National Science Foundation (SES-1026516), the Graduate School of the University of Wisconsin–Madison (through the Wisconsin Alumni Research Foundation gift), and the Korea Science Foundation (NRF-2010–330-B00169).

1. While the liberal arts means many things to many people, when I use the term, I mean a broad integrated education that includes coursework in the humanities, social sciences, and sciences.

2. The data for my analysis comes from reasonably thorough Google and Nexus searches. One issue here is that an absence in a database search does not, of course, mean that a university leader in one state has not responded to the attacks put forth by the governor of that state. But since I am interested in the breadth and persistence of the responses of university leaders, I feel confident that my search is adequate for my purposes here. Certainly for analytical purposes, the information I have gathered captures the varied dynamics in the apparent relationship between a state's flagship university and the governor of the state and provides adequate information for contemplating the kinds of strategies public university leaders might engage in to bolster the position of the liberal arts and the humanities on their campuses and in their states.

3. Zac Anderson, "Rick Scott Wants to Shift University Funding Away from Some Degrees," *Sarasota Herald Tribune*, October 10, 2011, available at http://politics.heraldtribune.com.

4. Ibid.

5. Ibid.

6. Qtd. in Nathan Crabbe, "Machen, Others Upset by Talk of Cutting Funding for Liberal Arts," *Gainsville.com*, October 11, 2011, available at http://www.gainesville.com (accessed September 1, 2013).

7. Qtd. in Anderson, "Rick Scott."

8. Ibid.

9. Ibid.

10. Lizette Alvarez, "Florida May Reduce Tuition for Select Majors," *New York Times*, December 9, 2012, available at http://www.nytimes.com (accessed September 1, 2013).

11. Bernie Machen, "All That and More: The True Purposes of College," Common Lecture, University of Florida, January 24, 2013. To date, Machen's pushback against Governor Scott's narrow conceptualization of higher education seems to have been successful. In 2014, the university announced a cost-sharing initiative with the state, which will allow the hiring of a number of new faculty members. While many of the new positions will be in clearly economically relevant sciences, the university will also be hiring faculty in African studies, creative writing, and social network analysis. See John O'Connor, "Seeking Top 10 Ranking, University of Florida Adds Staff," *State Impact*, January 9, 2014, available at http://stateimpact.npr.org (accessed June 8, 2014).

12. Holden Thorp, "Five Forces of Concern for Public Universities, Part 4: Liberal Arts Education and Access," Office of the Chancellor, University of North Carolina, November 2, 2012, available at http://holdenthorp.unc.edu (accessed August 15, 2013).

13. Tyler Kingkade, "Pat McCrory Lashes Out against 'Educational Elite' and Liberal Arts College Courses," *Huffington Post*, February 2, 2013, available at http://www.huffingtonpost.com (accessed August 18, 2013).

14. Ibid.

15. Brian Rosenberg, "Ignorance about Education," *Huffington Post*, January 30, 2013, available at http://www.huffingtonpost.com (accessed September 1, 2013).

16. Cullen Browder, "UNC System Could Lose Campuses," *WRAL.com*, March 21, 2013, available at http://www.wral.com (accessed September 1, 2013).

17. Jane Stancill and Anne Blythe, "UNC-CH Names Carol Folt First Female Chancellor," *NewsObserver.com*, April 13, 2013, available at http://www.newsobserver.com (accessed August 15, 2013).

18. Quoted in Amanda Albright, "Carol Holt Officially Installed as Chancellor Saturday," *dailytarheel.com*, October 13, 2013, available at http://www.dailytarheel.com (accessed June 8, 2014).

19. Rick Perry, "Separating Truth from Fiction in Higher Education Research," *Dallas News*, May 13, 2011, available at http://www.dallasnews.com (accessed August 18, 2013).

20. Kevin Kiley, "A $10,000 Platform," *Inside Higher Ed*, November 30, 2012, available at http://www.insidehighered.com (accessed August 16, 2013).

21. Ibid.

22. Justin Pope, "University of Texas, Rick Perry Clash Over the Future of Public Higher Education," *Huffington Post*, February 3, 2013, available at http://www.huffingtonpost.com (accessed August 16, 2013).

23. Chris Hooks, "Powers Deflects Talk of UT Conflict," *Texas Tribune*, April 6, 2013, available at http://www.texastribune.org (accessed August 16, 2013).

24. Randy Diehl and the Executive Leadership Team, College of Liberal Arts, "Maintaining Excellence and Efficiency at the University of Texas at Austin" (2011), available at http://7solutionsresponse.org/index.php?unit=home (accessed August 17, 2013).

25. Qtd. in Dee J. Hall and Samara Kalk Derby, "Gov. Scott Walker Unveils Agenda for Wisconsin during Speech in California," *Wisconsin State Journal*, November 19, 2012, available at http://host.madison.com (accessed July 10, 2014).

26. Daniel Bice, "Walker Promises Tax Reforms, School Funding Changes," *Milwaukee Journal Sentinel*, November 17, 2012, available at http://www.jsonline.com (accessed September 1, 2013).

27. Paul Fanlund, "David Ward on What Confronts the Next UW Chancellor," *Capital Times*, February 18, 2013, available at http://host.madison.com (accessed on August 18, 2013).

28. The University of Wisconsin's College of Letters and Sciences is embarking on an initiative to promote the career value of liberal arts education. The college recently published a piece directed to parents of current students. See "The Value of a Liberal Arts Degree," *Badger Parent* (April 2014), available at parent.wisc.edu/newsletter-story/the-value-of-a-liberal-arts-degree/ (accessed June 8, 2014).

29. See, for example, Martha Nussbaum, *Not for Sale: Why Democracy Needs the Humanities* (Princeton: Princeton University Press, 2010); and Mark Edmundson, *Why Teach? In Defense of a Real Education* (New York: Bloomsbury, 2013).

30. See amherst.edu/academiclife, accessed November 17, 2013.

31. "Biddy Martin on Amherst, Higher Education, and the Liberal Arts," available at http://parent.wisc.edu/newsletter-story/the-value-of-a-liberal-arts-degree/ (accessed November 19, 2013).

32. Richard Hofstadter, *Anti-Intellectualism in American Life* (New York: Knopf, 1963), 5.

33. Ibid., 2.

34. Kathy Wyer, "Survey: More Freshmen than Ever Say They Go to College to Get Better Jobs, Make More Money," *UCLA Newsroom*, January 23, 2013, available at http://newsroom.ucla.edu/releases/heri-freshman-survey-242619 (accessed November 17, 2013).

35. Vicki Sloan Williams, "Research Today: Attitudes toward Higher Education [and MOOCS]," Penn State Teaching and Learning with Technology (2013), available at http://tlt.psu.edu/2013/10/01/research-today-attitudes-toward-higher-education-and-moocs/ (accessed November 17, 2013).

36. See Leslie McCall and Lane Kenworthy, "Americans' Social Policy Preferences in an Era of Rising Inequality," *Perspectives on Politics* 7.3 (2009): 459–484; Jennifer Hochschild, *What's Fair: American Beliefs about Distributive Justice* (Cambridge, MA: Harvard University Press, 1981); and Martin Gilens, *Why Americans Hate Welfare: Race, Media, and the Politics of Antipoverty Policy* (Chicago: University of Chicago Press, 1999).

37. Hofstadter, *Anti-Intellectualism*, 33.

38. Steve Strauss, "Why I Hire English Majors," *Huffington Post*, June 23, 2013, available at http://www.huffingtonpost.com (accessed September 1, 2013).

39. Vivian Gaing, Lynne Guey, and Max Nisen, "16 Wildly Successful People Who Majored in English," *Business Insider*, May 13, 2013, available at http://www.businessinsider.com (accessed September 1, 2013).

40. Hart Research Associates, "It Takes More than a Major: Employer Priorities for College Learning and Student Success," Association of American Colleges and Universities (2013), available at http://aacu.org/sites/default/files/files/LEAP/2013_EmployerSurvey.pdf (accessed August 18, 2013).

41. See Williams, "Research Today."

42. Alexander Beecroft, "The Humanities: What Went Right?" *Chronicle of Higher Education*, July 3, 2013, available at http://chronicle.com (accessed September 1, 2013). A 2006 study by Goyette and Mullen suggests that majoring in the arts or sciences was not significantly negatively correlated with earnings, when controlling for demographic characteristics and educational attainment. In addition, although these authors do not have long-term employment data, consistent with other research, they conclude any difference in earnings between liberal arts and technical degrees diminishes over time. See Kimberly A. Goyette and Ann L. Mullen, "Who Studies the Arts and Sciences? Social Background and the Choice and Consequences of Undergraduate Field of Study," *Journal of Higher Education* 77.3 (May–June 2006): 497–538.

43. Richard Arum and Josipa Roksa, *Academically Adrift: Limited Learning on College Campuses* (Chicago: University of Chicago Press, 2011). Three decades ago, Forest's research also spoke to the cognitive virtues of liberal arts courses. Specifically, Forest found that students at institutions with a large proportion of required courses in arts and science fields experienced the greatest gains to critical thinking skills. See A. Forest, *Increasing Student Competence and Persistence: The Best Case for General Education* (Iowa City: American College Testing Program, 1982).

44. On "audit culture," see Marilyn Strathern, *Audit Cultures: Anthropological Studies in Accountability, Ethics, and the Academy* (New York: Routledge, 2000).

6 · SPEAKING THE LANGUAGES OF THE HUMANITIES

CHARLOTTE MELIN

In 1869, the first general report to the University of Minnesota regents made the case for establishment of what was essentially a humanities or liberal arts college—"a course of study best adapted to stimulate all the faculties of the mind, and to impart that breadth of information essential to every liberally educated man, should consist in proper proportion of linguistic, mathematical, physical and philosophical studies."[1] That notion of proportions is elegantly mirrored in the rhetoric, with the careful placement of referents to speculative fields (language and philosophy) bracketing those for the empirical disciplines (mathematics and physical sciences). Such precise symmetry emphasizes the importance of the humanities for the development of an educated citizenry from the perspective of time less remote than it at first appears. Today, we are abundantly familiar with such statements from strategic-planning documents, albeit with more inclusive language and judicious references to *liberal education requirements, student learning outcomes, global citizens,* and *lifelong learning.* Indeed, we still inhabit the disciplinary quarrels the document's authors registered in adding these words:

> Yet recognizing the fact that at the present time there are many conflicting views as to what is the proper proportion of these various branches of learning, in a general course of study, especially as to the comparative value of physical and linguistic studies, and of the modern and ancient languages, we recommend that there be organized several general courses of study . . . each one giving prominence to some one grand department of learning, without neglecting altogether either of the others.[2]

And so disciplinary competition began. Clearly, the humanities, and especially the languages,[3] have been entangled from the start in debates about the mission and purpose of land-grant institutions, or in words often attributed to Jean-Baptiste Alphonse Karr, *plus ça change, plus c'est la même chose.* My interest lies not in trying to resolve these tensions, but rather in asking how we use them to expand our vision.

Few institutions of higher education would accord the foreign languages such importance today, and as a discipline the languages are not alone in that predicament. On many campuses, the STEM fields dominate and continue to grow rapidly. While colleagues in those areas acknowledge the genuine need for humanities thinking and sympathize with our distress, they often occupy a privileged position. Moreover, within the humanities, social sciences increasingly seem to speak for the whole, while the languages, literatures, philosophy, religion, visual and performing arts shrink into self-inflicted silence. It is pointless to pursue internecine arguments about which humanities fields deserve to be strengthened under the circumstances, because if we do, we lose sight of the fact that all of them are jeopardized. What I want to point out in raising these issues is an obvious disparity, seen on my own campus and others. At the University of Minnesota, where strategic planning is now ambitiously focused on addressing society's grand challenges, "soft" humanities fields like the languages have negligible representation on the planning committees that are setting the agenda for the next decade. The sense of proportion, hard-won consensus, and intellectual balance laid out in the 1869 report has vanished in its original form. Missing from our current conversations is a commitment to ensuring that the university community has the tangible means to operate in our diverse and rapidly changing world. In the case of my own discipline, that means we have lost the presence of language as an intellectual force. The factors that account for this predicament are complex, but they point to a dire need for revitalization of foreign language education, especially at public institutions.

Many, of course, have preceded me in calls to revitalize the languages, including Janet Swaffar and Katherine Arens, Mark Roche, and Kate Paesani and Heather Willis Allen.[4] Colleagues outside the foreign languages are unlikely to know their work, and lamentably, too, many colleagues within language-related fields may not be familiar enough with their scholarship. We seem to assume that higher education can be constructed intuitively. It is simply easier to rely on general impressions rather than to do the hard work of considering colleagues' thoughtful recommendations. Yet here we are our own worst enemy: we gladly talk about our own esoteric research because it is familiar, ignoring or dismissing other research that could help us interpret the crisis at hand, notably the expanding field of Second Language Acquisition, which ties in directly with all that we do. Perhaps we assume that the status quo of disciplines will continue or that others will be our advocates, yet we fail to take care of the foreign languages in very fundamental ways.

Missing from even the most insightful discussions has been consideration of scalable, dynamic approaches to conceptualizing languages in higher education—approaches greatly needed at large, structurally complex, demographically diverse, research-intensive, land-grant institutions. It is an oversight we cannot afford, for our ability to address future challenges as a nation is at stake, just as it was when land-grant universities were founded. For public universities to live out their mission in the twenty-first century, it is vital to renew our commitment to the humanities, especially the study of language, culture, and texts in their historical and contemporary dimensions. Languages have high prestige and value for good reason. Language makes us human—it is essential to the discovery and circulation of knowledge. But such idealistic claims carry little weight in the current environment. If reports about the demise of the humanities are worrisome, the vulnerability of the foreign languages is all the more real, and exacerbated by complex factors.[5]

True, the 2009 MLA report on languages other than English reassured us that overall enrollments continue at an all-time high, with sustained growth in Spanish, Chinese, ASL (American Sign Language), Arabic, Korean, and certain LCTLs or less commonly taught languages.[6] In overall ranking as well, Spanish, French, and German continue to top the list.[7] The news briefly cheered colleagues in my own field, of course, when we learned that German had enjoyed enrollment increases of 3.5 percent from 2002 to 2006 and 2.2 percent from 2006 to 2009.[8]

But the fact remains that such modest enrollment gains offer no protection against larger fiscal challenges.[9] We face profound systemwide shifts in higher education that have serious implications for the foreign languages in particular. Local enrollment contractions (sometimes forced), heated discussion about foreign language requirements, and cost-cutting measures leading to highly publicized departmental closures confirm the perception that languages are expendable. Measuring this harsh climate in 2009, Linda Ray Pratt urged colleagues to "take a cold-eyed look" to the future, warning frankly that "the most vulnerable academic areas will be programs that have few majors or few student credit hours in the core curriculum," an assessment reinforced by her observation that "many modern language departments are already struggling to sustain enrollments in anything but Spanish and French."[10]

Since then, greater challenges have appeared. Double majors, long taken for granted by foreign language departments as a means to bolster enrollments, are becoming less feasible for students with credit-intensive majors (like STEM or pre-professional fields). While minors seem (at least anecdotally) to be on the increase, mechanisms for recognizing that departmental effort are inadequate.

Moreover, double majors make foreign languages and area studies vulnerable if administrators do not take them into account in relation to overall departmental contributions.[11] In addition, current and pending cuts in federal Title VI funding, which in the past bolstered the ability of land-grant universities to offer diverse languages, directly threaten both area studies and the foreign languages.[12]

For research universities, especially land-grant institutions, these trends have led to complicated challenges for graduate level foreign language programs. Decreases in language majors, rising student debt, and the inability to increase graduate student support to levels competitive with well-endowed private institutions make it difficult to attract top-quality graduate students in the foreign languages to public university programs. In the absence of sufficient support, our universities cannot compete with private universities that offer thousands of dollars more in support. As long as the humanities and foreign languages in particular are not a high priority, those programs have little hope for an increase in funds. Already for more than a decade at the University of Minnesota, graduate programs have "right-sized" graduate student admissions to a quota that could be financially covered by teaching assistantships and fellowships. They are also committed to limiting new cohorts to a number that reflects how many degree candidates are expected to find suitable jobs. These measures are an ethical response to the problems besetting graduate education. Nonetheless, and leaving aside the larger questions about the time it takes to get the PhD, it is obvious that foreign language departments are facing or will soon face an implosion of graduate programs with far-ranging consequences for language education as a whole, unless changes occur in the system.

These trends are also mirrored in the *MLA Job List*, which constitutes a source of data predictive of future staffing capacity for the humanities in higher education. One recent report showed a 32.5 percent decline in foreign language listings for 2011–2012 when compared with 2007–2008 levels.[13] Despite the limitations of the *Job List* (it does not attest to the expansion of adjunct staffing), it is obvious that shrinking numbers of permanent core faculty weaken the foreign languages. Land-grant universities are at the center of the vortex that these conditions create. At the University of Minnesota and many similar institutions, non-tenure-track faculty teach the majority of courses in foreign language programs and are responsible for the largest portion of department enrollments. In most cases, however, these colleagues hold appointments that are defined solely as teaching appointments, not in terms of everything that surrounds the educational process—planning, curriculum development, mentorship of graduate students, undergraduate advising, and ultimately research. That configuration of job expectations ignores, with immediate consequences, the complex responsibilities of teachers and skews the commitment of the university community to a mission of teaching, research, and service. As departments and tenured and tenure-track faculty are urged to pursue excellence in research to the exclusion of all else, less attention is accorded to teaching. Enrollments eventually suffer from this neglect, resulting in a further downward spiral. When the proportion of non-tenure-stream colleagues grows to make up for the poorly covered needs that remain, more disparities in the system result. The burden of operational work falls too disproportionately on the remaining faculty, who then surrender valuable research time to take on the extensive service and administrative commitments vital to the health of foreign language departments. Ultimately careers and departments suffer. One of the most concerning impacts of these trends is the resulting erosion of our capacity to advance intellectual values through a community of humanities faculty members who take responsibility for the interconnected work of teaching, research, and service—faculty who have an essential commitment to the broader mission that ensures the future vitality of foreign languages at land-grant institutions.

In light of these pressures, we need a paradigm shift that will enable institutions to address current challenges with solutions that affirm the centrality of language and culture to education—and that is where I will focus my attention in describing three pivotal issues. I begin with the context for the discussion of languages in the 2013 Commmission on the Humanities and Social Sciences report *The Heart of the Matter.* Following this background, I will propose a broader definition of the languages and their importance within the humanities. Finally, I will turn to the question of how we might newly conceive the role of languages at public, land-grant institutions in the twenty-first century.

THE SITUATION OF LANGUAGES AT LAND-GRANT UNIVERSITIES

Among the goals identified in *The Heart of the Matter*, the third, "Equip the nation for leadership in an interconnected world," speaks most directly to the role of languages in higher education. Its central justification has largely to do with economic factors and political exigencies, for as the report tells us: "Now more than ever the nation needs expertise in cultures, languages, and area studies to compete in a global economy and participate in an international community."[14]

To its credit, these matters are not the only ones that interest the report's authors. In addition to a rationale for languages that is tied to international security and competitiveness (55), the report cites reasons for learning languages related to our ability to see the world from different points of view (38), to grapple with ethical and moral questions (44), to develop critical intercultural skills (57), and to achieve many other benefits. The recommendations contained in *The Heart of the Matter* focus on four objectives:

- Promote language learning
- Expand education in international affairs and transnational studies
- Support study abroad and international exchange programs
- Develop a "Culture Corps," presumably an equivalent to Americorps or Teach for America (12)

Certainly we can agree that these are worthy goals, yet they are not unproblematical aspirations. Language learning cannot be fully promoted in the absence of long-term, time-intensive paths to achieving advanced levels of proficiency (such as the Flagship programs for critical languages), which are the foundation for international and transnational studies. Study-abroad options hinge on such highly variable factors as student interest and affordability, yet without such global mobility, learners cannot reach advanced levels of proficiency. A "Culture Corps" is a worthy goal, but such programs rely on the willingness of highly trained recent college graduates to dedicate themselves to public service for only minimal compensation. In addition, those willing individuals prepared to make such a commitment will need extensive language experience in real-world situations, something a traditional foreign language and literature curriculum, organized according to historical periods, may not be able to promise. Although the report strongly affirms the "importance of supporting the comprehensive nature of the research university," making a commitment to maintaining a diverse ecology of disciplines and fields at institutions of higher education is no simple matter (41). Here we can recognize enduring themes in current discussions of foreign languages: strategic importance, globalization, and presentism.

The MLA report "Foreign Languages and Higher Education: New Structures for a Changed World," published in 2007 and ever since *the* reference point for every discussion of foreign languages, resulted from the "language crisis" of 9/11.[15] The terrible events on that day revealed, among other things, the lack of capacity in the United States for communicating with other parts of the world, interpreting intelligence data, and being open to cultures beyond our borders. The resulting national security agenda focused on the instrumental value of language skill. Without dismissing that practical worth, the MLA report emphasized the need for learners to develop broader literacies reflecting "translingual and transcultural competence";[16] to that end it argued for a dismantlement of the "two-tiered" structure of many departments—the rift between language and literature (or other content) courses, or lower and upper division. While this division is less rigid than the report implies,[17] the concept helps us identify challenges that languages face within higher education as a whole. If languages are seen as merely a set of skills, it is difficult to argue that they make a broader intellectual contribution; if they are not integrated with intellectual work, they occupy a marginal position. In German we call this a *Teufelskreis*—a vicious circle.

That vicious circle is only one of several we face. The 2007 MLA report was swiftly eclipsed by the economic crisis of 2008, which froze the momentum that document was intended to create. Departments at public and land-grant universities seem to have been hit particularly hard as state budget shortfalls precipitated hiring freezes and restructuring. Data-driven curriculum management focusing on enrollments caught the languages in grinding systemwide collapse: as K–12 education cut languages to address budget shortfalls, language offerings at the postsecondary level were also compromised.[18] LCTLs, apart from the critical languages, struggled to survive,[19] and even federal efforts to increase language capacity (Title VI and Department of Defense funding) have had limited impact. Martha C. Nussbaum makes the case in *Not for Profit* that the United States desperately craves the imaginative powers of the humanities; whether or not we agree with her strategy for reinvigorating them, we recognize that it is difficult to promote their value in the present environment, especially when it involves the time-intensive work of learning another language.[20]

As William Rivers and John Robinson observe in a 2012 essay: "The past decade has seen the emergence of a consensus that the United States needs a more globally educated citizenry. . . . However, the decade's investments in foreign language instruction and programs by the U.S. government have effected marginal change on the educational system at best."[21] Arguably, this notion of a "globally educated citizenry" has become part of the problem. As programs of "Global Studies" have boomed, foreign language departments have often seen declines in majors. This shift may not have a direct cause-and-effect correlation, particularly when done right, because global or international studies do in fact promote language learning.[22] Yet outside of the liberal arts, it seems that "global" signals "taught in English." Globalization means that "the world is flat" (à la Thomas Friedman) and the universal language is English. Unfortunately, this focus on the "global" eclipses awareness of an emerging plurilingualism: the growth in multilingual communities in the United States due to recent immigration.[23]

Exacerbating the situation is a focus on the present. While history is not entirely dismissed, presentism fixes us on the immediate needs and interests of our students and society. Under this scenario, esoteric dead languages lose their status, with the practical result that the retirement of a faculty member specializing in such an area leads to the loss of an entire field. In terms of the categories proposed by the linguist Ferdinand de Saussure, *langue* and *parole*, we are left with only *parole*/speech detached from the larger, continuous flow in the system of *langue*/language.[24]

What I describe is, admittedly, a very schematic account of the current state of languages. It is tinged with pessimism that we can perhaps dispel by thinking about how languages and the humanities contribute to the creation and dissemination of new knowledge for the greatest good in society—the heart of the mission of land-grant universities. I propose that when we consider the role of languages in the twenty-first century, at least *four* distinct languages of the humanities are crucial to our enterprise: the languages of the present, of the past, of translation, and of plurilingualism. These ways of thinking about language overlap with notions of transcultural and translingual awareness, but challenge us to contemplate the dynamics of the educational system as a whole.

THE LANGUAGES OF THE HUMANITIES

In the academic year 2012–2013, I served on a college-level committee charged with looking at ways to strengthen foreign languages in the University of Minnesota's College of Liberal Arts (CLA). One of this committee's key charges was to develop a mission statement for the college. It expresses precisely what I advocate for public land-grant institutions in general:

> Language and communication are fundamental to human experience and in the globalized 21st century our learning and the creation of knowledge depend ever more profoundly on translingual and transcultural competence. The College of Liberal Arts is committed to fostering a community of undergraduate and graduate students, university faculty and staff, lifelong learners and global citizens prepared to address the global challenges of the future. To live out the land grant mission of the University in the 21st century, the College recognizes that the study of language, culture, and texts in their historical and contemporary dimensions must stand at the heart of liberal education. The College affirms that fundamental to the discovery and circulation of knowledge is the ability to communicate, read, and interpret. These capacities are grounded in language and nurtured in higher education through the convergence of research, teaching, and service. CLA is committed to maintaining access for students to educational pathways for the study of the rich heritage of diverse languages, to promoting mobility through study abroad and experiential opportunities, and to pioneering new forms of learning that lead to understanding of the practices and perspectives of other cultures.[25]

What this statement tries to capture is the scope of languages in higher education and our world today. As a heuristic exercise, such a mission statement requires us to think about the relation between languages and other parts of the university—beyond connections with fields of similarly minded colleagues where we have traditionally found allies: core disciplines like English and history.

The current emphasis on student learning outcomes (SLOs) and liberal education requirements, which is tied to calls for accountability, forces us to think about the role of languages in different ways. The 2009 Modern Language Association "Report to the Teagle Foundation on the Undergraduate Major in Language and Literature" eloquently responds to these challenges by articulating the intellectual value of the foreign langauge major.[26] On the ground, however, language departments find it difficult to envision how such values translate into educational practice, because the "two-tiered" structure is still tacitly entrenched.[27] Only by foregrounding the intellectual tools with which we actually equip our students do we arrive at a model for how the languages *should* relate to other disciplinary fields[28]—the purpose of the categories I have proposed for the languages of the present, the past, translation, and plurilingualism, to which we will turn now. Let us explore them in terms of their potential for land-grant universities in the twenty-first century:

- *The languages of the present*. Here we recognize that our students are learning languages to explore other cultures and gain access to knowledge. They may study abroad, engage in experiential learning, pursue internships that take them out into the world, and most of all, we hope they will become lifelong learners through these experiences who will continue to use their languages in the future.[29] On campus we also recognize that our intellectual community is thoroughly international. Likewise, we need to advocate for fields of knowledge—specifically Second Language Acquisition—that deserve a more prominent role in our institutions, because they advance the objective of expanding the capacity for languages throughout higher education. Colleagues in science fields frequently urge their students to look for cutting-edge research in other languages because they know not everything is translated into English. The languages of the present mean the languages of diplomatic negotiations, economic competitiveness, and innovation breakthroughs. They empower us to understand the perspectives and cultural practices of others, and to interpret them in ways vital to our future.[30]
- *The languages of the past*. Greek, Latin, Sanskrit, Middle High German, Anglo-Saxon—few of us have studied the "dead" languages, yet they surround us in the structure of knowledge production and university disciplines, in libraries, and living assumptions about our heritage. Together with the languages of the present, they connect us with history. The classical languages also remind us of our ethical responsibility to preserve currently endangered languages, through efforts like the *Ojibwe People's Dictionary* (at the University of Minnesota).[31] By including these aspects of language, we recognize that there is a connection between biological and cultural diversity and accelerating loss of both.[32]
- *The languages of translation*. Everywhere we rely on translations: books in translation, subtitled films, product instructions, Google Translate, and

BabelFish. Rarely do we stop to ask what translation means—whether it is accurate, what knowledge a translator needs to supply an adequate translation, or how language relates to textual meaning. Literature in translation enriches the teaching of a great many disciplines, offering us insight, however brief or fragmented, into otherwise inaccessible worlds. For professionals, linguistic precision is crucial: the Spanish-speaking health-care interpreter working at a local clinic conveys information that can be a matter of life and death, the court interpreter ensures a fair justice system, the field interpreter in a conflict zone delivers information of international consequence. Ask any colleague who has sought Institutional Review Board (IRB) approval for a research project and you will know that the approval protocol must ensure that subjects understand participation in their own language.[33]

- *The languages of plurilingualism.* While the 2007 MLA report persuasively urged translingual and transcultural competence as an aim, that aspiration has only been partly realized in higher education. It is, however, an even more urgent agenda today, given national political discussions of immigration reform, international mobility in education, and the land-grant mandate for educational access. The model for languages at universities in the past was a simple one: students learned *a* language in high school and continued with the same language. Even with the enhanced systemwide articulation that exists today, that model is woefully outdated. Heritage speakers, burgeoning immersion language education at the K–12 level, multilingual immigrants, and on-line learning complicate the paths of language education. To strengthen the educational access that land-grant universities represent, attention must be given to that system complexity.

ARGUMENTS FOR A NEW PARADIGM

It has often been observed that the liberal arts engage the "great questions."[34] All the more so the humanities, which provide us with the ability to notice what we encounter and put it into language, to tell stories (narratives) for interpreting the world, with tools for reflection that negotiate other perspectives.[35] The languages of the humanities are *the* vehicle for that process, despite their marginalization in current discussions. We need to resist both that marginalization and our own complacency about the status quo. When universities, such as my own, advocate the organization of research, teaching, and service as addressing "grand challenges," humanities colleagues may be reluctant to embrace the approach, because it feels like problem-solving simplification and empty rhetoric. Yet in the present situation, we in the foreign languages cannot afford to stand idly by as one opportunity for change after another passes.

Reshaping the structure of the major for my own department in a recent initiative, my colleagues and I sought a new paradigm for our work.[36] Rather than focusing on seat-time language requirements, a historical sequence of courses, or skills-defined competencies, we chose a different path: the intellectual tools that lie at the core of all that we do—teaching skill in language and textual analysis, understanding of context and media, and critical literacy in global perspective.[37] While it is not easy to make this shift, the survival of the languages at land-grant institutions depends on it.

For the foreign languages to survive and thrive at land-grant universities, we will need more than ever to cultivate an ability to imagine interdisciplinary partnerships that reach out across institutions and work to enhance the broad intellectual project we envision for ourselves as scholars of literature, culture, and language. Joint degree programs (such as the University of Rhode Island International Engineering Program), CIBER (Center for International Business Education and Research initiatives), and certificate programs (e.g., in languages for the health-care professions or translation and interpretation) offer pathways of undergraduate and professional studies that can exist only at research universities like ours. Growing interest in connecting foreign language teaching and learning with environmental and sustainability studies offers another way to build interdisciplinary collaborations that incorporate the study of literature and culture. Both models share a commitment to the deeper meaning of liberal education. Their curriculum is designed to familiarize students with cultural, environmental, and ethical perspectives available uniquely through the access that other languages give us. Its aim is multiple literacies. Such a curriculum consists not of courses in language study for instrumental purposes alone, but of education in the broadest possible way for understanding how language shapes the world we inhabit. The multifaceted foreign language curriculum of land-grant universities in the future needs to reflect such complexity and embrace the change that it brings.

In an essay by John Hudzik and Lou Anna K. Simon, "From a Land-Grant to a World-Grant Ideal," which appeared in the edited collection celebrating the sesquicentennial of the Morrill Act, the authors describe our institutions' mission in terms that speak directly to the role of languages in the humanities: "The land-grant concept foretold a trend in U.S. public higher education to constantly 'innovate' the university curriculum, research, and engagement by imparting a practical emphasis to higher education and extending its benefits beyond the elite social and economic classes. Connecting land-grant missions to global realities is not an end in itself but a means—the next step of innovation—to advance core values in a new environment."[38] Languages are vital to that innovation. Returning now to the State of Minnesota document I cited at the outset, we can see that "a course of study best adapted to stimulate all the faculties of the mind, and to impart that breadth of information essential to every liberally educated [*person*]" has, indeed, become today multiple courses of study. Yet to realize the mission of land-grant universities in the twenty-first century, we need to expand that conception again—to pursue breadth, access, and innovation by making full use of *all* the languages of the humanities.

NOTES

1. University of Minnesota, *Report of the Committee on Organization* (Minneapolis, 1869), 10, available at http://conservancy.umn.edu/bitstream/137221/1/Report_of_Committee_on _Organization.pdf/. The University of Minnesota was founded as a preparatory school in 1851 (before Minnesota became a state), closed during the Civil War, reopened in 1867 and was designated a land-grant (first president, William Watts Folwell inaugurated Dec. 1869). See University of Minnesota "History and Mission," http://www1.umn.edu/twincities/history -mission/index.html.

2. University of Minnesota, *Report of the Committee on Organization*, 10.

3. The term "languages" is used inclusively in this chapter to indicate foreign languages, second language studies, and the study of ancient languages. Sign language is offered as an option for fulfilling the language requirement at most land-grant universities.

4. See Janet Swaffar and Katherine Arens, *Remapping the Foreign Language Curriculum* (New York: Modern Language Association, 2005); Mark William Roche, *Why Choose the Liberal Arts?* (Notre Dame, IN: University of Notre Dame Press, 2010); and Kate Paesani and Heather Willis Allen, "Beyond the Language-Content Divide: Research on Advanced Foreign Language Instruction at the Postsecondary Level," Special Focus Issue, *Foreign Language Annals* 45.S1 (2012): S54–S75.

5. In particular, see the MLA blog "Mismeasuring the Humanities," http://mlaresearch .commons.mla.org/2013/07/02/mismeasuring-the-humanities/; "What's in a Number? MLA Posts on Measuring the Humanities," http://news.commons.mla.org/2013/07/08/ whats-in-a-number-mla-commons-posts-on-measuring-the-humanities/; "MLA Responds to Report on the Humanities and Social Sciences," http://news.commons.mla.org/2013/06/ 19/mla-responds-to-report-on-the-humanities-and-social-sciences/; and multiple related articles in the *Chronicle of Higher Education* issue from July 16, 2013.

6. See http://www.mla.org/pdf/2009_enrollment_survey.pdf.

7. Nelly Furman, David Goldberg, and Natalia Lusin, *Enrollments in Languages Other than English in United States Institutions of Higher Education, Fall 2009* (New York: Modern Language Association, 2010), 4, 13.

8. James J. Pancrazio, "The German Major in Today's Fiscal Climate," *ADFL Bulletin* 41.3 (2011): 38.

9. Furman, Goldberg, and Lusin, *Enrollments in Languages Other than English*, 19.

10. Linda Ray Pratt, "The Financial Landscape of Higher Education: Mapping a Rough Road Ahead," *ADFL Bulletin* 41.1 (2009): 13.

11. Natalia Lusin, "Curious Facts: Are You Counting Second Majors in Foreign Languages?" *ADFL Bulletin* 41.2 (2009):105–107.

12. Anna Grzymala-Busse, "Area-Studies Centers Are Vital but Vulnerable," *Chronicle of Higher Education*, November 14, 2013, available at http://chronicle.com.

13. MLA Office of Research 2012.

14. Commmission on the Humanities and Social Sciences, *The Heart of the Matter* (American Academy of Arts and Sciences, 2013), available at http://humanitiescommission.org/_pdf/hss _report.pdf (accessed August 21, 2013), 43. Further references to this report are in parentheses.

15. MLA Ad Hoc Committee on Foreign Languages, "Foreign Languages and Higher Education: New Structures for a Changed World," *Profession* (2007): 234.

16. Ibid., 237.

17. Cf. Glenn S. Levine, Charlotte Melin, Corrine Crane, Monika Chavez, and Thomas A. Lovik, "The Language Program Director in Curricular and Departmental Reform: A Response to the MLA Ad Hoc Report," *Profession* (2008): 240–254.

18. Russell A. Berman, "Foreign Languages and Student Learning in the Age of Accountability," *ADFL Bulletin* 42.1 (2012): 23–30.

19. Heritage languages traditionally associated with the populations of land-grant university states are endangered by this trend, despite apparently strong assurances that they will continue. Interestingly, at the University of Minnesota a faculty line for Scandinavian was mandated by the State of Minnesota in an early law: "It shall be the duty of the board of regents of the State University, as soon as practicable after the passage of this act, to appoint to said professorship [professorship of Scandinavian language and literature] some person learned in the Scandinavian language and literature, and at the same time skilled [in] and capable of teaching the dead languages, so called." See State of Minnesota, *General Laws* (St. Paul: J. W. Cunningham, State Printer, 1883), 197.

20. Martha C. Nussbaum, *Not for Profit: Why Democracy Needs the Humanities* (Princeton: Princeton University Press, 2010); see also Daniel Mark Fogel and Elizabeth Malson-Huddle, eds., *Precipice or Crossroads? Where America's Great Public Universities Stand and Where They Are Going Midway through Their Second Century* (Albany: State University of New York Press, 2012).

21. William P. Rivers and John P. Robinson, "The Unchanging American Capacity in Languages Other Than English: Speaking and Learning Languages Other than English, 2000–2008," *Modern Language Journal* 96 (2012): 369–379.

22. Jane Hacking, "Global Studies and Departmental Structures," *ADFL Bulletin* 42.2 (2013): 21–25. At the University of Minnesota, Global Studies majors have a higher requirement for language study than undergraduates in the College of Liberal Arts as a whole. Students must fulfill their requirement by completing four semesters of language study, plus an experiential requirement (minimum six weeks abroad or the equivalent). Unlike students in the College of Liberal Arts, they are also not allowed to "test out" of the required courses and cannot use previous language study to fulfill the requirement. For further details, see http://igs.cla.umn .edu/ugrad/majors.html.

23. Changing immigration patterns are dramatically reshaping the language profile of the United States, sometimes in unexpected ways. For example, in Minnesota (a state known for the strong Scandinavian heritage of its population), currently the largest group of Swedish speakers is the Somali community, because so many Somali immigrants arrived via a path that led through Sweden. This has led to reciprocal exchanges to share information about this process internationally; see http://minnesota.publicradio.org/display/web/2010/10/20/ somalis-sweden.

24. Ferdinand de Saussure, *Course in General Linguistics* (LaSalle, IL: Open Court, 1986).

25. The full-text document, "Second Language Acquisition Working Group Report," is available at http://ugp.cla.umn.edu/.

26. *Report to the Teagle Foundation on the Undergraduate Major in Language and Literature* (New York: Modern Language Association, 2009), available at http://www.mla.org/pdf/ 2008_mla_whitepaper.pdf/ (accessed July 18, 2013).

27. Cf. MLA Ad Hoc 2007. For an overview of the history of how this system evolved, see Rosemary G. Feal, "From the Editor," *Profession* (2012): 1–2.

28. See Charlotte Melin, "Program Sustainability through Interdisciplinary Networking: On Connecting Foreign Language Programs with Sustainability Studies and Other Fields," in *Transforming Postsecondary Foreign Language Teaching in the United States*, ed. Janet Swaffar and Per Urlaub (New York: Springer, 2014).

29. See Benjamin Rifkin, "Learners' Goals and Curricular Design: The Field's Response to the 2007 MLA Report on Foreign Langauge Education," *ADFL Bulletin* 42.1 (2012): 68–75.

30. *National Standards for Foreign Language Education*, American Council on the Teaching of Foreign Languages (2013), available at http://www.actfl.org/publications/all/national -standards-foreign-language-education (accessed November 15, 2013).

31. Access the *Ojibwe People's Dictionary* at http://ojibwe.lib.umn.edu/.

32. Cf. Tove Skutnabb-Kangas, Luisa Maffi, and David Harmon, *Sharing a World of Difference: The Earth's Linguistic, Cultural, and Biological Diversity* (Paris, France: UNESCO Publishing, 2003).

33. See the discussion of consent, language barriers, and research protocols, in section 4.11, at http://www.research.umn.edu/irb/guidance/guide4.html#.UhuS_b-d50Q.

34. Roche, *Why Choose the Liberal Arts?*, 15.

35. Daniel J. Philippon, "Sustainability and the Humanities: An Extensive Pleasure," *American Literary History* 24 (2012): 164–166.

36. For information about the redesigned major, see http://gsd.umn.edu/ugrad/major.html.

37. See Melin, "Program Sustainability through Interdisciplinary Networking."

38. John Hudzik and Lou Anna K. Simon, "From a Land-Grant to a World-Grant Ideal," in *Precipice or Crossroads?*, 160.

7 · GRADUATE TRAINING FOR A DIGITAL AND PUBLIC HUMANITIES

BETHANY NOWVISKIE

Today, some twenty years after its first formulation, there is little question of the validity of Jerome McGann's core and repeated argument: that humanities scholars and publics stand before a vast—indeed nearly wholesale—digital transformation of our various and shared cultural inheritance.[1] This transformation, more properly understood as a continual process of remediation, is fully under way. It opens new avenues for the work of the liberal arts in the public sphere: for our ability to access, to analyze and interpret, and, most importantly, to vouchsafe to future generations the words, images, sounds, and built and material objects that crystalize in our archives and that we carefully position to refract little, mirrorlike understandings of what it means, for the blink of an eye, to be human.

INTO THE GULF

Any deliberate reworking of both the fixed and fluid traces of human culture poses opportunity for humane reflection. This is because remediation, at its heart, is selective transformation—lossy and additive, a process akin to scholarly editing and interpretation—requiring the careful attention not only of content specialists, but also of specialists in technologies of information, past and present, and in knowledge representation: a community invested in the curation of things and the transmission and examination of the ideas those things represent. Ideally, the people engaged in this activity would be equipped by their humanities training with deep appreciation for the objects under their care. They should be versed in techniques that can amplify the faint voices still rattling around in them, and in best practices to facilitate new understandings from old stuff. This is because their work, at its heart, is to extend contextual, materialized, and historically situated knowledge to contemporary audiences, and to create spaces in which moderns can talk back to the past.

But it's increasingly evident that the cultural heritage enterprise is not all about engagement with history. Culture does not stop, and cultural heritage work is therefore both Janus-faced and Argus-eyed—which is to say, interestingly monstrous. Novel communications technologies and art forms generate a deluge of information in the present moment, a born-digital flood that pours into one welling up from our newly digitized past. It's a condition that requires librarians, archivists, and museum professionals to develop fresh modes of humanities data collection, comparison, and preservation, waist-deep in an unending stream—a stream in part directed by our publics, by the audience-participants who co-create and channel it. Meanwhile, the present moment invites scholars to examine, and to reject or embrace, modes of distant reading newly available in our "big data" age. Together, we experiment with our macroscopes, even as we to pay close attention to the smallest of objects, data points, and stories—and to too many metaphors and monsters at once—as scholars and archivists have always done.[2]

Under these conditions, no one seriously questions the validity of McGann's assertion that we stand at a technological and scholarly brink. But the growing question of the past two decades has been whether teaching and training programs in our public universities (private schools, by and large, never having led the way in the creation of new institutional forms for the digital humanities) adequately reflect the depth and breadth of the digital gulf before us, and whether we scholars—both as individual, free agents and as participants in a federated, broad, unwieldy, and rapidly changing system of public higher education—are prepared to mobilize and properly equip the next generation of specialist practitioners to move into the reaches of that gulf—actively, capably, and confidently.

The preparation of the next generation of scholar-practitioners is crucial, not just because positive opportunities for interpretive scholarship come with digital inquiry at scale, or with the knowledge-producing revelation of the unfamiliar that researchers invariably experience when confronted with a single artifact at its moment of digital conversion or reformation, deformation. And it's crucial not only because it will allow them to build new audiences for the public humanities; to blend technology training with a liberal arts education in ways beneficial to both sectors and to their own vocational prospects as students; to help present generations make good on significant past investments in the libraries, galleries, museums, and archives attached to public and land-grant universities; to network our federal and state cultural heritage institutions more effectively; and to ensure that our citizens have access to their publicly funded treasure-houses, now and into the future. No. The reason we must educate scholars and humanities students in the application of digital methods to humanities questions, and must equip them to craft digital tools and platforms of their own is this: a conversion and indeed culling of artistic and cultural content, and a comprehensive restructuring of the terms under which humanities scholarship can be conducted long into the future, is already happening. And it is happening largely without the active participation of practicing scholars.

McGann's direst warning (taken up by students and adherents like Johanna Drucker and Andrew Stauffer) does not go far enough. It has been this: "Expert scholars, engage, or librarians and academic IT staff will do it for you."[3] As a humanities researcher and a librarian working in information technology—even one who watches with concern as independent library holdings are converted to costly and ephemeral licensed content,[4] and as the "medium-rare" print collections of the nineteenth century are weeded or transported away—I say: losing control to thoughtful, struggling librarians and your university's in-house technical staff? You should be so lucky. Instead—as suggested by Siva Vaidhyanathan, Alan Liu, and many others,[5] and outlined with great clarity by Jeffrey Williams under the rubric of "Critical University Studies"—privatized, politicized, neoliberal forces, residing both beyond and (complicitly or uneasily) within the academy, already possess and work to reframe our research infrastructure.[6] They are, in fact, the commercial, corporate, and casualizing forces with which librarians and humanities-trained IT staff struggle on behalf of scholars every day—and against which we too rarely work together. These forces diminish the capacity of our faculty, weaken its agency, and drive instrumental decisions that bear upon the things we hold in common and hold dear: the preservation of pluralistic cultural content and our ease of access to it; the ethics and thoughtful practice of teaching and learning; our public support for its audience; and the shape and scope of our infrastructure for scholarly communication and humanities data, big and small.

We do stand at the edge of a gulf. It's one that most of us will not enter or cross. But our challenge (and one from which, on the whole, humanities faculty have shamefully turned away) is to replace ourselves as men and women of letters with the cohorts of scholar-practitioners now called to construct brilliant and fundamentally different architectures within that space—to make a new habitat for the liberal arts and to develop its new technological habitus—to build and to fight, or be lost.

DE-STIGMATIZING ALTERNATIVES

If we (who have by and large been trained for a different world) are to face this challenge, we must ask ourselves painful questions. What messages about the future of the academy do we overtly send to devoted students of the humanities? And what systemic or perhaps even unintended guidance do we offer a generation that looks to us for mentorship and models? Taken as an aggregate, graduate programs urge hordes of students down a single, well-trodden, and vanishingly narrow employment path. We can no longer believe they'll all continue on that track. Do we believe that they should? Of the ones who attempt to go where we are sending them, how many will arrive? And in what condition, and at what cost? In what relation will they stand to the unlucky majority—in a system ever more obviously driven by privilege and luck than by merit? Are we content with the odds they face—with our returns on investment—when we regard our job-seeking protégés both as individuals and as a collective? And why are we, on the whole, so hapless in our engagement with this problem? Why so willing—as evinced through our daily actions in graduate teaching and counseling—to squander public resources, institutional energies, and private lives, preparing students for careers that no longer exist?

The perceived need for cheap teaching labor at R1s (an especial driver of the size of graduate English programs, which staff intro composition courses across the university); the desire of tenured and tenure-track faculty to avoid teaching low-level courses and instead offer sophisticated graduate seminars in their areas of expertise; their natural impulse to mentor students along career paths similar to the one they have followed; the protectionism evident in their policing of boundaries and upholding of "placement" rankings; and their deep resistance to program reductions, out of well-placed but ineffectual rage at the notion that only an "oversupply" of PhDs, has created our present adjunct crisis: all of these (outlined, among other issues, in a recent report from the Modern Language Association's task force on doctoral study reform) must be let go.[7] In their place, we must institute and support programs—not just in our academic departments, but throughout the whole of the cultural heritage enterprise—that drive devoted students of the humanities toward stable careers addressing our critical moment of phase-change in humanities collections and corpora. To do that, we must ask ourselves what factors inhibit us, as leaders in state-supported higher education, from pointing out the varied spaces, outside and within the academy but certainly beyond our current conception of the professoriate, where the public so clearly needs humanities-trained scholar-practitioners to labor and explore? Why are we so slow to shore those spaces up? And what dangers will we face as we reconfigure our own practices and disciplines more appropriately for the projects ahead?

In late 2009, I co-opted a throwaway term, used by a colleague at the National Endowment for the Humanities to describe his oddball career as an "alternative academic," and I began writing, organizing, and convening conversations at the heart of what became an "alt-ac" movement.[8] For me, this simple awareness-raising activity was meant to provoke conversation among PhD-holding professionals already working off the straight and narrow path to tenure—though not as struggling adjunct instructors or what we euphemistically call independent scholars, the only two non-tenure-track academic identities then normative in humanities discourse. And yet so many people held hybrid positions—like my own. In addition to my duties as a librarian and digital humanities center director, I research and publish in my field, take on leadership roles in a number of scholarly professional associations, mentor and advise graduate students, and occasionally teach. By the time I defended my dissertation in the country's top-ranked public English department, in 2004, I had known for several years that I would not pursue tenure-track employment—yet, by 2009, the only common descriptor for my full-time, non-tenure-track library faculty position at a flagship research school was . . . nonacademic. By pointing out the incongruity of that term in social media, I struck a nerve.

#Alt-Academy, the open-access collection of twenty-four essays by thirty-six authors that followed from MediaCommons Press, framed the exploration of alternative academic careers as a voluntary and valid choice (though rarely an easy path) for scholars motivated to work in fields like digital humanities research, scholarly communication, higher ed administration, and cultural heritage.[9] The #Alt- in our title was offered as a signal not of divergence from the scholarly mainstream, but of solidarity with it: we saw ourselves as academics working in a new scholarly mode. And the publication had a dual audience. First, it spoke to humanities graduate students considering or actively pursuing careers that would call on their training in far more practical ways than their academic mentors had likely anticipated. And faculty were themselves our second audience—people who had long, though perhaps unthinkingly, conveyed a damaging message about the status and desirability of alt-ac careers, both to their protégés and to their colleagues, deans, and provosts.

The negativity that tenured faculty still overwhelmingly broadcast about work in public humanities and cultural heritage travels down to students through the academic hierarchy in numerous unsubtle ways, which don't bear rehearsing. But it's worth pointing out that the message travels laterally and upward as well—most notably in our continued, striking complicity with the basing of departmental rankings on outmoded notions of student "placement." When we permit academic departments to be ranked and valued on their tenure-track faculty placements, we encourage our colleagues and academic leaders to see all other paths as roads to perdition. Why would we set up signposts there? Why would we widen and tend those ways? When we rank and value academic departments on their tenure-track faculty placements, we deeply inscribe the message that careers in the public and digital humanities—in libraries, museums, and archives, in private foundations or public agencies of the arts and humanities, or in technology and administration—are a distant second or third option: a ratty safety net for middling scholars who have tried and failed.

Half a decade on, although the problem of rankings and attendant, internalized value-statements has not been addressed, grad students are in a different place. Alt-ac punditry and even paid consultancy is so well established as to have become a cottage industry—so awareness of alternatives is no longer an issue. Anger and desperation has grown among the cohort of post-economic-crash grad students who have been unable to secure tenure-track employment. But the many professionals who made voluntary moves early on, and who embraced alt-ac's reframing of the "nonacademic," continue to describe their vocations as callings, in compelling ways far beyond the original publication act of #Alt-Academy. Their working lives demonstrate a richness of possibility our collection only gestured at. Likewise, the blossoming of worldwide interprofessional humanities conferences and unconferences (like the annual Digital Humanities gathering and grassroots THATCamp movement) puts an increasing number of scholars and students into contact with library, museum, and humanities technology professionals whose work is differently structured but who share common intellectual interests and research problems. In casting a spotlight on problems of contingent labor in the academy, groups like the Modern Language Association have illuminated options beyond adjunct teaching. And while the academic job market continues ever poor, the twittering blogosphere in which it is lamented and dissected goes strong. Open conversations about the former, within the latter, serve to de-stigmatize work off the tenure track.

So does organized action and the targeted support of funders like the Mellon Foundation. Recently, the American Council of Learned Societies moved beyond its "New Faculty Fellows" initiative (commonly known as the ACLS "Save Your Ass/Wait Out the Market" fellowship), to create a "Public Fellows" program, placing recent PhDs with nonprofits and public agencies that put their humanities training to pragmatic use. The Council on Library and Information Resources (CLIR) has expanded its transformative fellowship program, which has placed postdocs in academic libraries since 2003, to target particular areas of hybrid scholarly/archival expertise, such as medieval and early modern data curation. And with Mellon Foundation support through the Scholarly Communication Institute at the University of Virginia, the international Consortium of Humanities Centers and Institutes (CHCI) has begun partnering with center-Net, a worldwide band of digital humanities centers, to develop pilot programs for training graduate students "in and for the digital age." At the same time and through the same SCI support, the UVa Library Scholars' Lab (which I direct) established the Praxis Program, conducted a survey on grad student prepared- ness for alternative academic careers, and developed an international Praxis Network. Our local Praxis Program is a concentrated pedagogical experiment at the University of Virginia, and the Network is its super-set: a showcase of in- progress, new-model structural approaches to methodological training in the humanities.[10]

As a model and experiment, the UVa Praxis Program is extracurricular— embedded in the Scholars' Lab, a working DH center—and collaborative in nature; indeed, in some ways it is self-consciously about the cultural and affec- tive challenges to interdisciplinary and interprofessional collaboration in a university setting.[11] Now in its fourth year as a cohort-based internship pro- gram, Praxis attempts to be critically informed about the present state of the disciplines and, above all, generative of positive, concrete interventions and thought-experiments in particular areas of humanities discourse and technol- ogy. These interventions operate within a specific theoretical horizon and are based in projects rather than prose—but research outcomes are not the key product of the program. People are. The six graduate fellows chosen annually for the Praxis Program come together as a single team, across disciplines (in the space of its first three years, representing eight different academic departments at UVa), to build a humanities toolset or undertake a shared venture. The curric- ulum is adjusted yearly in order to keep up with technological advances, match the needs and interests of the student cohort, and equip them properly for the particular digital humanities project they choose to undertake. That said, some units of the year-long seminar invariably recur. Our Praxis Program students learn to conduct work that is iterative and public, expressive of a core value on open access and open source, and broadly pitched rather than narrowly special- ist. Discussion of intellectual property and the challenges to interdisciplinary collaboration happens each year, and we marry specific instruction in digital tools, programming languages, versioning, and software development practices with lessons in design thinking, wireframing and user experience, project man- agement, funding and sustainability, and public engagement in social media. The Praxis Program also situates itself in a world where every academic field must engage self-consciously with cross-cutting theories and practices of information design—that is, with the tenets of knowledge representation across disciplines.

It's a quirky program and, because it was designed to draw on local strengths and expertise within a particular university and library context, it is perhaps only replicable in part. But by turn, our larger Praxis Network means to inspire administrative thinking toward the rich variety of programmatic responses that will be necessary in order to transform graduate education. To do that, it pro- vides mix-and-match templates. Eight programs, like-minded with our own but differently structured, form the core of the Network. They come together from public and private institutions across the United States, Canada, the United Kingdom, and New Zealand and include programs at the University of Virginia, Duke University, Michigan State University, the CUNY Graduate Center, Hope College, Brock University, University College London, and the University of Christchurch. Each of the Praxis Network's eight programs attracts students who wish to engage deeply with humanities research problems through digital vectors and methods. The six graduate programs in the Network mean to produce expert scholars, capable of working at the leading edge of their fields, yet who are not allergic to a whiff of what many might consider vocational training. Their graduates are prepared to take up a variety of roles in and around the academy, and bring a hybrid sensibility even to traditionally structured faculty positions. The Praxis Network drive to equip humanities-trained grad students for alt-ac positions is aligned with Kathleen Woodward's call, in Chapter 3 of this volume, to de-stigmatize community college teaching and rescue the very concept of vocational training from the contempt of scholars: "The study of the humanities and the development of skills for the workplace should not be understood as being in opposition to each other. That would entail a dubious argument at best. Pragmatically, it is foolish, perhaps even suicidal."[12]

So we do not lack for experiments. Nor do we want for pronouncements and role models. In recent years, an increasing number of academics have left tenured positions to assume high-profile leadership roles in scholarly professional associations, new-model presses, or cultural heritage organizations. Among professional societies, the American Historical Association exhorts its members to support public history as a first choice for graduate students, urging No More Plan B, and the MLA has also made extensive recommendations for doctoral study reform in departments of modern language and literature. Finally, the word from higher-ed commentators is now less often a totalizing, conversation-ending "Just don't go," than an exhortation to go smarter, go deeper.[13] All of these things make it easier for graduate students of the humanities to admit it—even just to admit it—when they begin to form a more expansive conception of their futures than their academic departments are set up to support. Taken together, these developments make it harder for the notion that academics can "fail," or that careers can be "thrown away on service," so neatly to compute.

Perhaps I belabor my point, that individual and systemic status-seeking has served as a prime inhibitor to our disciplines' investment in a more public-spirited mission for graduate education. But just as the American digital humanities had its start as instructional technology and "humanities computing" research endeavors almost exclusively in state schools like Virginia, Maryland, Nebraska, George Mason University, Michigan State, and Illinois—places less bound by tradition or more prone to take a reputational risk than their private counterparts—so, too, might a new call originate: for public universities conscious of an obligation to the common good to articulate their kinship with public humanities agencies and institutions; to lobby for federal and state funding not only for their own missions but for the aligned missions of these institutions; to help to build them up as an integrated network; to better support the libraries and humanities centers in their own midst; and to prepare graduate students for deeply necessary, broad-based work in digital cultural heritage. (On the possibility of higher education's recommitment to the public good, and on the systemic consequences of policies and rhetorical practices that have "redefined education as a consumer service, which enjoins a commercial transaction rather than another kind of human interchange," see Jeffrey Williams's discussion of "Critical University Studies" in the present volume.)[14]

The message we've sent to several generations of emerging scholars ("a tenure-track job at an R1 or a prestigious, private liberal arts college is success; all else is failure") is akin to the ones we too clearly send ourselves: that the academy is a contest; that grad programs should compete not in the tangible skills they provide to students, but in the heft of their citation networks, the superiority of their placement rankings, and the degree of their prestige. That it's permissible to create a binary training system in which our students become either superstars or waste product. That we will not be impoverished by the consequent narrowing of graduate training to a privileged few of independent means. That it's valid to call "impact" the totting-up of publications in dwindling formats for narrowing, subdisciplinary expert audiences. That twenty-first-century humanities disciplines should be more about the cultivation of private sensibility than about the instigation of public action. That it's in any way okay to measure institutional value by ranking our ability to self-replicate.

AN EXERCISE FOR PROBLEM SOLVERS

Conversation at the University of Illinois symposium that inspired this volume struggled above all with one question: whether we are right to imagine (or reimagine) the humanities as a problem-solving enterprise—rather than one, as Kathleen Woodward writes, dedicated not to answering but simply to raising questions and always stringently avoiding the "charge of presentism." I support her declaration that the humanities can "no longer shrink from the language of problem-solving."[15] Indeed, we can no longer shrink from action. Investment in a more public-spirited mission for graduate education in the digital age will quickly demonstrate that problem-solving lies within our domain. I will close by offering a few of the most obvious problems humanities faculty and administrators must address.

First: the problem of personnel. Who among us is best positioned to provide grounded training in digital tools and methods? Who is equipped to mentor students as they heed the call to bring humanities perspectives to bear on the mass digitization of our cultural commonwealth?[16] Not, in large part, the faculty we now recruit and tenure, who are not rewarded for—and are in fact actively warned against—engaging in the kind of "risky" work that leads to expertise in digital methods. Might we adjust the norms by which digital scholars are evaluated? Ought we to do so? If so, how quickly?[17] Meantime, it grows increasingly plain that we should expand our notion of a university's teaching and mentoring staff to include (as UVa's Praxis Program does) the humanities-trained personnel already working among us in digitally inflected, so-called alt-ac roles—personnel plainly more qualified to teach digital humanities methods than many faculty who have been warned away from the field as a distraction from their books. But there may have been losses among the gains of these alt-ac scholars' practical experience. Have they been too long absent from daily discourse and pedagogical advances in their disciplines? What do they now know that they may be unprepared to teach? Digital humanities practitioners are certain to have developed tacit understandings and unexamined practices that—to be fully considered and conveyed to students—would require the provision of time and space for reflection characteristic of faculty roles, but not commonly allotted to staff.[18] How will we overcome structural problems relating to the involvement in pedagogy and collaborative research of people working in libraries, presses, administrative offices, humanities centers, and campus IT—to their intellectual property rights, for instance, or to the ways their labor is accounted for and rewarded? How will we ensure, in other words, their ability to contribute without being exploited? How will we help them create collegial—not service-based—relationships with faculty partners, as a way of integrating them with respect and bringing their skills more fully into new humanities teaching programs?

Next, if we succeed in training our graduate students differently and well, are they certain to find employment? The answer, in short, is no—not yet to an extent adequate to the monumental curatorial and remediation task at hand, and certainly not at a level that "solves" the jobs crisis for un- and underemployed humanities PhDs. (I will, however, close this essay with a ridiculous and deadly serious proposal that might.) In the meantime, though, for positions currently advertised and opening, a call like mine might be seen as little more than a colonization of the territory of schools of library science and information—whose teachers and students actually know what they're doing in the sphere of cultural heritage and digital knowledge representation.[19] Humanities programs must not step into and painfully disrupt these areas, without adequate reflection on what they do and don't bring to the table. Thoughtful engagement by scholars and cultural heritage practitioners placed into collegial contact by programs like those of ACLS and CLIR are key, and universities that have an enviable opportunity to forge partnerships between humanities departments and schools of library and information science should lead the way. And it is no coincidence that universities investing in I-schools are overwhelmingly publicly funded. Such investments indicate these universities' awareness of their obligation to provide vocational training to students and to contribute to the greater good.[20]

In the meantime, we must acknowledge that our demographics are bad. Imbalances in gender, race, class, sexual orientation, and ethnicity among people working in tech-oriented humanities fields have arguably reinforced a digital archival focus on canonical texts and reified homogenous perspectives. Who is privileged to speak, produce, experiment, and create change with new media and new technology? These imbalances stem, of course, from disasters in public, secondary STEM education—a problem that humanities scholars too often lazily and self-defeatingly imagine as being out of higher ed's control.[21] (Frustratingly, we shift and shirk our collective responsibility for getting at the root of the "pipeline" problem, at the same time we too frequently waste our energies on infighting over its aftereffects—its impact on high-end humanities research culture.) Inclusivity initiatives at tech conferences and library and digital humanities professional associations are a step in the right direction, but they necessarily treat the symptoms of imbalance and not the disease.

And further: are we crazy to valorize hybrid, mix-and-match, alt-ac employment models at a moment when adjunct labor runs rampant and administrative bloat casts shadows everywhere? Has, as Martha Nell Smith suggests, the rise of DH centers employing humanities professionals outside the structure of academic departments contributed to the erosion of tenure? (I see greater causes elsewhere, but this niche is as susceptible to systemic changes as any other.) To be sure, the organization, academic focus, and leadership of digital centers, and the level of "contingency" of individual alt-ac positions within them varies widely.[22] The value, potential for distorting impact, and general applicability of tenure models to library, administrative, and alt-ac positions is an area of much debate. And in truth, the tenure concern of a collectivist imagination may not rest overmuch in protections for the individual—in employment stability at the solitary-scholar level, that is—as in the public-spirited protection of a committed institutional, residential faculty, fully embedded in a community where it can develop and articulate its own agendas. Already, too many outspoken digital scholarship staff members are collaborators on controversial projects and unprotected exercisers of academic freedom. Can we move that needle, perhaps through policy revisions and the deeper inclusion of alt-ac professionals in institutional governance structures? Should we create more of these unprotected positions before we do? Where can we look for models? And is this devil's bargain—chiefly, our ability to position a greater ratio of still-practicing scholars where they can serve archival and public humanities missions within universities—worth the institutional and personal risk?

Some have sensed a related danger: that overeager promotion of "capital-DH" Digital Humanities fosters misunderstanding among administrators and governing boards, of the role of technology vis-à-vis research and teaching in the liberal arts. In recent years, some have taken DH as an aggressive new academic discipline, rather than as what most longtime practitioners agree it is: a set of overlapping professional communities, involved in exploring a loose constellation of evolving, often incongruent digital methods. (Witness the recent, anomalous posting of ill-defined professorships in Digital Humanities and equally surprising surprise, a cycle or two later, that more such unicorns are not called for.[23]) Even the DH that many of us understand as an international community of practice—dating to the smallish, everyone-knows-everyone joint ACH/ALLC conferences of past decades—falters under conditions of rapid expansion and increasingly rich diversity of method. Are we helping our deans, provosts, chancellors, and politically appointed governing boards to "get it"—or has our own eagerness for funding, mild social media celebrity, and a modicum of glitz distracted us as they have moved quickly, taking our willingness to experiment with new research methods as an opening to increase pedagogical efficiency, perform so-called strategic dynamism, and—above all—to strengthen "the brand"?

And one last, dark concern. When I began working in new-model humanities education and alt-ac advocacy several years ago, I felt I was fighting for the current generation of grad students. At the local level, this conviction holds. In the Scholars' Lab, we work for the betterment of the individual graduate students who come our way—conscious that they are laboring within larger systems that are broken and that can wound them. We want to broaden their options and help them build the technical and conceptual skills that will enable their active engagement with the humanities well into its digital future. We hope to render them more capable of constructing new systems and of resisting inappropriate ones, from wherever they may land. Our own placement record for former graduate fellows is remarkable. Students go on to faculty appointments, sometimes in new, interdisciplinary fields, but always into positions for which they are recruited as a result of their digital humanities experience. Many others (perhaps the majority) decide along the way to pursue a hybrid, alt-ac, or public humanities career and are likewise heavily recruited to start or help grow digital scholarship centers or library-based services, or to lead public arts and humanities projects. Still, most days, we're not sure if we work in preventative medicine or the emergency room.

But as we field questions from scholars and administrators who find inspiration in our Praxis Program and seek to replicate it elsewhere, I grow troubled.

Graduate students at the University of Virginia already enter the job market with a competitive advantage. If the kind of thing we do at the Scholars' Lab spreads far and wide as a primary response to the problem—that is, if efforts in humanities education reform focus not on deep structural and curricular interventions, but on increasing the capacity of malingering PhD programs to produce alt-ac staff alongside scores of freeway flyers and a few lucky college professors—at scale, ours is no longer a preventative or life-saving exercise. Spread systemwide, our extracurricular work becomes merely palliative, a kind of hospice care for the humanities.

Do not, therefore, confuse the sharing of stop-gap, renegade, extramural, and tacked-on models for methodological training—or the growing surge in interest and advocacy for bettered working conditions for humanities professionals off the tenure track—with a suggestion that conventionally structured PhD programs can become magical pathways to fulfilling alternative academic careers. We need a bolder and broader answer—maybe even originating from outside our universities. We are producing a lost generation of graduate students at the same time that we fail to acknowledge the dangerous under-involvement of humanities scholars in digital remediation and data curation.

Yet these are not problems to be solved from the supply-side of our economic equation. They are problems that demand a very literal New Deal for the Humanities. We need a government Works Progress Administration for jobs creation in the GLAM sector, to fill our Galleries, Libraries, Archives, and Museums with devoted and deeply scholarly workers at the digital brink. Public humanities in the second decade of the twenty-first century needs its own WPA Library Extension Program—its Historical Records Survey, its Federal Writers Project. We need our WPA Museums Projects, our New Deal Archaeology. To weather and guide the digital transformations ahead, public humanities today needs its Federal Project Number One.

Naturally, a concept like this seems even more a pipe dream in a time of widespread austerity measures, threats to public funding for the arts and humanities, and government shutdowns. Employees of public research institutions have also seen a long, slow decline in public support. (Last fiscal year, for instance, a mere 5.8 percent of the University of Virginia's total budget came from state general-fund appropriations. Adjusting for inflation, Virginians have seen a 51 percent drop in per-student state support since the year 1990.) Yet a pipe dream can provoke more productive thought experiments.

Consider the consequences of a New Deal for GLAM—and not alone for the stuff, for the objects of digital curation and research—but for their surrounding social and economic systems. What would happen if humanities faculty and academic librarians joined public lobbying organizations like the National Humanities Alliance in full force to articulate our startling societal need, gather data for analysis, and compellingly present the economic feasibility of major invest-ments in cultural infrastructure? For one thing, we could handily change the self-defeating internal evaluation criteria driving our junior colleagues to avoid work that smacks of service (yet which often leads to productive involvement in university governance). It would also palpably demonstrate—at a meaning-ful moment for public sector cultural heritage workers—the academy's under-standing of and appreciation for the indispensable GLAM institutions on which humanities work depends. Retooling higher education to support large-scale WPA-like GLAM subsidies might beautifully require pushing down serious humanities concentration and training to the undergraduate level—in the way that engineering schools, education schools, and nursing schools prepare col-lege students for meaningful and marketable careers. Imagine history, literature, language, and anthropology programs so competitive that matriculation would require our students to pass the equivalent of a "pre-med" student's organic chemistry. The expectation that public and digital humanities job preparation would require facility with interpretation and languages of various sorts, com-fort with ambiguity, and a broad basis of humanistic learning on which to build, might lead to open rebellion against the SOL-driven American primary and sec-ondary education that sends us students so unprepared. And further positive and revelatory consequences might be imagined.

Barring a real New Deal, however, we must give our undergraduate students less of a raw one, in the form of better counseling. Faculty should begin to push would-be humanities PhDs instead toward master's-level programs that will refine their ability to do digital cultural heritage and provide excellent intern-ships and career counseling. (These exist already and, where they do not, could be developed in concert with schools of library and information science, busi-ness schools, ed schools, and schools of public policy and law.) We must charge our colleagues not to let undergraduate advisees slide toward overcrowded, bootless professor prep, at the same time that we demonstrate our own commit-ment to the altered teaching assignments that would come from such a shift, and work to align tenure and promotion guidelines with the reality of academic labor and scholarly communication. And we should ensure that all this does not read to administrators and funders as a quiet diminishment of our PhD programs—but rather a right-sizing and vibrant refocusing of them, so that they can better produce the much-needed future faculty who will join and revitalize the profes-soriate at replacement levels, not at a glut. We need to acknowledge that we make the adjunct crisis by continuing to make and employ adjuncts, and that we are losing control of our humanities archive and infrastructure at its most critical moment since the birth of print by not asserting control.

There are dangers and complexities plainly inherent in embracing a new attitude toward graduate humanities education, with all of its sequelae and the conception of a grand, generational "project" for scholar-practitioners it implies. But it would be more dangerous to ignore the issues that drive us to that embrace. Our shared cultural heritage is even now being remediated and winnowed out, with or without humanities expertise. The public university is being reshaped in response to corporate and political pressure, with or without the placement of our own in positions of influence within those zones. Our elected officials, governing boards, and fellow tax-paying citizens are assessing the value of the humanities—based on the stories and the data we make available to them, and the degree to which we help these things inspire and capture their imaginations. The digital and public future of the humanities will play out as it may—with or without concerted action from us. Let it be with.

NOTES

1. See McGann's "Culture and Technology: The Way We Live Now, What Is to Be Done?" in *New Literary History* 36:1 (Winter 2005) and "The Future Is Digital," in *Journal of Victorian Culture* 13:1 (Spring 2008).

2. For the notion of the "macroscope," see *The Historian's Macroscope: Big Digital History*, by Shawn Graham, Ian Milligan, and Scott Weingart (in progress: http://www.themacroscope .org). *Neatline*, a digital project from the University of Virginia Scholars' Lab, asserts the continuing value of "small data" in a big data world: http://neatline.org/.

3. Johanna Drucker, "Blind Spots," *Chronicle of Higher Education*, April 3, 2009; Andrew Stauffer, "The Troubled Future of the Nineteenth-Century Book," *Chronicle of Higher Education*, December 11, 2011.

4. For a brief summary of this issue, see Nowviskie, "Fight Club Soap," http://nowviskie.org/ 2010/fight-club-soap/.

5. Siva Vaidhyanathan, *The Googlization of Everything: (And Why We Should Worry)* (Berkeley: University of California Press, 2011); Alan Liu, "The State of the Digital Humanities: A Report and a Critique," *Arts and Humanities in Higher Education* (February/April 2012).

6. See Jeffrey Williams, "The Need for Critical University Studies," Chapter 9 in this volume.

7. *Report of the Task Force on Doctoral Study in Modern Languages and Literature* (New York: Modern Language Association, 2014): http://www.mla.org/report_doctoral_study_2014.

8. See "#alt-ac origin stories" for the genesis of the name and hashtag in a Twitter conversation: http://storify.com/nowviskie/altac-origin-stories.

9. *#Alt-Academy:* http://mediacommons.futureofthebook.org/alt-ac/.

10. See http://praxis.scholarslab.org/ and http://praxis-network.org/.

11. See John McGowan's persuasive description of these in the context of "science envy" in "Can the Humanities Save Medicine and Vice Versa?" Chapter 8 in this volume.

12. Kathleen Woodward, "We Are All Nontraditional Learners Now: Community Colleges, Long-Life Learning, and Problem-Solving Humanities" Chapter 3 in this volume.

13. Anthony Grafton and James Grossman, "No More Plan B: A Very Modest Proposal for Graduate Programs in History," *Perspectives on History* (American Historical Association, October 2011). Thomas H. Benton (William Pannapacker), "Graduate School in the Humanities: Just Don't Go," *Chronicle of Higher Education*, January 30, 2009.

14. Chapter 9, Jeffrey Williams, "The Need for Critical University Studies."

15. Woodward, "We Are All Nontraditional Learners Now."

16. See the 2006 report of the ACLS Commission on Cyberinfrastructure, chaired by John M. Unsworth, "Our Cultural Commonwealth," available: http://www.acls.org/programs/Default.aspx?id=644.

17. For an examination of these concerns in the field of language and literature, see the reports of the 2011 and 2012 NINES summer NEH institutes on evaluating digital scholarship (available: http://institutes.nines.org) and MLA's "Guidelines for Evaluating Work in Digital Humanities and Digital Media," revised 2012 and available: http://www.mla.org/guidelines _evaluation_digital.

18. For a treatment of these issues see "Speaking in Code" a 2013 software developers' summit at the University of Virginia Library (http://codespeak.scholarslab.org), as well as "Off the Tracks: Laying New Lines for Digital Humanities Scholars," a 2011 workshop at the University of Maryland (http://mith.umd.edu/offthetracks/), both supported by the National Endowment for the Humanities.

19. See Gavia Libraria (the Library Loon), "Poaching Jobs," March 16, 2013. Available: http:// gavialib.com/2013/03/poaching-jobs/.

20. "Directory of ALA-Accredited Master's Programs in Library and Information Studies." http://www.ala.org/accreditedprograms/directory.

21. Chad Sansing, "Hacking Admissions Standards," May 25, 2010. Classroots.org and Hacking the Academy (online edition). Available: http://classroots.org/2010/05/25/hacking -admissions-standards/.

22. A recent blog post by Miriam Posner highlights perhaps the most abusive kind: the staff position that involves so much teaching that it becomes virtually indistinguishable from a faculty position, except in terms of status, stability, voice in governance, and ownership of intellectual property: "Don't cry for me, ASA. As I said, I love my job, and I'm well-suited to it. But I do hope to give you pause as you consider what a university would look like if it were populated by many *more* people like me: flexible employees, carrying out a great deal of administrative work, whose time is managed by someone else, who do research when they can carve out the time, whose work belongs to someone else, and who have no voice in faculty governance. The picture begins to look a lot like a corporation." "What Alt-Ac Can Do and What It Can't," November 25, 2013. Available: http://miriamposner.com/blog/what-alt -ac-can-do-and-what-it-cant/. On the issue of intellectual property, see my 2009 MLA talk, "Monopolies of Invention." http://nowviskie.org/2009/monopolies-of-invention/.

23. See Roopika Risam, "Where Have All the DH Jobs Gone?" September 15, 2013. Available: http://roopikarisam.com/2013/09/15/where-have-all-the-dh-jobs-gone/.

8 · CAN THE HUMANITIES SAVE MEDICINE, AND VICE VERSA?

JOHN McGOWAN

The term "medical humanities" has been coined to cover a wide field of research and pedagogical initiatives, some over forty years old, others just emerging. In their text *Medical Humanities* (2002), M. Evans and I. Finlay describe one broad rationale for the term and the field it names.

> Since medicine is concerned . . . with responding to our illnesses, our physical incapacities and our bodily suffering, then it could not consist of the natural biological sciences alone. . . . [T]he intellectual resources for clinical medicine must be drawn from . . . the social and behavioural sciences and the liberal humanities disciplines [which] . . . represent distinct ways of recording and interpreting human experience, including the experiences of health and illness, of seeking and undergoing . . . and providing . . . medical care.[1]

The medical humanities include a research and a curricular agenda, even in aspiring to influence, inform, and improve clinical practice. On the research side, medical humanists write about the history of medical practice and medical diagnosis, study illness narratives from various cultures and eras, explore the societal contexts in which meanings and practices arise, and ponder ethical questions that impact how and when patients should be treated. The diverse array of humanistic perspectives is brought to bear on fundamental questions of meaning and value raised by illness and therapeutics. As with any emerging field, new research protocols within the medical humanities are in flux, which makes for exciting times, but also puts a premium on collective conversation and reflection. On the curricular side, medical humanities pushes for a place in medical schools. The most robust curricular growth has come in undergraduate colleges of arts and sciences, where new majors and minors in the field have been created in the past eight years at Vanderbilt, Columbia, and the University of North Carolina, Chapel Hill, among other schools.

In fact, the medical humanities include many people trained and practicing in the health sciences. It is inherently an interdisciplinary endeavor. Medical practitioners have turned to the humanities because of a felt inadequacy within the health sciences to teach us all we need to know to care for patients. Humanists look to medicine as one place where momentous questions are encountered quite literally in the flesh. The medical humanities depend on conversations and collaborations across disciplines that directly impact how medicine is understood and practiced.

In June 2013 I was among over four hundred attendees of a conference in London celebrating twenty-five years of "narrative medicine." The conference featured the wide variety of participants that has become characteristic of the field, with health-care professionals from various disciplines sharing the platform with anthropologists, philosophers, historians, and literary critics. And there was very little of the incomprehension or condescension that characterizes so much cross-disciplinary encounters. Pretty much everyone there was singing the same tune, which was basically that attention to patients' narratives was a key to better medical care and that providing opportunities for medical professionals and for families of patients to tell their stories was crucial to sustaining the mental and emotional health of those receiving care and of those giving care.

This unfamiliar unanimity in an academic conversation is largely explained by the overwhelming sense on the part of all the participants in medical humanities that they are fighting an uphill battle, that they are a minority within a huge system that finds their concerns and viewpoints beside the point. For medical practitioners, the humanities offer a critique of a health-care system that is increasingly bureaucratic, impersonal, and driven by economic imperatives. A certain kind of sociological critique could doubtless explain the interest in medical humanities among doctors as reflecting a professional anxiety about their growing loss of autonomy in a "system" that has all but eliminated small, independent private practices, that dictates acceptable diagnoses as well as the time to spend with each patient, and that rewards specialization in ways that work against any ongoing or substantial relationship with patients. The humanities are a rallying point for health-care professionals who are protesting the view that medicine is only a science and never an art, and the attempt to establish streamlined, efficient processing of patients. But before we too hastily characterize the turn to the "je ne sais quoi" that the humanities so helpfully provide as the mere attempt to retain professional privilege and pride, we would do well to remember that patients are as unhappy with contemporary medical practices as are many doctors and nurses. All the complexities of human interactions that the humanities endeavor to track, from the interpretation of communicative acts to the difficulties of encounters across cultures, are part and parcel of the clinical encounter. Until the medical system finds a way to eliminate "seeing patients" as part of medical care, the skills the humanities endeavor to teach will remain relevant to the quality of health care.

So medical professionals are increasingly turning to the humanities to support their attempts to reform a health-care system that all too often treats the human factor as noise. Don't listen to what the patient tells you about how she feels; just go by what the machine (the EKG, the MRI, the blood test) tells you. As one speaker at the London conference put it, the doctor is trained to replace x (what the patient says) with y (the real diagnosis, the medical name for the condition). What would it mean to take patients' self-reports seriously, to truly involve patients in their own medical care, to place the communicative interaction between patient and care provider at the center of medical practice?

All this can be catnip to humanists. Here we have scientists—if not natural scientists, at least health scientists—using the humanities as a rallying cry for a reformist agenda that aligns itself remarkably well with humanists' own concerns and worries. The pressure, especially at public universities, to deliver more degrees at lesser cost mirrors efforts to increase the efficiency of patient management, while the "corporatization" of the university is another instance of the ways that medical decisions are driven by what health insurance will or will not pay for. More specifically, the suspicion among some doctors of interpretive or diagnostic models that say x must really be understood as y echoes the critique of critique, the suspicion of the hermeneutics of suspicion, finding voice in various corners of the humanities recently.[2]

This is not the place to offer a full-blown analysis of why critique seems to have lost favor after its long run, but two contributing factors are directly relevant to the issue of medical humanities. First, there is currently a general, dare we call it "democratic," sensibility among those in the "helping professions"— education, health care, social work—toward deemphasizing expert hierarchies in favor of participatory or collaborative modes of interaction. Active learning and group work in our humanities classrooms bears a family resemblance to the involvement of patients and family members in making health-care decisions. Instead of handing over a ready-made truth, one that nonexperts will likely never grasp on their own, the new modes contend that the lessons that will stick, that will actually influence behavior, are the ones a self participates in constructing instead of having received from on high. Thus, a utilitarian justification—better outcomes—is tied to a more abstract commitment to an egalitarian, democratic ethos.

Secondly, critique can, from a certain angle, look like science envy, even if of a peculiar sort. When the critic says that the judicial system is really only a way to protect the interests of the powerful, a definitive truth claim is made, one that strives to unearth hard facts akin to the chemist's claim that water, no matter what it appears to be, is really two hydrogen atoms bound to an oxygen atom. At stake, ultimately, is what counts as evidence and what does not. As a reform movement within the health sciences, medical humanities is, interestingly, aimed at the hegemony of "evidence-based medicine," at the presumption that only the results of double-blind clinical trials count as knowledge. The medical humanists—like all humanists at all times?—insist that there is more under heaven and earth than can be accounted for by the dominant natural philosophies of our time. And like humanists, these reformers are continually on the defensive, continually fighting an uphill battle when insisting that the soft methods of the humanities uncover information of material consequence even as that information often does not register on our sophisticated instruments. Perhaps the humanities are doomed, in our culture at least, to be the realm of that which cannot be measured, and, hence, of that which is always prone to be overlooked. In other words, we humanists just need to learn how to live on the defensive because there is no way for us to take the offensive. If such a scenario is our destined playing field, then either attempts to emulate the sciences or raucous denunciations of science and all of its works will be two oft-repeated moves. I think both moves are misguided.

These sweeping speculations aside, it is noteworthy that the health-care folks come to the humanists precisely to find a way to talk about things that don't factor in as hard evidence, while humanists can, at times, head toward medicine in the hope of becoming more scientific. Of course, each side in this partnership needs to beware of romanticizing the other. Humanists can be turned off by scientists who are looking for touchy-feely escapes from blood tests and MRIs, while scientists will be wary of humanists looking for simple answers and the imagined camaraderie of the lab. Human seekers of knowledge of whatever stripe are not, it turns out, going to abandon the frustrating realms of uncertainty and contingency by becoming more scientific; the various purveyors of objective approaches to the human science—among whom, despite all their differences, I would number New Critics, structuralists, rational-choice theorists, and the purveyors of critique—were (are) all deluded to think that objectivity could be brought to the humanities and social sciences by aping the methods of science, not because they failed to grasp some essential undecidability in the humanities, but because they misunderstood science. They never took in what Charles Sanders Peirce had understood by 1880: namely, that science itself deals in probabilities, not certainties, and that scientific facts are assembled through intersubjective processes that make "fallibilism" an irreducible ingredient in all scientific assertions.[3]

There are, however, more-plausible reasons for science envy, I believe. Dwelling on those reasons provides a way to reflect on the difficulties currently facing the humanities—and suggests why a pursuit like medical humanities does offer some possible pathways through or beyond current impasses. The reasons to which I now turn are institutional and sociological, not epistemological or (god forbid!) metaphysical. It's not about the nature of the universe or of facts; it's about the way we organize the socially interactive processes of education and research. And, crucially, it's about authority. What claims and practices are heeded in our society—and why? I think anyone reading this would likely agree that the sciences have more authority in our society than the humanities do. And even if a few would contest that claim, no one would deny that the sciences are better funded at our research universities. NSF and NIH dwarf NEH and NEA. Science envy might well begin and end with the fact that the scientists can compete for the big bucks.

But we humanists would be better served by considering the ways science has garnered such respect. Scientists, while certainly competitive, generally understand themselves as contributing to a collective enterprise, to the advancement of knowledge in their chosen field. And that orientation to the collective is reflected in their collaborative work habits. Scientists rarely work alone; they form teams, which capitalize on the different expertise of the various members. And (ideally at least) their knowledge claims are judged by a community that accepts or rejects those claims on the basis of subjecting them to various tests. There is a fairly formal process by which something becomes received knowledge—and once it does become received knowledge, that claim is not usually (there are exceptions) associated with an individual. Science does not collect its received knowledge in Norton anthologies organized by the names of the authors of each relevant theory or piece of information.

Contrast this approach to standard practices in the humanities. Each researcher is pressed to make an original contribution, which in practice seems to mean showing that everyone else in the whole tradition got something terribly wrong or overlooked some matter of supreme importance. Schools of thought do form—psychoanalysis, new historicism, narratology—but true distinction awaits only those who disagree with everyone. The humanities look to outsiders like squabbles in which no conclusion is ever reached. Even our bromides—like the ones about how we teach critical thinking or about the benefits of agonistic dialogue—are delivered half-heartedly to general audiences as we bite our tongues to prevent ourselves from pronouncing all the caveats by which we would like to qualify these statements. Science envy, it seems to me, would serve the humanities well if it pushed us to try to assemble the received knowledge of our field, toward more collaborative modes of work, and toward a more robust ability to speak collectively as humanists about the methods and aims of our practices. I am suggesting that Thomas Kuhn was right to say that something like "normal science" exists, and that Chemistry 101 and the textbook used to teach it varies little from one university to the next. No such unanimity reigns in "Introduction to Literary Studies." I do think we humanists manage, almost in spite of ourselves, to inculcate what I have been calling a humanities sensibility. But I know from concrete experience that most of our English majors have only the vaguest idea of the dominant paradigms or protocols in the field. And that's because their various courses in the subject have offered them a dizzying array of approaches to the subject matter (which itself can vary wildly). If only for the purposes of explaining ourselves to noninsiders, it would be a good thing if the various humanities disciplines could agree on a simple definition, a mission statement if you will. Biology and chemistry, as contrasted to English and sociology, are much closer to being able to articulate such a coherent and succinct statement of their basic enterprise. I know that setting the MLA to such a task entails a sea-change in sensibility, not just some Andy Hardy–like effort to put on a show. But if humanists begin working with scientists in truly collaborative and interdisciplinary projects like those that characterize the medical humanities, maybe such a change will happen.

The sciences also garner authority because of their real-world impact. They are not merely an academic pursuit. Let me quickly admit the problems here. Certain scientific questions also are endangered if utilitarian pressures trump every other consideration on our campuses. The sciences and the humanities both have a real and lasting stake in fighting against shortsighted obsessions with returns on investment. So perhaps it makes more sense to say that the health sciences, as contrasted to the research sciences, are more obviously directed to real-world results than the humanities. The humanities currently feel a strong need to claim (demonstrate? But how?) some kind of influence in the world. The American Academy of Arts and Sciences report, *The Heart of the Matter*, runs directly into this difficulty.[4] The report forthrightly declares that "evidence of the particular needs of the humanities and social sciences now reaches us from every sector" (9); the evidence then cited points to the shrinking investment in humanities and social sciences education, especially in K–12 schooling, but also at universities. And we are solemnly told that "each of these pieces of evidence suggests a problem; together, they suggest a pattern that will have grave, long-term consequences for the nation" (9). But evidence that would support this claim about "grave, long-term consequences" is not forthcoming. The report asserts, again and again, a connection between competence in the humanities and social sciences and "foster[ing] a society that is innovative, competitive, and strong" (11), but never manages to move beyond assertion to anything that would substantiate the existence of such a connection. I highlight this deficiency not to mock the report, or to claim the fault could be easily corrected, but to indicate how truly difficult it is to provide evidence (or even arguments) about the value of the humanities that go beyond vague platitudes unlikely to satisfy the hostile or indifferent. The best the report can offer is the consoling information that most of the public still supports "the concept of a liberal education," while 51 percent of employers are willing to call it "very important," with another 43 percent deeming it "fairly important," while 74 percent of the general public "would recommend the concept of a liberal education to their own child or a young person they know" (33). As always with such surveys, it is difficult to know how to understand such generalized statements of support when confronted with the hard evidence the report has already cited of a diminishing investment by our society in humanities and social science education.

The medical humanities are attractive in part because they do offer a path toward supporting claims about the beneficial results of the humanities in practice. Researchers in the field are conducting clinical trials that measure the therapeutic impact of concrete practices inspired by models of social interaction and narratological techniques for telling and interpreting stories.[5] More broadly, apart from any specific humanities-inspired technique or humanities- interpretive heuristic, the medical humanities forefronts a humanities sensibility as much as any particular piece of humanities knowledge. The health-care professionals are saying that attention to the specifics of human interactions leads to better outcomes.

Of course, for humanists to ride this pony we need to overcome our trained suspicion of the soft side of the humanities, of sentimentalism and humanism. Maybe it would help if we humanists could understand those ingrained suspicions as the unhelpful consequences of a certain version of science envy. We think we need to be tough-minded to earn our place at the research university—and beyond. In any event, what I would love to see is a more unapologetic common commitment by humanists to the insistence that a humanistic sensibility leads not only to better concrete outcomes in the hospital or the workplace, but also to a world that is closer to one people would actually choose to live in. Issues of value are central to the humanities, including the issue of what kinds of lives humans should get the opportunity to live. We humanists need to find a better way to come to terms with what I would argue is the inescapable value-laden nature of our field. On the one hand, much work in literary studies (to take just one example) denounces the practices of global capitalism and neo-imperialism ad nauseum, while on the other hand the same critics suspect any effort to describe what a satisfying human life might look like is squishy sanctimoniousness. We seem caught between some kind of unacknowledged obeisance to notions of objectivity that rule out value judgments in favor of factual assertions, even as we indulge in massive bouts of self-righteous crypto-normativism. Yes, I am exaggerating here, but I think practitioners in the field will understand to what I refer. Perhaps it's an issue of scale: denouncing global capitalism has no bite because it reaches to the broad and far away, while grappling with the moral complexities of what is right in front of us and perhaps amenable to our intervention is harder to do. The health-care providers who turn to the humanities are not only working to sustain the lives of their patients but are also focused on preserving their dignity and personhood in a system that often seems dedicated to destroying both. That's a real-world impact I think we humanists should find easy to endorse.

But enough abstractions. I direct a humanities institute and, thus, am often called upon to offer sermons on the value of the liberal arts. Most English—and history and religious studies—professors know every word I will say before I open my mouth. And I know from experience that my platitudes are reassuring to the nonacademic audiences to which I deliver them, but not exciting. What really grabs my listeners' attention is when I tell them about specific things the faculty at UNC are teaching and writing about. The work of humanists becomes self-evidently interesting and important when I talk about the history professor who is studying how the League of Nations created our current map of the Middle East in the 1920s or about the American studies professor who is uncovering the stories, songs, and legends of the various people (from escaped slaves to Civil War deserters to land speculators) who populated North Carolina's Great Dismal Swamp.

So here are two medical humanities projects at UNC. In the first one, a team comprised of a geriatric nursing student, a geriatric resident, a grad student in social work, a grad student in pharmacology, and a humanities student (either undergrad or grad) visit (along with a supervising professor from the medical school's Department of Gerontology) an elderly person or couple who still live at home. During the visit, the team collects as much information as possible about the daily routines that ensure the patient's wellbeing and the daily challenges the patient faces. After the visit, the team meets to recommend a "care plan" that ensures that all of the patients' needs can be met and is aimed toward allowing the patient(s) to remain at home as long as possible. The team meetings have generated the pedagogical byproduct of making it obvious how professional training has already influenced what each of the team members sees. Thus, issues of attention and interpretation inevitably come to the fore. The humanities student's familiarity with such issues, and, crucially, comfort with conflicting interpretations, has, time and again, proved useful to the team's creating a care plan that all can endorse as comprehensive and holistic.

The second example is a research project, with possible clinical benefits pending the results.[6] Various claims have been made about how different mental exercises help stave off elderly dementia. A research team at UNC is going to collect memoirs from residents in an elder-care facility. One group of residents will tell their stories to a researcher who will be recording the session. Another group of residents will write their memories down. The study aims, most simply, to see if there is any difference in mental capacity between the group that writes and the one that doesn't and a third group that has not transmitted their memories in either form (with the testing coming at three-month intervals over a year's time). In short, the study aims to test a claim often made in "narrative medicine" about the efficacy of stories and to see whether relating as opposed to writing makes any difference. Is there real evidence, not just anecdotal reports, about the efficacy of this kind of intervention in the care of the elderly? This study will also produce the beginnings of a database of stories, one that can be used for a variety of different purposes by future researchers. And, of course, a major question is also whether the simple fact that someone is paying attention, has asked for these patients' stories, is therapeutic in itself.

These examples suggest what the humanities can contribute to medical practice and research. The claim is that the characteristic methods of the humanities—which include attention to context, questions of meaning and value, and a focus on intersubjective interactions and individual motivations—encourage us to attend to worldly factors that pertain to human wellbeing. I think there is something fairly concrete that can be called "the humanities sensibility" and, perhaps, it is most easily recognized when humanists work alongside non-humanists. In such cases, what the humanities bring to the table is evident—and there are ways to study the concrete difference such practices make. The effort to establish the presence of the humanities and their characteristic methods in more social sites, like the hospital, can be a source not only of inspiration and delight, but also of hard evidence for the argument that the humanities matter, that they do make our lives better. We might just find our jaded (even cynical) professionalism revitalized. If I might presume to offer a nostrum for the reenchantment of the humanities: more-collaborative work plus a more-missionary zeal for cultivating everywhere and everywhen the humanities sensibility.

The second consequence of what I've been saying is that the humanities are inevitably, and perhaps even primarily, wrapped up in education. A sensibility is learned through immersion in an environment, through practice and through imitation. The humanities have had a good long run of dominating American education from kindergarten through the second year of college. The liberal arts bias of our curriculum prior to the point where the college major is chosen is a major explanation for the presence of those humanistically inclined health scientists in our hospitals and med schools. The battle to retain the liberal arts is most crucially a battle over general education, not about specific majors. Liberal arts education cannot stand still. We must embrace wide experimentation in new content, new classroom practices, and new curricular models. It's the sensibility we should be trying to preserve and extend, not some specific canon or teaching method or institutional arrangement. Concretely, I think that means the humanities, especially, should be much less focused on the major, and much more interested in getting its hands on all the students who pass through our universities and colleges. It is great that medical schools are now interested in admitting students with English and philosophy majors, but it would be even better if we had biology and chemistry majors who had imbibed the spirit of the liberal arts during their college days.

This educational mission is especially crucial for our public universities. I assume my audience is all too familiar with the pressures currently facing public education, from kindergarten all the way through to doctoral programs. Just as the doctors are being pushed to process patients more efficiently, educators in publicly financed schools are being pressured to deliver results (as measured by test scores and degrees) at a lower cost per student. I heard one college administrator recently say that he hated the term "public Ivy" to describe the most elite public research universities. The Ivy League schools, he said, operate on an absolutely different model than the public universities, even the most elite ones. At the Ivies, we see massive resources devoted to educating a small number of students. At the publics, even the wealthiest ones, we get, instead, massive resources devoted to educating large numbers of students. What we might call the Big Ten model. In our time of growing economic and social inequality, the great danger is that the superb education our public universities have made available to large numbers over the past sixty years will be diminished in quality even as it reaches fewer students. A gap will open between the private and the public universities, a gap that will mirror and exacerbate the other equality gaps in American society. The crisis currently facing the public universities is an issue both of continued access to higher education by nonelite students (where being elite is a matter of economic status and of the kinds of educational experiences that were available during the K–12 years) and of maintaining educational quality as state support steadily, but surely, drains away.

The humanities have a particular dog in this fight because, just as I have already discussed in relation to medical practice, the humanities insist that beneficial educational outcomes rely heavily on small-scale, personal relationships between teacher and student. Here, too, there is good hard evidence to cite about the positive effects of small classes, geared toward the solicitation of student input orally and in frequent writing assignments.[7] Surprisingly, the American Academy of Arts and Sciences report has nothing to say on educational techniques or about the fact that its call for making "communication— reading, writing, and speaking—a fundamental element of education" (23) has direct consequences on how schools teach and on the kinds of resources needed to get the recommended results. We reach here familiar dilemmas infecting the ideal of mass education, with the humanities occupying a time-honored, but nonetheless vital, commitment to introducing qualitative concerns into the quantitative calculus of degrees conferred. More baldly, the humanities' task is to call attention relentlessly to the chasm between an ever-present rhetoric of providing a superb public education for all and the ever-decreasing share of public resources our society is willing to devote to that education. Good education, like good health care, does not come cheap, because it is work that requires lots of human-to-human face time. Our elites know this as they flee our public schools when it comes to educating their own children and hurry off to high-priced specialists when their own health is at stake.

The humanities, then, are well positioned because of their sensibility and their historical commitment to small-scale educational interactions to be at the center of reform efforts at our public universities, just as the humanities are crucial to reform efforts within the health-care system. At our public universities especially, I think this conversation about educational models should be general, not just about what happens in English, art history, and philosophy classes. Thus, in tune with my earlier comments about infusing the humanities sensibility throughout the curriculum, the humanities' perspective on educational methods should aspire to impact how we teach everything. The focus should be on what produces the best results, not on specific subject matter. (And this means accepting that no one method is suitable for every subject matter, nor is any single method effective for every student.) If our current economic situation continues (i.e., a growing gap between the very rich and everyone else, coupled with sluggish job growth that makes it especially difficult for the young to break into the job market), I think we should expect that many students and their families, especially the kinds of less-affluent students likely to attend our public universities, will see any humanities major as an unaffordable luxury. If the humanities are to thrive on our public campuses, then the humanities must attend more consistently to general education than to attempting to prop up and defend specific humanities disciplines and majors.

I will close by moving from these speculations about the prospects of America's public universities and the role a humanities sensibility might play in the current landscape to mundane matters of institutional formation. The medical humanities in our med schools is, among other things, a curricular reform movement. Its proponents are working to change the criteria for admission to med school, the courses med students take once admitted, and the defined outcomes for which medical education aims. The resistance to such reforms is strong, but progress has been made. Seventy-five percent of medical schools now require at least one humanities course of their students, while the national accreditation bodies for med schools are rewriting their templates for evaluation of medical education.

On the undergraduate level, new majors and/or minors in medical humanities are part of the huge growth in interdisciplinary majors that have students take courses in various departments to complete their course of study. Despite their demonstrated popularity with students, universities, which are all mostly wedded to the departmental organization developed during the twentieth century, have been largely flummoxed by the development of such programs. Thus, we are having trouble at UNC bringing the Anthropology Department on board for a proposed undergraduate major in medical humanities. That department has long had a robust interest in medical anthropology, attracts a significant number of majors based on its strength in that field, and justifies hiring new professors of medical anthropology based on those enrollments. Hence it fears it will lose out if these students are lured away to an interdisciplinary major. And we get no help from the College of Arts and Sciences when such issues (and fears) arise. The college generally acts as if interdisciplinary majors are just more trouble than they are worth; it only approves them when the professors and departments involved manage to come to an agreement themselves. And if it's bad enough for the college when a student's major course work cannot be credited to a specific department, just imagine the total nightmare we have created in our attempts to cross the lines between the College of Arts and Sciences and the School of Medicine. At UNC, we are trying to get medical school professors and students into the same classroom as humanities professors and undergraduates. You would think we were trying to bring peace to the Middle East. In my more frustrated moments, I have come to believe that courses exist only for accounting purposes, a classic case of the tail wagging the dog. The demands for internal transfers of funds trump educational justifications almost every time.

These institutional issues explain why humanities centers are often central to fostering medical humanities at a large research university. A center like UNC's Institute for the Arts and Humanities does not owe allegiance to any department and thus can broker deals that it also facilitates by providing seed money for courses and other experiments. But seed money lasts only so long. Getting something actually instituted takes eons; at UNC our Global Studies major, with over eight hundred students, still exists on the beg, steal, and borrow model, with only two full-time professors serving all those students. The courses those Global Studies majors take in history, anthropology, political science, Asian studies, and the like barely count at all, and the number of majors hasn't pushed the college to create a Global Studies department even as they are not money in the bank for the various departments that do teach them. So anthropology's fears about joining a medical humanities major are not misplaced. One problem, of course, is that we seem stuck in a model of department or bust. Universities are not going to be supple or truly interdisciplinary until they can organize themselves in nondepartmental forms. Fields of study are fluid; they come and go;

and the paths a student might take through the whole demesne of knowledge are infinite (as are the paths taken by our most imaginative professors). Binding students to the mast of the major, with its ten required courses, leaves them unable to shape what they study and what they learn on the journey through college. A student goes to study in Argentina, then comes home and scrambles to get the courses for her major instead of being able to build on the Latin American experience. We have an assembly-line model where we already possess the intellectual resources to offer a much more customized education. We shouldn't process students the way that insurance companies want doctors to process patients. A broader, less major-focused, humanities does allow us to mobilize the astounding resources we have assembled at a place like UNC to better serve our students. The institutional barriers to achieving such educational results are maddening, but should remain a constant focus of all reform efforts. Every university on the planet claims it aspires to be interdisciplinary. We should hold universities accountable to such rhetoric, just as we try to hold our society accountable to its rhetoric about providing a quality education for all.

But let me end by being really optimistic. The humanities are going to save medicine by giving us a health-care system in which both patients and health-care professionals can find satisfying ways toward wellbeing. Medicine is going to save the humanities by offering us models of collaborative research practices, by providing a site at which the humanities have demonstrable real-world impact, and by reminding humanists about their common commitment to a humanities sensibility. And, finally, medical humanities as a hybrid interdisciplinary enterprise is going to save the university by making it change its institutional structures and accounting procedures to better accommodate the kinds of trans-domain education and research that best suits our society's current needs and our students' and professors' interests (in every sense of that word).

NOTES

1. Martyn Evans and Ilora G. Finlay, eds., *Medical Humanities* (London: BMJ Books, 2002), 2.

2. For examples of literary critics questioning the practices of critique, see Rita Felski, "After Suspicion," *Profession* (2009): 28–35; and Michael Bérubé, *The Left at War* (New York: New York University Press, 2009). Bruno Latour has offered a particularly influential statement of the turn away from critique in his essay, "Why Has Critique Run Out of Steam? From Matters of Fact to Matters of Concern," *Critical Inquiry* 30 (2004): 225–248.

3. For Peirce's understanding of science as a collective enterprise that deals in probabilities not certainties, see chapters 8 ("How to Make Our Ideas Clear"), and 10 ("The Probability of Induction") in *The Essential Peirce: Selected Philosophical Writings*, Vol. 1 *(1867–1893)*, ed. Nathan Houser and Christian Kloesel (Bloomington: Indiana University Press, 1992).

4. *The Heart of the Matter: Report of the Commission on the Humanities and Social Sciences* (Cambridge, MA: American Academy of Arts and Sciences, 2013). I have used the print

edition and have provided page references parenthetically in the text of my essay. The report is also available online at http://www.amacad.org.

5. Rita Charon and Peter Wyer, "Narrative Evidence Based Medicine," *The Lancet* 371 (January 2008): 296–297. Accessed online at http://www.thelancet.com/journals/lancet/article/PIIS0140-6736%2808%2960156-7/fulltext.

6. The study described here is supported by a grant from the Mellon Foundation administered by the Consortium of Humanities Centers and Institutes. The study will be conducted during the 2015 calendar year.

7. Richard Arum and Josipa Roksa, *Academically Adrift: Limited Learning on College Campuses* (Chicago: University of Chicago Press, 2010), provides one wide-ranging study that finds only small classes, with extensive reading and writing assignments and specific instructor feedback, have a demonstrable impact on learning outcomes.

9 · THE NEED FOR CRITICAL UNIVERSITY STUDIES

JEFFREY J. WILLIAMS

This chapter outlines a new field of criticism, Critical University Studies, that targets the corporatization of American higher education over the past three decades, relinquishing much of its public promise, often at the expense of students and faculty. While its focus is not the humanities per se, I sketch the context that has brought the humanities to their current state. Moreover, Critical University Studies often comes from those in the humanities, and the humanities have classically been the place where we consider ideas of the university.

To offer a comparative sense, I look at the moment following World War II alongside our own. Postwar policies carried out what I identify as a liberal humanism—enacting liberal state support for public services like education as well as encouraging a liberal pursuit of study. This ushered in the mass expansion of higher education, opening it to unprecedented numbers of people, as well as the peak of the humanities—in number of students as well as prestige. In contrast, the period beginning in the 1970s turned toward neoliberal policies, draining public support and shifting costs to private individuals, notably in the exponential rise of tuition, as well as the mercantilization of research and other aspects of the academic multiplex. This spurred an antihumanism, reorienting the goal of education to job training, technological development, and monetary profit rather than human exploration or flourishing.

One result has been the deepening stratification of higher education. Postwar policy aimed at equality for all students, providing quality education across the spectrum of institutions, state and private, large and small, universities to community colleges. Now we have steeper tiers among institutions, with bespoke education and intensive human contact at the high end, but progressively more mechanized schooling for the mass, epitomized by the recent turn to online education. Advertised as a great cost reducer, online dehumanizes higher education, degrading teaching labor, evacuating human contact, and accepting a substandard practice.

One aim of Critical University Studies is not only to diagnose the problems of contemporary higher education but also to push for its more truly public promise. Particularly for those of us in the humanities, it's tempting to default to the idea that the humanities exist for their own self-fulfilling good. More compellingly, they contribute to a fuller democratic vision of human endeavor and human flourishing, beyond merely getting and spending and having ever-new devices to spend on.

FROM LIBERAL HUMANISM TO
NEOLIBERAL ANTIHUMANISM

In the era after World War II, higher education in the United States was reconfigured as an instrument of equality. One of the central documents setting out postwar policy was *Higher Education for American Democracy: A Report of the President's Commission on Higher Education*, more commonly known as the Truman Report, which was authorized by President Harry Truman in 1946 and appeared in 1947. It advocated for racial, ethnic, and gender as well as economic equality. Tempered by the war just concluded, the document offered not bromides but frank criticisms, stating that American accomplishments "stop far short of our purpose. The discrepancies between America's democratic creed and how Americans live are still many and serious, [and] our society is plagued with inequalities, even in so fundamental a right as education."[1] To remedy them, it featured a series of calls for action, among them a call for free tuition in the first two years of college at public institutions and financial assistance for those with need beyond that, and it culminated with this declaration: "The time has come to make public education at all levels equally accessible to all, without regard to race, creed, sex, or national origin."[2]

The report also charged American colleges and universities to teach "an active appreciation of different cultures and other peoples" and "a sympathetic understanding of the values and aspirations that move men in the vast areas of eastern Europe, Asia, Africa, South America, and the islands of the sea."[3] In this regard, it forwarded a version of cosmopolitanism, holding that education "help our own citizens as well as other peoples to move from the provincial and insular mind to the international mind."[4] One consequence was that foreign language programs saw unprecedented support, and the report ushered in the heyday of comparative literature.[5] Likewise, English and the other humanities flourished, with a rise in majors through the 1970s.

A third goal that the report set out was that higher education bring "creative imagination and trained intelligence to the solution of social problems and to the administration of public affairs."[6] In doing so, it adapted the Jeffersonian idea that higher education form well-rounded citizen-statesmen who would carry out the aims of democratic government. Accordingly, the expansion of the American university fed directly into the growth of the liberal welfare state in the postwar period, culminating with Lyndon Johnson's Great Society.

Of course, the report did not magically accomplish its goals in one fell swoop. It was still two decades before the Civil Rights Act, so it was only one step forward on the bridge of equality. Its aims also became entwined with the Cold War, so it was not entirely pure in its international aspirations. And it ushered in the "agencies, and bureaus, and technicians" of the welfare state, institutional checks on the "variousness and complexity" of life that Lionel Trilling worried about in the preface to *The Liberal Imagination.*[7] Still, by most empirical markers, the policy succeeded, as higher education welcomed unprecedented numbers of students from various classes, enrollments rising from about 1.4 million in 1940 to 6 million in 1960. Public institutions in particular mushroomed, resulting in what historians call the Golden Age of American higher education.[8] The Golden Age was built with state funding and federal initiatives through the era, such as the subsequent National Defense Education Act of 1958 and National Education Act of 1965. As R. C. Lewontin observes in "The Cold War and the Transformation of the Academy," the Cold War paradoxically created the conditions for public funding of social entitlements despite a traditional American aversion to taxes and such social programs.[9]

We might call postwar educational policy *liberal humanism.* It was liberal in several senses: in the political sense, instituting a kind of equalization or redistribution, a signature of the liberal welfare state; liberal in a Jeffersonian sense, to encourage public service and promulgate a more democratic society; and liberal in the educational sense, encouraging the liberal pursuit of knowledge, extending beyond parochial concerns to the world. It was humanistic because it cultivated the humanities as a base of higher education; it promoted wide cultural knowledge and understanding; and, more generally, it placed primary value on the flourishing of human lives over other measures.

The Golden Age subsided in the 1970s, and since the 1980s higher education has experienced a turning tide, with public funding shrinking, tuitions rising precipitously, and student debt skyrocketing to pay it. This has not been an inevitable, natural event of economic weather; the economy thrived through the Bill Clinton years and at several other points. Rather, it was the deliberate implementation of policy, notably the deregulation of loans and the relentless push to cut social entitlements such as welfare and education beginning with the Ronald Reagan–Margaret Thatcher revolution of the early 1980s.

In our period, American higher education has been recast in terms not of equality and cosmopolitanism but of consumer choice and market competition. For instance, in 1989 President George H. W. Bush advocated his Educational Excellence Act solely in terms of economic aims, declaring that "educational achievement promotes sustained economic growth, enhances the nation's competitive position in world markets, increases productivity, and leads to higher incomes."[10] This vision informs almost all subsequent policy, including the Spellings Commission Report under President George W. Bush, which stresses "accountability" and calls for a national testing system; and *The Heart of the Matter*, which, while focused on the humanities, takes competitiveness to be one of the primary goals of the humanities. It also informs the push for mechanized (online) education, or what Clayton Christensen calls "the innovative university," as I'll discuss below.[11]

This line of policy adopts the neoliberal principle that public services should be privatized and on a market basis. The central concern is not equality but freedom of choice. Accordingly, it has redefined education as a consumer service, which enjoins a commercial transaction rather than another kind of human interchange, and makes citizenship a private matter.[12] Rather than paid from the tax base as a collective social responsibility, the cost of college education has been progressively shifted to individuals as their private responsibility, in the form of high fees and debt. Likewise, rather than keeping a firewall between the profit-seeking market and nonprofit institutions of higher learning, the new policy has turned wholeheartedly to the commercialization of research and other parts of the academic multiplex. In addition, instead of a body of scholars governing its mission, corporate-style, it has adopted vertical management and the casualization of a majority of faculty.

The precipitous rise in college student loan debt is neoliberalism in action. Sometimes student debt is framed as a new problem that resulted from the financial crisis of 2007–2008, but actually it arose in the 1980s. In 1982, the average federal student loan debt for a graduating senior was about $2,000—not negligible, but that adjusts to about $4,650 in 2012 dollars. By 1992, the average jumped to $9,000 ($14,500 in 2012 dollars), in 2002 to $19,000 ($24,050), and in 2012, by my estimate, about $28,000.[13] (That doesn't include private loans, which have risen exponentially over the last decade.) It has also created lucrative new financial markets, with high profits for Sallie Mae and other student loan holders and servicers. (Sallie Mae had been a governmental body but was privatized through the late 1990s, seeing strong profits since.) Rather than the Golden Age, we have entered the Debt Age of American higher education.

According to current empirical markers, there is a widening gulf of inequality in US society, and higher education has become an instrument of inequality for many students under the weight of debt or simply prevented them from attending,[14] for their parents who might have to remortgage the house to send them to college, and for faculty, who have become deeply stratified, with those on top doing fairly well but the other three quarters now in substandard, contingent, and sometimes poverty-wage positions. Instead of a job crisis, we are confronting an inequality crisis. Similarly, for student debtors, we are undergoing not a tuition crisis but an inequality crisis.

We might call the policy of our current period *neoliberal antihumanism*. It is neoliberal because it reconceives higher education as a mercantile market rather than a public realm apart from the market; it reconfigures those attending as job seekers rather than as citizens; and it aims for an edge in global competition rather than cultural understanding and sympathy. It is antihumanist because it minimizes the humanistic base of higher education as negligible rather than central; conceives learning as a question of job skills rather than human exploration or democratic training; and believes learning can be as well done via machines as by human contact.

Postwar policy alleviated some of the disparities of class. This new line of neoliberal policy reinstalls them.

THE NEED FOR CRITICAL UNIVERSITY STUDIES

In the face of these changes, over the past two decades a new movement in criticism has gathered momentum, analyzing the policies, practices, and problems of contemporary higher education. As a shorthand, I have called it Critical University Studies.[15] In part, it arises from the tradition of literary and cultural theory that has addressed sociocultural problems, but it is not just a new way to speak about or do scholarly work. Like Critical Legal Studies, it analyzes how our social institutions foster injustice or perpetuate inequality, and it advocates for their fuller democratic possibilities. Thus its aim is, besides exposition and analysis, confrontation and opposition to the current neoliberal turn in higher education.

There is of course a long tradition of criticism of American higher education that we could date back to colonial times—for instance, early debates over state support, religious influence, and curriculum. The modern radical tradition starts with works like Thorstein Veblen's *The Higher Learning in America* and Upton Sinclair's *The Goose-Step* in the early twentieth century, responding to the first Gilded Age, and continues through 1960s critiques like Robert Paul Wolff's *The Ideal of the University* and sixties-inspired initiatives like the Critical Pedagogy movement.[16] Critical University Studies responds to our recent conditions, mustering a rising generation of critics who have experienced these changes.

To give it a name recognizes that Critical University Studies has some coherence, as well as points to a meeting place for those considering similar kinds of work. "Critical" indicates its unapologetic confrontation of current policies and practices, particularly as they fail the goals of equality, similar to approaches like Critical Legal Studies, Critical Race Studies, and Critical Development Studies. It also suggests its standing outside most conventional scholarship, for instance in education, that deals with particular field issues or tacitly supports contemporary practices.[17] "Studies" picks up its topical character, focused on a particular problem in higher education but drawing on work from any relevant field to address it, without limiting itself to particular disciplinary warrants. "University" suggests its general frame of reference, continuing the tradition of "the idea of the university" as well as examining contemporary instances.

Critical University Studies comes from those in literary and cultural studies, where there is a long tradition examining the idea of the university, as well as from those in education, public policy, sociology, history, and other fields. It is not only academic, and part of its resonance comes from its organic connections to graduate student unionization and contingent faculty movements. That is probably a significant reason why it draws literary and cultural critics, since those in English and foreign language departments typically do a great deal of elementary teaching (rather than, say, working in a lab or on a particular funded project under one professor) and lead union efforts.

While the neoliberal turn emerged in the 1980s, criticism of it did not gain traction until the 1990s, as scholars began realizing what was happening. (In the 1980s influential commentators like William Bowen were still predicting rosy prospects for the 1990s.) It first looked at the development of the "corporate university" in exposés like Lawrence Soley's *Leasing the Ivory Tower: The Corporate Takeover of Academia* (1995), continuing through David Noble's *Digital Diploma Mills: The Automation of Higher Education* (2001) and Jennifer Washburn's *University, Inc.: The Corporate Corruption of Higher Education* (2005). Alongside those, it provided in-depth scholarly analysis in Sheila Slaughter's series of books, beginning with Slaughter and Larry L. Leslie's *Academic Capitalism: Politics, Policies, and the Entrepreneurial University* (1997), which examined "technology-transfer" to businesses and the rise of corporate managerial policies in place of traditional faculty governance.[18]

A major wing of Critical University Studies has targeted the deteriorating conditions of academic labor. Coming out of the graduate student union movement, Marc Bousquet has been one of the most original voices on the exploitation of graduate students, culminating in his book *How the University Works: Higher Education and the Low-Wage Nation* (2006), as well as essays and entries on his blog, howtheuniversityworks.org. A growing wave of criticism has come from the adjunct, contingent faculty, and New Faculty Majority movements, some of which is encapsulated in Joe Berry's *Reclaiming the Ivory Tower: Organizing Adjuncts to Change Higher Education* (2005). Life is not necessarily rosy for tenure-stream faculty, either, and another aspect of the critical perspective on labor focuses on the rise in service, notably in Katie Hogan and Michele Masse's *Over Ten Million Served: Gendered Service in Language and Literature Workplaces* (2010), and the proportionate ballooning of administration over faculty, in Benjamin Ginsberg's *The Fall of the Faculty: The Rise of the All-Administrative University and Why It Matters* (2011).

Since the mid-2000s, a prominent line of Critical University Studies has been to illuminate the position of students, notably student debt, in a number of my own essays such as "The Pedagogy of Debt" and "Student Debt and the Spirit of Indenture" and, in the past couple of years, blowing up online through groups such as Student Loan Justice and Out with Student Debt.[19] In addition, Bousquet has called attention to the flip side of debt, the precipitous rise in student work ("Take Your Ritalin and Shut Up"), and public-policy expert Tamara Draut has pointed to the "The Growing College Gap," as proportionately fewer minority students now attend college than in the 1970s.[20] We tend to think we've conquered such problems, but they are actually intensifying.

An important wave of recent work has defended public higher education and made proposals to reinvigorate it, notably Christopher Newfield in *Unmaking the Public University: The Forty-Year Assault on the Middle Class* (2008), as well as in his blog, "Remaking the University" or utotherescue.blogspot.com, which has been on the vanguard of exposing the real costs of current practices. He has been joined by union leader and scholar Robert Samuels, whose *Why Public Higher Education Should Be Free: How to Decrease Cost and Increase Quality at American Universities* (2013) makes a powerful argument for free tuition.

In my view, this work's particular strength lies in turning the tools of criticism to direct use, debunking commonplace views that have policy implications and political consequences. For instance, contrary to the notion that research supports other parts of the university, Newfield shows that it often occurs at the expense of teaching, especially in the humanities, and in fact surpluses from the humanities frequently support engineering and sciences. Or several of us each debunk the idea that the university has a benevolent relationship to students; rather, graduate students are frequently used as cheap labor, and undergraduates are captive objects of exorbitant banking profits.

In some ways Critical University Studies has succeeded literary theory as a nexus of intellectual energy. Postmodern theory often looked reflexively at the way knowledge is constructed; this new vein looks reflexively at "the knowledge factory" itself (as Stanley Aronowitz has called it), examining it as both a discursive and a material phenomenon.[21] But it adds empirical study of and reportage on the actual conditions of higher education, and makes proposals to change them.

Because both scrutinize central social institutions and join criticism with politics, a comparison between Critical University Studies and Critical Legal

Studies might give a fuller sense of the former. Critical Legal Studies, or CLS as it was called, was initiated in the late 1970s and established during the 1980s among a group of legal scholars in the United States who aimed to show that the law was not neutral or impartial, but served dominant social and economic interests.[22] CUS is similar in turning a cold eye on higher education and foregrounding its inherent politics, particularly how it is a site of struggle between private commercial interests and more public ones.

Another similarity is that CLS and CUS argue against academic practice as usual. CLS distinguished itself from standard legal history, arguing that law was an instrument of its social structure, as well as tried to find ways that law might contribute to more equality. CUS distinguishes itself from the standard history of education or the palliative tradition of "the idea of the university," analyzing how higher education is an instrument of its social structure, and figuring out how it might contribute to more equality.

Their differences also help pinpoint CUS. CLS was formed by scholars largely from the sixties generation and reflected concerns of the civil rights and antiwar movements. Emerging twenty or thirty years later, CUS enlists those from subsequent cohorts, responding to the draining of social institutions since the 1970s, as I mentioned above. CLS was a critique of complacent midcentury liberalism, whereas CUS is a critique of neoliberalism and the conservative ascendency.

Both CLS and CUS assume not merely an academic but an activist dimension. CLS, however, usually came from those at elite institutions, notably Harvard and Yale, and aimed to effect change through legal education. It embraced literary theory—as Hutchinson puts it, it formed "an outpost of critical theory," stressing indeterminacy in legal language. CUS comes from a more diffuse group of people, from a range of institutions and in diverse positions, for the most part from public colleges and universities, and aims to change policy through direct action in unions or the student loan movement, as well as in reportage, analysis, and pragmatic proposals. It dwells less in the realm of high theory and is more rooted in contemporary practices and policies.

In philosophical terms, CLS was generally realist rather than idealist in orientation, studying how the law operates in practice. It emphasized what the legal theorist Mark Kelman called "law-in-action" rather than "law-in-books." Similarly, CUS is realist rather than idealist, studying concrete instances and uses of higher education. Taking a note from Kelman, I would emphasize that CUS is "criticism-in-action" or "theory-in-action." It might draw on some of the procedures of critical theory to expose ideology, but it connects them to the institution under our feet. Or, in the case of online, at our fingertips.

CHALLENGES TO EQUALITY

The challenges facing Critical University Studies seem, if anything, more pronounced as American higher education continues its shift to privatization and its neoliberal phase. In part through the work of CUS, there is more awareness of issues such as corporatization, casualization, and student debt. The latter two explicitly show how inequality affects the primary constituents of the university, faculty and students. Rather than a body of scholars with roughly equivalent rights, now there is a deeply stratified system of academic labor, with the majority of faculty contingent, with little formal job security, inferior or absent benefits, and often poverty-level wages. As I have suggested elsewhere, other professions, such as medicine, exemplify how we might build a different, fairer system of academic labor, although most likely any positive change will come from the bottom up rather than from the top down. Groups such as the New Faculty Majority present one possibility for those in contingent positions to organize and redeem some control of their labor.

Regarding students, college-loan debt is one of the pressing social issues of our time, one that will mark current and coming generations through their middle age and, in many cases, old age. Sometimes the culprit is identified as the rise of tuition, as if colleges have just become greedy. But the spike in tuition ties directly to the public defunding of higher education,[23] as well as to the overriding commercialization of college life. In addition, debt conjoins with the rise in student work hours, now estimated at twenty-five hours per week for students in state schools, since both represent ways for students to pay the individualized cost of education.

The best remedy, in my view, is free tuition at public colleges and universities, first proposed by Adolph Reed as part of an initiative of the Labor Party in the 1990s, and recently forwarded by Robert Samuels.[24] The brilliance of the proposal is its simplicity as well as fairness: it would alleviate charges of "class warfare" and any such discrimination. This might initially seem a pie-in-the-sky idea, but Samuels shows how the cost of instruction has often been siphoned off by research and administrative costs, and in fact that it is affordable. Also, there would be considerable savings through the abolition of the federal student loan program, which offers large subsidies to banking in the form of interest and fees, and other administrative costs sucked up in loan servicing.[25]

A major challenge that has crystallized in the past decade is what Andrew Ross has called "the rise of the global university," which entails primarily the export of American higher education. One could see this as a further stage in corporatization: after the phase of entrepreneurial corporatization, it seems that American universities are moving to imperialist corporatization, gaining high revenues overseas, frequently in straight cash deals and without government oversight or tax. This trend has been promoted as altruistic but is usually a profit-seeking endeavor through which US or European universities sell their brands and services.

For instance, the university where I teach, Carnegie Mellon, has recently agreed to provide an engineering program for Rwanda, a plan that met with controversy because of the human rights abuses of the Rwandan regime that signed the deal. That was troubling enough, but underneath lay a fundamental problem. Even if Rwanda were an exemplary state, the deal was foremost a cash transaction, Carnegie Mellon receiving $95,000,000 for providing faculty and programs. Carnegie Mellon operated as any profit-seeking company would—which is good for their coffers, but is that the role a nonprofit university should have? Moreover, rather than gaining a niche for our schools in underdeveloped regions, shouldn't the goal of such an exchange be for Rwanda to develop its own universities?

This is an issue of equality because it exploits global inequality, as richer first-world institutions make deals much to their advantage with less powerful or developed nations. It has spurred a new gold rush, as administrators spy wealth in the Middle East, Asia, and Africa, and its impetus is largely commercial, covered in the thin veneer of classical rationales of higher education.

Finally, perhaps the most prominent challenge is online education, promoted in many quarters as auguring wholesale, even revolutionary change. Like globalization, it is advertised as an altruistic good, spreading education presumably everywhere, but it actually institutionalizes inequitable access, under the banner of technological innovation.

The inequality of access is a central premise of Clayton Christensen and Henry Eyring's *The Innovative University*.[26] Christensen is the guru of modern business education who coined the mantra "disruptive innovation," and he is perhaps the most influential thinker championing online higher education. In *The Innovative University* and various op-eds, he assumes that universities operate as American car companies did in the 1970s, set in their ways and resistant to change, thus ripe for disruption. *The Innovative University* acknowledges that places like Harvard are superior, but sees higher education as a straightforward consumer purchase rather than a right or public instrument of equality. Thus, Harvard is a luxury good, like going to Bloomingdale's, but most of the rest of us have Walmart, so we are not deprived. Christensen puts this in cheery promotional rhetoric, praising the convenience of online providers such as DeVry or Southern New Hampshire University.[27] Like Walmart superstores, they are open twenty-four hours a day.

If you are buying a shirt, one from Bloomingdale's and one from Walmart will clothe you. However, if we consider higher education a public good and a right for those qualified, this is a deprivation, reinforcing rather than relieving inequality. It is not that everyone can go to Harvard, but the impetus of the postwar period was to make public education commensurate with one that you might receive at Harvard. Berkeley was the Harvard of the West; and the school where I got my PhD, Stony Brook, aimed to be the "Berkeley of the East." Though Ivies had more prestige, there was greater parity among schools and effort to offer commensurate education to all, from community colleges in California to graduate schools in New York. Now we have too often given up that democratic expectation and accepted the inevitability of inequality.

The simple exchange model of the market frame obscures the other functions of higher education. In general, Christensen and Eyring see higher education primarily as a qualification or training for a job, minimizing the other uses that the Truman Report casts as primary, such as cultural understanding or civic service, not to mention alleviating inequality. Their frame largely ignores the political dimension of education. For instance, they note that tuitions have risen over the past few decades and assume it's simply a market adjustment due to rising costs,[28] instead of looking at the fact that tuitions rose in direct correlation with the decrease of public support. Their one-stroke market model fails to account for politics, but politics has clearly played a major role in the affordability of tuition, and the consequences of that. The market model makes it all seem like a mechanical process, rather than a fungible human process.

Because *The Innovative University* has been so influential, I think it's necessary to note a few other problems. By basic academic standards, it is shoddy in its research, if not intellectually dishonest. Overall, Christensen and Eyring start with the assumption that universities are set in their ways, invoking the metaphor that it has a DNA or set structure. But that's a myth: the actual history of American higher education shows a great deal of change, from the small religious college to the expanding state university of the late nineteenth century, and from the mid-twentieth-century institution open to mass education to our contemporary diversity of schools. If there is one principle of the American institution, it is adaptability.[29]

Along with its shallow history, *The Innovative University* regularly relies on questionable sources. For instance, it remarks on the success of DeVry University, a for-profit technical college, and takes as evidence of its "rigorous standards" a DeVry Internet posting and a report from the business consultant McKinsey.[30] The book tends to make its surmises on this superficial basis, with a kind of business report cheerleading rhetoric, and does not investigate any deeper, as one would expect of academic analysis.

Another questionable claim is what online will do for students. At one point, Christensen and Eyring point out how wonderful one online university is because instructors occasionally talk on the phone to students.[31] Even if online has some positive potential, it is indeed stretched to see this as an asset comparable to face-to-face instruction, but they wash over that quibble with more cheerleading. They also note that students like Facebook so will naturally want to have higher education in this fashion.[32] But this cliché ignores two key problems: first, recent studies have shown that electronic participation, which promotes multitasking, diffuses attention and actually is inefficient and less effective than traditional modes.[33] Also, it's a myth that students want online: according to student representatives in California, students in fact don't want online but face-to-face education.[34] Not to mention simple common sense: this is candy reasoning—if students want to eat candy, should we then encourage it? That's a key problem with consumerist models of higher education. Higher education does not depend on students' desires, but on what our culture has historically deemed useful and essential to know, and what experts know that students have little idea of.

From a business frame, a major impediment, and what Christensen wishes to disrupt, is faculty control. Though himself a longtime professor, he displaces faculty from their role as legislators of the university to common employees for hire. Looming in the background of his metaphor of "DNA" is faculty, whom he sees as impediments to change—that is, they are resistant to mercantile initiatives. He does not see that they might represent a different interest, of educational expertise or of public interest; rather, he only recognizes that salient decisions are made top-down and administrative.[35]

In the current climate of boosterism for online education, to question online often provokes charges that one is a Luddite. But we need more-serious questions about what online can do and cannot do, and more-trenchant examination of its possibilities and problems. As a corollary, part of my point in going through Christensen's claims at length is to show the necessity of critical inquiry, which is a fundamental humanistic value.

A more searching account of the possibilities of online education comes from a group called the Open Learning Initiative (OLI).[36] They are interested in investigating how online might be used to improve teaching, and they did an experimental study with an introductory statistics course. Ordinarily students attend a lecture of, say, 200 students, and then take exams. In place of the lecture, a cohort of students did much of their basic course work online and then met in small sessions twice a week for fifty minutes with the professor to discuss the lecture material. They found that students in this cohort did significantly better on their exams and retained the material at a better rate.

One lesson of OLI is that online does not dispense with teachers; if anything, it probably featured more direct and individualized contact. What it replaces are lectures. Though one can attend memorable lectures, we should have no particular nostalgia for lectures, which were installed on the factory model, arising in the nineteenth century as universities first experienced expanded numbers of students. (Before the Civil War, colleges were more like small prep schools, with only a few professors.) In other words, the promise of online might simply be that it adds another format to our repertoire—in place of or supplementing large introductory lecture courses, where students are sometimes lost. Thus it might not revolutionize education; in some ways OLI returns to the traditional model of the tutorial, working best with face-to-face contact. The greatest effect of online might be on textbooks—which will probably develop into multimedia packages.

OLI does not take a critical perspective in the sense of CUS, but it does bring up a dimension that we might learn from: we indeed should experiment and try to find better teaching methods. However, the criterion should not primarily be a business decision, but a pedagogical one. Also, we should be well aware of online's limitations. Large introductory lecture courses like statistics call for a different pedagogy than, say, most courses in the humanities, when a significant part of learning might be the experience of the professor's method in framing and addressing questions.

Given the problems that higher education now confronts, what would a new Truman Commission call for? We hear a lot about "innovation," which sounds as if it is an unalloyed good. Who would claim to be against innovation? Yet we should ask the fundamental question, what good is innovation if it brings us inequality? Rather, a goal of higher education should still be to abate inequality, so we need to reinforce rather than withdraw support for free public education, open to all.

NOTES

1. *Higher Education for American Democracy: A Report of the President's Commission on Higher Education* [Truman Report], Vol. 1, *Establishing the Goals* (New York: Harper, 1947), 12 and 13.
2. Ibid., 38.
3. Ibid., 14 and 17.
4. Ibid., 15.
5. This call received a notable boost after *Sputnik* in 1957; see, for instance, Joseph Axelrod and Donald M. Bigelow, *Resources for Language and Area Studies: A Report on an Inventory of the Language and Area Centers Supported by the National Defense Education Act of 1958* (Washington, DC: American Council on Education, 1962).
6. Truman Report, 8.
7. Lionel Trilling, *The Liberal Imagination: Essays on Literature and Society* (New York: Harcourt Brace Jovanovich, 1950), xii.
8. See Geiger's account of the Golden Age—and also qualifications about it—in *Research and Relevant Knowledge: American Research Universities since World War II* (New York: Oxford University Press, 1993), ch. 7.
9. See R. C. Lewontin, "The Cold War and the Transformation of the Academy," in *The Cold War & the University: Toward an Intellectual History of the Postwar Years*, by Noam Chomsky,

Laura Nader, Immanuel Wallerstein, Richard C. Lewontin, and Richard Ohmann (New York: New Press, 1997), 1–34.

10. Qtd. in Richard Ohmann, "A Kinder, Gentler Nation: Education and Rhetoric in the Bush Era," *JAC* 10.2 (1990): 220.

11. Christensen extends his argument from his best-selling business advice book, *The Innovator's Dilemma: The Revolutionary Book that Will Change the Way You Do Business* (New York: Harper, 2000), in a number of mainstream articles, and his book, co-written with Henry J. Eyring, *The Innovative University: Changing the DNA of Higher Education from the Inside Out* (San Francisco: Jossey-Bass, 2011).

12. Lauren Berlant also shows how citizenship has been privatized during this period, although she primarily focuses on the way it evokes personal intimacy, rather than the more material factors I describe; see *The Queen of America Goes to Washington City: Essays on Sex and Citizenship* (Durham, NC: Duke University Press, 1997).

13. I gather my statistics from the *Digest of Education Statistics*, the data compiled annually by the US Department of Education and published by the National Center for Education Statistics and online at http://nces.ed.gov/programs/digest.

14. Tamara Draut notes the disturbing trend that fewer minority students now go to college than in the 1970s, a choice that is largely correlated with income; see "The Growing College Gap," in *Inequality Matters: The Growing Economic Divide in America and Its Poisonous Consequences*, ed. James Lardner and David A. Smith (New York: New Press, 2005), 89–101.

15. My term is in homage to the 1984 essay "The Need for Cultural Studies," by Henry Giroux, David Shumway, Paul Smith, and James Sosnoski, in *Dalhousie Review* 64.2.

16. Heather Steffen, with whom I've collaborated in marking the field of Critical University Studies, has illuminated the history of radical criticism, looking at figures such as Sinclair and groups such as the 1920s Student League; see her "Intellectual Proletarians in the 20th Century," *Chronicle of Higher Education*, November 28, 2011.

17. I should note that in Europe some critics within the discipline of education have called for Critical Higher Education Studies. It deals particularly with internationalization after the Bologna Process, which attempted to standardize measures in the diverse systems across Europe.

18. Sheila Slaughter and Larry L. Leslie, *Academic Capitalism: Politics, Policies, and the Entrepreneurial University* (Baltimore: Johns Hopkins University Press, 1997).

19. See Jeffrey J. Williams, "The Pedagogy of Debt," *College Literature* 33 (2006): 155–169; and "Student Debt and the Spirit of Indenture," *Dissent* (Fall 2008): 73–78.

20. Marc Bousquet, "Take Your Ritalin and Shut Up," *South Atlantic Quarterly* 108 (2009): 623–649; and Tamara Draut, "The Growing College Gap," in *Inequality Matters*, 89–101.

21. See Stanley Aronowitz, *The Knowledge Factory: Dismantling the Corporate University and Creating True Higher Learning* (Boston: Beacon Press, 2001).

22. See Mark Kelman, *A Guide to Critical Legal Studies* (Cambridge, MA: Harvard University Press, 1987). As Kelman describes, CLS sees law as "an instrument of social, economic and political denomination, both in the sense of furthering the concrete interests of the denominators *and* in that of legitimating the existing order" (297). He also recounts the initial organizing letter of January 17, 1977, for a "proposal for a gathering of colleagues who are pursuing a critical approach toward the study of law in society." For a useful anthology covering early work defining Critical Legal Studies, see Allan C. Hutchinson, ed., *Critical Legal Studies* (Totowa, NJ: Rowman and Littlefield, 1989).

23. See Michael J. Rizzo, "State Preferences for Higher Education Spending: A Panel Data Analysis, 1977–2001," in *What's Happening to Public Higher Education? The Shifting Financial Burden*, ed. Ronald G. Ehrenberg (Baltimore: Johns Hopkins University Press, 2006), 3–35.

24. Adolph Reed, Jr., "A GI Bill for Everybody," *Dissent* (Fall 2001): 53–58; Robert Samuels, *Why Public Higher Education Should Be Free: How to Decrease Cost and Increase Quality at American Universities* (New Brunswick, NJ: Rutgers University Press, 2013).

25. See Jordan Weissmann, "Here's Exactly How Much the Government Would Have to Spend to Make Public College Tuition-Free," *TheAtlantic*.com, January 3, 2014, available at theatlantic.com. Weissman reports that it would cost the federal government less than $40 billion to pay all tuition at public colleges. (Public schools collected about $60 billion in tuition in 2012, and the federal government already pays over $20 billion in grants; added to that, there are many other costs the federal government pays that would be lessened.)

26. Christensen and Eyring, *The Innovative University*.

27. The latter has an unaccredited business program that Christensen praises for its bucking "the trend" (344). It is a rhetorical sleight of hand to consider accreditation as a "trend," as if visceral fashion, rather than a profession standard.

28. Christensen and Eyring, *The Innovative University*, 13.

29. See my "Post-Welfare State University," *American Literary History* 18 (2006): 190–216.

30. Christensen and Eyring, *The Innovative University*, 25.

31. Ibid., 337.

32. Ibid., 325.

33. See Bob Samuels, "Being Present," *Inside Higher Ed*, January 24, 2013, available at http://www.insidehighered.com.

34. See Christopher Newfield, "Whose Online? What Online?," *Remaking the University* [blog], January 16, 2013, available at http://utotherescue.blogspot.com/2013/01/whose-online-what-online.html.

35. In invoking his mechanical model of the market, Christiansen claims that "Another source of online course improvement is market competition among instructors" (Christensen and Eyring, *The Innovative University*, 328). This totally evacuates the sense of professional judgment—that is, the best assessment of professional value would be from those in a profession. (Think of how it would be if medical doctors operated on this basis.) Not to mention that there is already a great deal of competition for jobs.

36. See Marsha Lovett, Oded Meyer, and Candace Thille, "The Open Learning Initiative: Measuring the Effectiveness of the OLI Statistics Course in Accelerating Student Learning," *Journal of Interactive Media in Education* (2008): 1–16, available at http://jime.open.ac.uk/2008/14. OLI is based at Carnegie Mellon, although I only know of it through their publications.

10· WHAT ARE THE HUMANITIES FOR?

Rebuilding the Public University

CHRISTOPHER NEWFIELD

Before a recent talk, someone approached me with the observation, "You're the guy who says we're destroying our public universities." I laughed and replied, "I'm now the guy who says that we succeeded." When I find myself caught in a humorless joke like this, I know I am dealing with something I care enormously about that seems to be in irreversible decline. In the case of public universities, the decline is perverse, since they seem not just unable but unwilling to save themselves. Given their inertia, public universities will have an easier time moving forward if they start from the idea that public universities as we knew them are dead.

Obviously, the institutions and their activities carry on—the building mortgages, the student activities, the administrative hiring, the sports programs, and the academic labor. But their *public* missions do not. Each year, millions of students attend formally public colleges and universities that support a share of their budget with taxpayer funds, and yet, on several counts, they are no longer truly public. The most prominent among them get a small and shrinking proportion of their funding from the state; their leaders no longer express public purposes that transcend individual or economic self-interest; their policy choices are dominated by private-sector economic beliefs; and they no longer present themselves as forming the destiny of humanity, which lies necessarily over the horizon of current debates. The mid-twentieth-century public university, in short, is dead.

This chapter addresses the connection between the humanities and the project of rebuilding the public university. My title notwithstanding, I will focus on this issue, and will not cover the range of purposes of humanities-based research and teaching.[1]

WHAT DOES PUBLIC MEAN?

University officials have, if anything, increased their emphasis on the word "public" in their justifications of policy and their explanations of the mission. But they have at the same time defined public down. At UC Berkeley, top officials have taken to equating "public" with having a high percentage of low-income students. Citing Pell Grant statistics lends the appearance of sustaining a social justice mission, though all the while the campus is replacing resident students with nonresidents, severing staff from faculty by putting staff into "shared services" tanks—which strips academic content from administration—and steering academic departments toward "unit-level entrepreneurialism."[2] University administrations cannot actually support public service missions while forcing frontline educational units to divide their attention between education and growing their own revenue streams, yet that is exactly what they are trying to do. One function of these careless and misleading definitions of "public" is that they disguise privatization—a term that, at the University of California, we are generally not welcome to use.

So let me define the term public as it has functioned in the great university systems in states as otherwise different as Texas and California and Wisconsin and Iowa.

First, public meant *mass* access. The term *access* meant that you could afford to go, and wouldn't run up debt. No one imagined that student debt would become a major outcome of attending university or a major profit center for the financial industry. Access meant more fundamentally that you could get into the public university—that you would actually be admitted to it. UC campuses were all close to open admission into the early 1970s, and most accepted all applicants who met baseline requirements. In contrast, in 2014, Berkeley and UCLA rejected more than 80 percent of their applicants. My own Santa Barbara campus now rejects two-thirds of its applicants. A high percentage of rejects are qualified, so we have the spectacle of public universities asking for public funds while rejecting most of the public trying to get into them. Public research universities are increasingly like elite private universities in their propensity for excluding applicants, but privates don't then turn around and ask for public operating money, and of course public universities do.

Second, the *public* in public universities meant mass *quality*. The great flagships—including Ann Arbor, Austin, Berkeley, Bloomington, Chapel Hill,

Columbus, Iowa City, Madison, Urbana-Champaign—did not take a back seat in quality to Ivy League universities but competed with them and, in emerging fields in particular, often won; the publics offered quality on a scale that private universities could not match and never would. That was in research. In teaching, the public idea was to elevate the individual capabilities of huge numbers of students. Public universities didn't reject everyone who wasn't already on a high level. They took nearly all comers and then improved them after they got in. No offense to Stanford or Harvard, but these universities minimize their public impact by accepting and improving only those students who are already at the top of the achievement pyramid before they've attended their first class. In contrast, there has been enormous public impact in taking mid-level achievers and making them good or great. Mass quality in public universities has meant reducing the mediocrity of the masses—taking the vast majority of we allegedly mediocre folks and our middling backgrounds, average levels of ambition and not-so-great personal focus, and making us really good at some things. Mass quality has consisted of *Bildung*—personal development, a model that Sheldon Rothblatt places in historical context in this volume[3]—on a mass, even unprecedented scale. Of course, this was presumed to lead to economic development, as the Morrill land-grant legislation demanded, and as politicians invariably insist upon. But the means and also the tacit end was instruction that combined subject mastery with individual cultivation. When they functioned well, public universities taught content while doing liberal-arts style work on what we might now call "creative capabilities," to adapt a general concept of Martha Nussbaum's.[4] Intellectual content and personal identity were addressed together.

Third, the *public* in public universities meant sociocultural inclusion: women, people of color, and religious minorities were included (via struggle, over time) and sometimes even actively welcomed and valued.[5] The most important form of integration was racial, but in a land with what one recent cultural geographer calls the eleven nations of North America, public universities also established conditions of general cross-cultural equality.[6] Assimilation to WASP norms became decreasingly the university's operative assumption.

This was a long, slow road. As Michael Meranze reports, African Americans and Latinos did not catch up with 1967 white college participation rates until 1994 and 2009, respectively, and by those years white participation had leapt ahead.[7] Although the distance traveled was small, the integrationist direction was clear. Public universities were important sites of postsegregationist experience, which was the foundation for racial equality in a near-future society. Racial equality was honored in the breach, but it was honored. It persisted in a double bind: the university could not fulfill an egalitarian vision, yet it could not settle for *not* fulfilling it.

We don't yet live in that integrated future. We still have ongoing, enormous problems of racial climate on campuses coast to coast, and, as Yolanda Moses notes in these pages, universities have yet to incorporate diversity into their vision of academic excellence.[8] If we ask whether African Americans feel as if UCLA or Michigan Ann Arbor belongs to them as much as to others, the answer today is no. If we ask whether California's or Michigan's colleges offer structurally equal opportunity to all racial groups, the answer is no again. But *public* did start officially to mean antiexclusion on the basis of race, culture, or other identity, with the outcome being the possibility, for the first time in US history, of a solidarity society formed by what we now call the 99 percent.

I offer a summary table (Table 10.1) that shows, from left to right, social challenges in the 1950s and 1960s, the traditional mainstream position, the public university's general, if often implicit, stance, and finally, the *non*conservative middle class that the public university was producing—to the pleasure of most people and the horror of certain economic and political elites. My point is clear in the title. The United States faced challenges in the political, economic, and cultural domains (rows 1–3 respectively). By the 1960s, traditional conservatism (column 2) no longer offered functional responses, even though the majority of the middle class remained loyal to them. My claim here—argued at length in *Unmaking the Public University*—is that the public university offered meaningful problem-solving in these three dimensions where the political right and center were failing (column 3). The society imagined by the "nonconservative middle class" represented a major expansion of democracy in those three zones (column 4). The mass white-collar middle class (John Kenneth Galbraith's "technostructure") began to take for granted a kind of bourgeois labor theory of value that entitled it to much of the proceeds of the new wealth they traced back to their own expertise: the theory of human capital was a leading neoclassical articulation of this view.[9]

TABLE 10.1   Public University for Mass ("Middle Class") Democracy

Challenge	Traditional middle class	Public university	Nonconservative middle class
Multiracial mass democracy	Experts follow elites	Free/open access	Majoritarian democracy
Early decline of profits; unhappy workforce	Management vs. labor; managers loyal to elites	*Bildung*—deep personal development	Value created by skilled white-collar degrees
Racial equality in post-WASP society	Cultures are unequal; assimilate to Anglo-Euro	Egalitarian inclusion & diversified curriculum	Postsegregation; emergent cultural equality

But where are these goals today? Are we still evolving public universities that offer open access at little or no cost, focus on *Bildung* or personal development as much as or more than on economic outcomes, and constantly adapt their curricula not just to discuss but to achieve racial equality?

THE PUBLIC'S MATERIAL CONDITIONS

In addition to enjoying a non-hostile environment public universities also needed certain material conditions. For starters, even the research campuses in public-university systems needed to have a strong instructional focus. Their students were generally not the specially customized type who get admitted to Yale and Duke. Public-university students had potential but it was more often not yet developed. They were not second-tier minds, but their minds were more dependent on higher education for their equal development. So lots of public-university teaching needed to be done.

This wasn't easy, since funds were always limited, and public research universities had faculty who necessarily spent much or most of their time in libraries and laboratories at a distance from undergraduates. Public research was vital. It was not (and is not) to be compromised. But even as public universities limited teaching expectations so that research could happen, they also grew graduate programs and mixed mass instruction with seminars to allow a decent amount of face-to-face, active learning. My university system was particularly aggressive in bragging about its low student-faculty ratio, which averaged 17:1 or so well into the 1980s. In the 2000s, the Office of the President was still insisting that undergraduates were being taught to do research and to enlarge the knowledge base. In other words, undergraduate instructional quality was part of the core of the public mission. Instructional quality was measured, implicitly, not simply by where students ended up intellectually, but by how far they had traveled with us from first to final year.

Public universities had to conduct high-end research while working on the individual cultivation of what we might call *ordinary smart people*, which meant justifying the way universities took taxpayer money and failed to generate products or profits in private-sector terms. Higher education is like public health in that the costs of a truly protective system are high and must be shared across the entire population that benefits. The funding had to be public because individuals simply don't use their private funds to support (a) lots of other people who are (b) not necessarily like them and who are, in addition (c) not visibly great. The enormous social benefits of university education cannot be made visible via orthodox market calculations. Only public funds will support the instruction of the majority, to help all of us move from the ordinary promise in which 99 percent of us live our first two decades into an even higher, even more capable state.

Certainly I don't claim that public universities realized these goals. But they once came within a country mile and, although most institutions still try, they are not now funded or politically supported to offer top quality on the necessary scale. But for decades, real success was achieved locally, in every state, and to such an extent that they remained general aspirations. The goals and intermittent achievements formed a gravitational field that kept everyone's feet pointed more or less in the same direction.

Here's a modification of the previous table that adds the public university *means* for achieving these public ends (Table 10.2). These means appear in column 2. The outcome, in the right-hand column, is a broad mainstream social formation that supports mass democracy, inclusively defined via both "deep freedom" and egalitarianism.[10] Open access to higher education encouraged majoritarianism (row 1), or more specifically the felt individual capability to participate fully and equally in a complex, generally alienating society. Democracy really happens only when ordinary people are on the same footing as elites, not only in representational power, but also in their capacity to be full agents, as Doris Sommer explains at length.[11] Similarly, Helen Small rejects the "guardianship model" of democracy— that which is dependent on the expert practice of the "professional few"—and advocates as a more sustainable understanding of the humanities' contribution to the "sufficiently educated practice of the many."[12] I think of this as a "good enough creativity" that can have a transformative effect when distributed across society.

Cultural equality across race (row 3) became a regulative norm of democratic, middle-class capitalism, again, honored in the breach. The public university also supported the enormous expansion of what came to be called intellectual capital, which depended on a partnership between social investment and individual learning effort in K–12 and higher education.[13] This was broadly supported

TABLE 10.2   Means of Mass Democracy

Challenge	Public university means	Public university	Nonconservative middle class
Multiracial mass democracy	High public funding	Free/open access	Majoritarian democracy
Early decline of profits; unhappy workforce	Mass active learning, research learning	*Bildung*—deep personal development	Value created by skilled white-collar degrees
Racial equality in post-WASP society	Advanced student services linked to society	Egalitarian inclusion & diversified curriculum	Postsegregation; emergent cultural equality

as both the fountainhead of national wealth and of a good individual life. The college-educated middle-class formed a "technostructure" that meant knowledge workers would have economic stability and authority that paralleled their cultural openness and democratic power.[14]

By the early 1970s, the term *public* in public university pointed towards racially egalitarian mass *Bildung*. This implied a strong democratizing effect in multiple dimensions of common life and sounded proto-revolutionary to conservatives.

THE GREAT SURRENDER

As the decade wore on, the goals I've described came under increasingly systematic attack and were discredited in many segments of the wider society. This is the story of the culture wars that I told in *Unmaking the Public University*. What also happened is that universities adjusted themselves to meet these critiques at least halfway. Senior managers made a set of decisions that became regularized across the country. In isolation, each decision was most likely quite sensible— like a "temporary" dialing up of nonresident admissions to augment revenues "until public funding recovers." But the interactive effects have been terrible, and the public university trapped itself in a *privatization cycle* that has damaged access, affordability, quality, and the public mission. Elsewhere I detail the university decisions that have fed this downward spiral loop, which has helped to lock in those cuts and to impoverish the social impact of these institutions.[15]

Column 2 in the next table pulls out three features of the doom loop (Table 10.3). Public-university officials have given up on high public funding (column 2, row 1). For years, public officials suggested that they were mostly soaking corporate research sponsors and wealthy donors, but the post-2007 period has brought to everyone's attention that the only meaningful private source for covering

TABLE 10.3   University's Internal Contribution to Decline

Public university	Public university officials	Public university means	Embattled nonconservative middl class
~~Free/open access~~	High private revenues	~~High public funding~~	Majoritarian democracy?
Bildung—deep personal development deemphasized	Deskilling knowledge work: adjuncting-MOOCs	Reduced mass active learning and research learning	Value created by skilled white-collar degrees?
Egalitarian inclusion & diversified curriculum under siege	Anti-egalitarian demotion of sociocultural (non-STEM) knowledge	Advanced student services less linked to society	Postsegregation; emergent cultural equality?

public-university operations is the regular tuition increase—averaging 4.2 percent per year above inflation since 2002–2003.[16] At the same time, the shift from permanent to contingent faculty (column 2, row 2) has convinced much of the country that college teaching doesn't require tenure and long-range skill development, and that this is yet another public good that the public doesn't really need to support. Finally, public-university leaders have put the sociocultural, literary, and artistic fields in the back seat, while science, technology, engineering, and mathematical disciplines (STEM) sit up front, and have first crack at resources (column 2, row 3). Whether one is talking about confronting racial resegregation, reducing economic inequality, or orienting national politics towards mitigating climate change, US solutions are largely sociocultural. Yet university leaders have decided to shortchange these forms of expertise.

The tragic irony of these adaptive strategies is that public universities have not been rewarded for compromising themselves. To the contrary, many years after a financial crisis that first surfaced in 2007, higher education's financial situation is more precarious than ever. First, public funding per student remains nearly 30 percent below its level in the late 1980s, after adjusting for inflation, while state lawmakers promise that funding will never return to "where it was before."[17] Second, the tuition escape hatch is being nailed shut: the national student debt crisis has put unprecedented—and justified—pressure on universities not to raise tuition to make up for lost state funds.

Third, the bloom is off those alternative funding roses of the 1980s, 1990s, and 2000s—federal research grants and philanthropy. For different reasons, neither has compensated, nor will ever compensate, for public funding cuts. Fourth, the recent technological ride to the financial rescue has collapsed, by which I mean MOOCs (massive open online courses), which were to use Silicon Valley genius to eliminate college's "cost disease" by replacing people with machines, as in manufacturing. That higher ed had already spent thirty years cheapening its workforce with contingent faculty escaped the notice of those advocating ed-tech cost savings as a panacea. So fifth, public-university officials are pushing harder on ever more marginal strategies, the most familiar being to increase nonresident student enrollments so as to capture doubled or tripled fees. Universities are also trying to goose more royalties out of patenting programs and have increased institutional borrowing: for example, the University of California's debt doubled in the five years following the crisis's first appearance.

In short, public universities continue to move through the stations of the privatization cycle that has simultaneously undermined fiscal solvency and damaged the public educational mission. Thanks in large part to the university's own decisions to let go or dial back core resources (Table 10.3, column 2), they have reduced their most popular results (Table 10.3, column 3). Today, many if not most voters see public universities as fiscally unstable *and* overpriced *and* debt-creating *and* not really preparing students for work. Few have much faith in the diminished university bridge between social challenges and nonconservative solutions. And why should they? Where is the inspiring public educational mission that could make an increasingly sub-middle-class US population want to reinvest in public universities as places that imagine a society, built on current conditions, that is both just and enlightened? The great public missions need to be reinvented; what we have done instead is narrow the full public mission to supporting industry and spreading quantitative skills, which in fact won't help the economy as advertised.

THE RECOVERY TO COME

It is hard for me to skip past my doom loop of privatization and move on to what is to be done. But we need to fix the present untenable situation, so I'll now make suggestions for this. They do come back around to the humanities.

First, admit we have a problem. All recovery programs begin like this. University officials need to admit that in recent decades they have locked in major mistakes and misled many people including students, parents, faculty political allies, and themselves. They must especially stop saying private funds—gifts, tuition hikes, etc.—can ever replace public funding cuts. This encourages legislators to cut, while making allies think that public funding wasn't all that special. We tenure-track faculty members need also to admit that overall we have gone along for the ride rather than openly espousing counternarratives. Both major political parties agree on austerity measures, because neither they nor the public act as if they know what "public" means in "public university" besides "lots of low-income students." There is plenty of fessing up to go around, plenty of self-awareness to be achieved.

Second, university officials must state directly and openly that the cuts aren't part of a business cycle, but reflect a systematic restructuring of US society. US corporate, financial, and political elites have canceled the productivity bargain that underlay middle-class capitalism. The productivity bargain was that if you invest time and effort to increase your personal productivity by graduating from university, you would be rewarded with a standard of living to match. As you became more productive, your wages would increase. The expansion of the middle class reflected the increasing value of college-graduate labor. The bargain has been gradually withdrawn over the course of the past four decades. The economist Lawrence Mishel bleakly summarizes his conclusions: "The hourly compensation of a typical worker grew in tandem with productivity from 1948–1973. . . . After 1973, productivity grew strongly, especially after 1995, while the typical worker's compensation was relatively stagnant. This divergence of pay and productivity has meant that many workers were not benefitting from productivity growth—the economy could afford higher pay but it was not providing it."[18] University leaders have tended to hide the fact—even from themselves—that learning no longer equals earning.[19] They probably know, but do not say, that a university degree is less the promise of a good life than the opening ante into a competition in which global university enrollments have doubled in ten years and in which the new global standard for knowledge workers is not high-skill, high-wage jobs, but high-skill, low-wage jobs. Public-university folk need to state this out loud. Some graduates of the most selective private universities can scramble to the new "commanding heights" of the knowledge economy and accumulate huge salaries or fortunes by acquiring various ownership and control rights through exclusive organizational positions. But this is not a future available to the intelligent multitude emerging from our thousands of public colleges and universities. University leaders must now proclaim to the working- and middle-class majority that they and their children and their institutions of upward mobility, their public universities, have been jointly selected for downgrading. I would love to hear the head of a major public research university teaching politicians and donors that presumed levels of social mobility and innovation will no longer happen without full public funding recovery for public universities.

Our actual situation is pushing public-university systems past lobbying political leaders who have cut university funding for thirty years, towards building social movements, in which universities make direct appeals to the underserved portion of the public by spelling out how they are being underserved. Public-university officials need to be clear that their schools, which created the mass middle class, can't appeal for proper funding to elites who don't want a mass middle class anymore. The left-hand column of the next table links the post-productivity era to our university issues (see Table 10.4). Public universities no longer have the means (columns 2 and 3) to take negative impacts on core middle-class constituencies (column 1) and turn them into a multiracial egalitarian democracy in which college-educated workers keep the increased value they produce (column 4).

TABLE 10.4   Public Universities under Post-Middle-Class Conditions

Challenge: going post–middle class	Public university means	Public university	Embattled nonconserva-tive middle class
Post-democracy; plutocracy	~~High public funding~~	~~Free/open access~~	Majoritarian democracy?
"Global auction": high skills can go with low wages	Reduced mass active learning and research learning	Bildung—deep personal development deemphasized	Value created by skilled white-collar degrees?
Naturalization of all kinds of inequality (race, class, nation)	Advanced student services less linked to society	Egalitarian inclusion & diversified curriculum under siege	Postsegregation; emergent cultural equality?

Instead, universities increasingly transmit those negative impacts. University officials need to tell this story. A public university that does not level with the middle class about the nation's post middle-class policies will never attract new middle-class interest or support.

The idea that the United States is plutocratic or post-middle-class got a huge boost from the frenzied welcome accorded the English translation of Thomas Piketty's *Capital in the Twenty-First Century*. Piketty's deep historical data were widely assumed to show that, in capitalism, "there is no general tendency towards greater economic equality."[20] The egalitarian period that grew public universities was not the rule, Piketty confirmed, but an exception driven by unusually rapid economic growth after the Second World War. Public universities need to understand—and then shout from the rooftops—that there is no free-market logic that will bring back public universities or the middle class.

To put this another way, rebuilding public funding for public universities now requires jettisoning traditional strategies of patience and accommodation for confrontation with both major parties. To extend Daniel Kleinman's observations in this volume, public-university leaders can now succeed only by generating political and social movements that will change economic ground rules, ground rules that have for decades been damaging their resource base and their students, rather than by nurturing relationships with influential players.[21] The university needs to make itself chief architect on a national project whose mainstream branch could be called "rebuilding a middle-class society"—on an egalitarian model.

HUMANITIES *BILDUNG* VERSUS SCHUMPETERIAN INNOVATION

The next measure is to rebuild budgetary support for the academic humanities in a specific mode—as a domain that has for centuries been carving out visions of human development that do *not* require what Joseph A. Schumpeter called "creative destruction."[22] Although less referenced in recent years, Schumpeter remains the presiding deity over US—and Western—innovation culture. His influence in the United States has run through business intellectuals like Thomas A. Stewart, who applied a narrow, Schumpeterian notion of innovation in the 1990s in coining the concept of "knowledge management," and Clayton Christensen, who, as Jeffrey Williams notes in his essay in this volume, became one of the Western world's most influential capitalist thinkers through his notion of "disruptive innovation."[23] Schumpeter became the Marx of twentieth-century capitalism by putting technological innovation at the center of the economic system. His cultural influence has also been enormous, since the theory of entrepreneurial dynamism redefined capitalists as fountainheads of innovation and all new economic value rather than as bulwarks of tradition and reaction. For Schumpeter, progress required not the toleration but the embrace of economic, social, and cultural destruction—Detroit today illustrates a process that he thought inevitable and progressive.

I'll reduce the logic of Schumpeter's innovation culture to a few stylized steps. First, technology is the central driver behind the growth of capitalism, not labor or capital as such. Second, technological innovation comes from the individual entrepreneur, not from owners, workers, government, anybody's craft skill, or the effects of collaboration. Third, social relations and governance are mostly, even inherently, anti-innovative, so innovators must disrupt bureaucracy, unions, social movements, faculty senates, and democracy. In addition, wealth inequality is explained and justified by the enormous resources and continuous risk in any true innovation process. Monopoly market positions are the natural effect of a superior innovation. The only legitimate mitigation of a monopoly is an even better innovation: regulation for social or humanitarian purposes is not legitimate (or efficient). Finally, real innovation always involves replacing human labor with technology—including replacing "creative" labor. In short, human or culture factors are, for Schumpeter, obstacles to capitalist dynamism. Human labor is always in the crosshairs: progress cannot exist without its endless subordination. The same goes for the humanities. Modern economies could sideline or dispense with their historical function of encouraging the "illimitable freedom of the human mind," to quote Thomas Jefferson on the purpose of universities, since the human mind in all its psychological and social relationality doesn't lead to and in fact slows down technological innovation.

Schumpeterian innovation (S-innovation) takes the elements of the current post-middle-class trend and transforms them into economic law. Our current innovation system rationalizes the excess political influence of the very wealthy by casting them, in general, as made up of entrepreneurial innovators (see Table 10.5, column 2, row 1). Schumpeterian innovation justifies the contingent status of many or most highly skilled professionals by asserting that they are too far from the process of value creation (which is almost always technical, as Thomas Stewart insisted) (column 2, row 2). S-innovation also demands assimilation to tech culture, which is inhabited by a superior breed of entrepreneurs who orchestrate programmers and venture capitalists, though the members of this new breed are not WASPs or racially homogenous (even as they are overwhelmingly male). The public university, seen here (columns 2 and 3), has enfeebled its countervailing tendencies of open access, personal development for all, and egalitarian inclusion. It has weakened them to the point that they cannot form authorized countertendencies as was the case in earlier decades. We are getting the interaction of columns 1 and 4, over the dying corpse of 2 and 3, which is of course a recipe for further descent into what we might call innovation plutocracy.

TABLE 10.5   Permanent Crisis via Diminished Humanities

Challenge: going post–middle class	Public university means	Public university	S-Innovation
Post-democracy; plutocracy	~~High public funding~~	~~Free/open access~~	Minoritarian democracy of tech talented tenth-metrics not development
"Global auction": high skills can go with low wages	Reduced mass active learning, research learning	Bildung—deep personal development deemphasized	Plutonomy with precarity
Naturalization of all kinds of inequality (race, class, nation)	Advanced student services less linked to society	Egalitarian inclusion & diversified curriculum under siege	Assimilate to innovation culture (Spencerian technogenesis)

Economic development is less sustainable when a society devotes itself, as ours has, to diminishing not just the academic humanities but also the deep forces they represent. I've mentioned three that have been on and off the table for decades. One is the experience that democratic power sharing increases intelligence and effectiveness: we will need this understanding more than ever in a world of seven to ten billion people, even as for now we are reverting to elitist models of ability and to authoritarian definitions of effective governance. A second humanistic force is the understanding of the transformative power of advanced skill or craft capabilities—in the face of our increased efforts to replace (not supplement) skills with technology and with systems management. A third force is the capacity for communication and negotiation across a culturally fractalized and staggeringly complex planet. This requires knowledge deployed with egalitarian mutuality, and yet we are defunding exactly the fields that deliver this. Reversing the diminishment of humanities knowledge hinges on public universities openly confronting the limits of Schumpeterian innovation.

I schematize the basic elements of a successful version of this confrontation (see Table 10.6). The humanities disciplines (column 3) can repurpose the innovation system I just summarized (column 2). Humanities faculty members are relatively familiar with the items in the first and third rows: the broad distribution of intelligence in the population, and the priority of situated experience to a culture's assumption of its superiority to others. The second row requires that the humanities articulate their interpretative and communicative practices as forms of craft agency that can intervene in the economy. This is going to be more difficult for us. I posit here that we are living through the fatigue of energy-intensive, labor-replacing Western capitalism that has depended both on military superiority, whose returns have been diminishing for decades, and on

TABLE 10.6   Recovery via Humanities as Practical Arts

Challenge: going post–middle class	S-Innovation	Strong humanities	Public university
Post-democracy; plutocracy	Minoritarian rule of tech's talented tenth	Mass intellectual-ity: participation of 100%	Free/open access
"Global auction": high skills can lead to low wages	Plutonomy with precarity	"Industrious revolution" based on diverse craft capabilities, cultural agency	Bildung—deep personal development
Naturalization of all kinds of inequality (race, class, nation)	Assimilate to innova-tion culture	Egalitarian non-assimilationist pluralisms of specific experience	Egalitarian inclu-sion & diversified curriculum

the replacement of labor with technology. We are starting to develop better concepts to describe emerging modes of human effectiveness: Doris Sommer's concept of cultural agency; Gayatri Chakravorty Spivak's notion of reading as translation in which the "trace of the other" appears in a "site of conflict"; Kaoru Sugihara and Giovanni Arrighi's notion of the "*industrious* revolution" that began in East Asia long ago and is spreading out of it.[24] When these conceptual developments are under way, they will rehumanize higher education and the wider society again, as they have done in different waves in the past.

I'll end on quasi-technical but nonetheless momentous institutional notes. The fourth measure is full costing for extramurally funded research. STEM research, usually misread as a profit center, loses large amounts of money for research universities both public and private. An example that my research suggests is typical of research universities appears in a profit-and-loss chart from Arizona State University (see Figure 10.1). Here we see that the big research revenue fields—engineering, natural sciences, life sciences—apparently run up even bigger costs: their net revenues are negative. Cross-subsidies generally run from cheap high-enrollment fields, particularly the social sciences but also the humanities, toward fields with expensive research, like most of STEM. I'm one of those STEM lovers who think we need more basic scientific research not less, but it needs to be fully funded. The current situation means that humanities and social sciences cannot use a large piece of their teaching revenues to invest in upgrading teaching or supporting research in their own disciplines, for central administrations use their surpluses to fill budgetary holes elsewhere. The sociocultural and artistic disciplines are simply too poor to go on subsidizing STEM disciplines as we have. By one means or another, humanities subsidies of STEM has to stop.

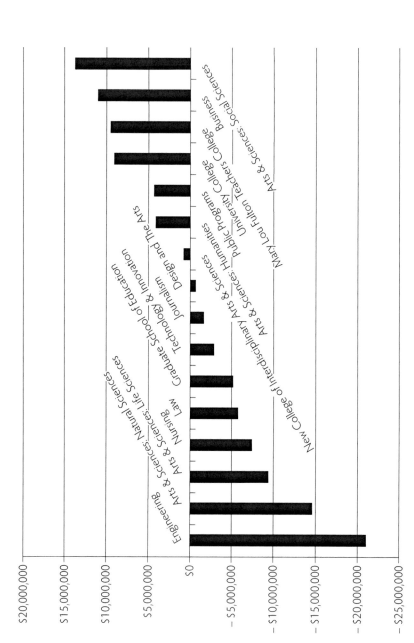

FIGURE 10.1. Difference between Revenue and Direct Expenses by College, Arizona State University, 2010

The fifth and final step involves refocusing universities toward their core missions of research and teaching. The genius of the university was to unite these functions—discovery, invention, creative practice, explaining, reformulating, disseminating. A "professor" was someone who read, thought, wrote, discovered, invented, and taught all these things. Thirty years of privatization, focused on cutting labor costs, has produced a dissociation of educational sensibility between professors and managers that damages academic labor and educational quality for students. Here's one illustration, from AAUP's recent salaries report, aptly titled "Losing Focus" (see Figure 10.2). For thirty-five years, universities have grown mostly in nonacademic managerial staff. They have paid for this in part by hiring contingent faculty to replace full-time faculty. Both part-time and full-time non-tenure-track faculty have grown faster than tenure-track faculty by an order of magnitude: twelve times faster for part-time faculty, eleven times faster for full-time non-tenure-track faculty. The fastest growth has been in "full-time nonfaculty professional" employees, most of them front-line and middle managers. Managers have grown faster than tenured and tenure-track faculty by a factor of sixteen. Management has been made larger and more secure, while academics have been made (relatively) smaller and more contingent.

By pulling work time and payroll away from teaching and research, this seismic shift in hiring has redefined what the university is and what its people

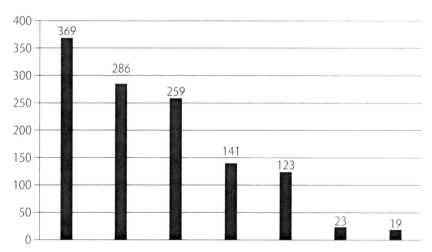

FIGURE 10.2. Percentage Change in Number of Employees in Higher Education Institution, by Category of Employee, 1975 and 1976 to 2011
SOURCE: John W. Curtis and Saranna Thornton, "Losing Focus: The Annual Report on the Economic Status of the Profession, 2013–14," Academe (March 2014), available at http://aaup.org/sites/default/files/files/2014%20salary%20report/Figure%201.pdf [accessed May 21, 2014].

primarily do. In the midst of this confusion of purpose, adjuncting (the practice, not the people) has put the long-term health of every intellectual discipline at risk, while routinizing universities' exploitation of the people on whom their future reputation depends. More broadly, this massive employment shift has been diluting the university's public impacts and robbing it of its social identity. As the university comes to talk and act like any other corporation, fewer people know why it is special enough to deserve meaningful public support.

This loss of educational focus and its functional twin, administrative bloat, need to be reversed. Current trends—new federal-level interest in the plight of contingent faculty, and growing contingent faculty unionizing efforts—suggest that management's disproportionate growth is coming to an end. The growth ratios shown here must now be inverted: full-time faculties need to be rebuilt.[25]

The five measures I've described can be summarized as follows:

1. Proclaim that accepting public funding cuts and tuition hikes has been a disastrous mistake.
2. Admit the university no longer offers students direct entrance to a prosperous middle-class, and has a new and broader public purpose.
3. Define that public purpose as supporting non-Schumpeterian, sustainable innovation.
4. Support cultural disciplines through the full costing of extramurally funded research
5. Support higher-order teaching, including research-based learning, by de-bureaucratizing the university, and converting adjuncts and nonfaculty professionals to full-time teaching and research staff.

The first three measures involve repositioning the university, actively and openly, on the side of the majority of their graduates to whom they no longer offer economic guarantees. The last two give the university the research and teaching capacities to make good on their new contribution to evolving societies. My answer to what the humanities are for is that they are for putting mass *Bildung* back at the center of the postcapitalist university that is now in the early agonies of birth. The public university is dead. Long live the public university.

NOTES

1. Two other recent books that I think of as companions to my work here are Helen Small, *The Value of the Humanities* (Oxford, UK: Oxford University Press, 2013), which analyzes the five major types of value-claims for these disciplines; and Doris Sommer, *The Work of Art in*

the World (Durham, NC: Duke University Press, 2014), which links the humanities to socially transformative art practices.

2. George W. Breslauer, "UC Berkeley's Adaptations to the Crisis of Public Higher Education in the US: Privatization? Commercialization? Or Hybridization?" available at http://cshe .berkeley.edu/sites/default/files/shared/publications/docs/ROPS.CSHE_.17.13.Breslauer .BerkeleyAdaptions.12.11.2013.pdf [accessed May 3, 2014].

3. See Sheldon Rothblatt, Chapter 2, "Old Wine in New Bottles, or New Wine in Old Bottles?"

4. In Martha C. Nussbaum, *Not For Profit: Why Democracy Needs the Humanities*, 1st ed. (Princeton: Princeton University Press, 2010), the author discusses "cultivating capabilities" that are essential to democratic public life. For example, Chapter 3 offers a useful discussion of psychological capabilities that allow the negotiation of group differences without the resort to violence. A follow-up work, Martha C. Nussbaum, *Creating Capabilities: The Human Development Approach*, reprint ed. (Cambridge, MA: Belknap Press, 2013), describes the "Capabilities Approach" to human and social development. "Creative capabilities" is a summary term that Nussbaum does not use in her description of the major "capabilities." Most relevantly here, she insists that "the attitude toward people's basic capabilities is not a meritocratic one—more innately skilled people get better treatment—but, if anything, the opposite: those who need more help to get above the threshold get more help" (*Creating Capabilities*, 24).

5. Michael Meranze summarizes the growth as follows: "Whereas in 1969–70 men still outnumbered women by approximately 1.5 million, in 1979–1980 women finally attended colleges and universities in higher numbers: 5,887,022 women enrolled in the fall of 1979 compared to 5,682,877 men. . . . this explosion did not extend equally to students of color. While the number of minority students did increase, they did so at a much smaller rate. . . . The story of higher education in the aftermath of World War II, then, was one of a partially increased democratization; one never fully achieved but significant nonetheless" (Michael Meranze, "Humanities Out of Joint," unpublished manuscript).

6. Colin Woodward, *American Nations: A History of the Eleven Rival Regional Cultures of North America* (New York: Penguin, 2011).

7. Meranze, "Humanities Out of Joint."

8. See Yolanda Moses, Chapter 4, "Humanities and Inclusion."

9. Gary S. Becker, *Human Capital: A Theoretical and Empirical Analysis, with Special Reference to Education* (Chicago: University of Chicago Press, 1964).

10. For the former term, see Roberto Mangabeira Unger, "Deep Freedom: Why the Left Should Abandon Equality," Institute for Public Policy Research (October 24, 2013), available at http://www.ippr.org/juncture/deep-freedom-why-the-left-should-abandon-equality [accessed May 3, 2014].

11. See Sommer, *The Work of Art in the World*.

12. Small, *Value of the Humanities*, 142.

13. One of the architects of modern conservative economics, Milton Friedman, verified that societies cannot depend on price signals to develop human capital to the proper level. Calculations he did with Simon Kuznets suggested a "sizable underinvestment in human beings" (Milton Friedman, "The Role of Government in Education" [1955]) available at http:// faculty.smu.edu/millimet/classes/eco4361/readings/friedman%201955.pdf [accessed July 15, 2014]). While supporting government-funded vouchers to students rather than direct grants from governments to universities, Friedman acknowledged that individual educational effort and reward had to be supplemented with public funds.

14. John Kenneth Galbraith, *The New Industrial State* (New York: Houghton Mifflin, 1967), ch. 6.

15. Christopher Newfield, *Drive Through College: Higher Education and the End of American Social Decline* (forthcoming 2015).

16. College Board, *Trends in College Pricing 2013*, 3, available at trends.collegeboard.org/sites/default/files/college-pricing-2013-full-report.pdf [accessed May 2, 2014].

17. State Higher Education Finance Officers, *State Higher Education Finance FY 2013*, figure http://trends.collegeboard.org/sites/default/files/college-pricing-2013-full-report.pdf; Cory Weinberg, "Some Colleges Get a Pinch Instead of a Punch from State Governments," *Chronicle of Higher Education*, August 19, 2013, available at http://chronicle.com [accessed August 29, 2013].

18. Lawrence Mishel, "The Wedges between Productivity and Median Compensation Growth," Economic Policy Institute (April 26, 2012), available at http://www.epi.org/publication/ib330-productivity-vs-compensation/ [accessed January 4, 2013].

19. Phillip Brown, Hugh Lauder, and David Ashton, *The Global Auction: The Broken Promises of Education, Jobs, and Incomes* (Oxford: Oxford University Press, 2010), Kindle Locations 134–139.

20. Martin Wolf, review of *Capital in the Twenty-First Century*, by Thomas Piketty, in *Financial Times*, April 15, 2014, available at http://www.ft.com.

21. See Daniel Kleinman, Chapter 5, "Sticking Up for Liberal Arts and Humanities Education," on university administrators' defenses of the humanities in the face of political pressure.

22. Joseph A. Schumpeter, *Capitalism, Socialism, and Democracy*, 3rd ed. (New York: Harper Perennial Modern Classics, 2008), 82–83.

23. Thomas A. Stewart, *Intellectual Capital* (New York: Doubleday Business, 1997); Clayton M. Christensen and Michael E. Raynor, *The Innovator's Solution: Creating and Sustaining Successful Growth*, 1st ed. (Cambridge, MA: Harvard Business School Press, 2003). See Jeffrey Williams, Chapter 9, "The Need for Critical University Studies."

24. Gayatri Chakravorty Spivak, *An Aesthetic Education in the Era of Globalization* (Cambridge, MA: Harvard University Press, 2012), 270; Giovanni Arrighi, *Adam Smith in Beijing* (New York: Verso, 2007), ch. 1.

25. I am *not* proposing mass layoffs of nonfaculty professional staff. I am talking about the *conversion* of staff to direct involvement in teaching and research—for example, through the creation of research-learning groups in which staff would work with faculty to guide student research. Money saved via the reduction of non-academic functions would be shifted toward academic staff—allowing a net increase in instructional staff and contingent faculty members to become permanent.

AFTERWORD

GORDON HUTNER AND FEISAL G. MOHAMED

We began planning this volume in the wake of Occupy and while celebrating significant anniversaries of the first Morrill Act and the GI Bill, a moment that for reasons we could not have anticipated proved to be particularly fortuitous: had we held our proceedings a year later, in September 2014, our participants would have met on an embattled campus, where humanities professors are newly demoralized, a campus that thousands of academics from across the nation, indeed around the world, have pledged to boycott, accepting no offers to speak and declining to review tenure and promotion candidates. Our efforts to hold a conference, like those of other Illinois colleagues, might well have come to naught if one speaker after another withdrew.

The cause of this new demoralization is widely known. Having accepted a job offer as associate professor in the American Indian Studies Program at the University of Illinois, Steven Salaita was notified by Chancellor Phyllis Wise on August 1, 2014, roughly two weeks before he was officially to start his job, that she would not forward his appointment to the Board of Trustees for final approval. She consulted no academic office involved in the hire: not the department, the College of Liberal Arts and Sciences, or the provost. The reason for this extraordinary action, the chancellor held, was the purported "incivility" of Salaita's posts on Twitter, particularly during the conflict between Israel and Gaza during that summer. Despite immediate and widespread outrage in the academic community, Chancellor Wise was unbending, supported both by President Robert Easter and the Board of Trustees, which ultimately cast an 8–1 vote against the appointment at a meeting that fall. Evidence of communication between the chancellor's office, the development branch of the university, and several donors leading up to the August 1 decision has since come to light.[1]

For the purposes of this volume, we offer no opinion on this professor's writings, academic, journalistic, or social.[2] More relevant to our aims are the institutional issues that this episode casts in high relief. As Roger Geiger's chapter notes, this is not the first time in Illinois's history that upper administration has involved itself in the faculty's political views: a former president, David Kinley, strove in the 1920s to keep socialists from creeping into the fold. To this example we might add more: in the late 1940s, the state's Broyles Commission required all public employees, including faculty, to take a "non-Communist" oath; a biology professor, Leo F. Koch, who proselytized for premarital sex and trial marriages in the pages of the student newspaper, was dismissed in 1960 for views that President David Dodds Henry called "offensive and repugnant."[3] The symmetries are inexact, but a general tendency is clearly discernible: screening the political and moral views of faculty creates a climate of real or perceived intellectual intolerance and elicits derisive laughter from the backward glance of history.

The Salaita unhiring was actually the university's second politically motivated dismissal in a span of six months. The previous one concerned James Kilgore, a former member of the Symbionese Liberation Army who had been convicted as an accessory to murder during a bank robbery and who, after many years on the lam, ultimately served his sentence. Along the way, Kilgore had become a scholar and novelist and, more lately, a much-respected member of the non-tenure-track faculty in the Center for African Studies. An August 2014 report by the provost's hiring process review committee showed that all departments in which Kilgore had held appointments followed accepted procedures. Nor had he made any secret of his past, going well beyond legal obligations of disclosure. Ultimately, the chancellor and trustees cleared Kilgore for reappointment at the university.[4]

Both episodes followed closely on the heels of negative publicity in the local newspaper, Champaign's *News-Gazette*, which, arguably, had been at odds with the university at least since American Indian Studies led a campaign to remove the ceremonial "Chief Illiniwek" as a presence at university events or an emblem on university paraphernalia. Only the threat of NCAA sanctions against universities using stereotypical racial mascots finally quickened Illinois into action, exacerbating any normal register of distrust between town and gown. So when Salaita was being hired in the same program, and was being challenged from other quarters as an anti-Semite, the newspaper could scarcely resist the story as another example of the wayward thinking of professors, and perhaps, since American Indian Studies was involved, the paper proceeded with a little more zeal than usual. The newspaper seemed alternately amused and disgusted by the credentials of an English professor (of Arab-American literature) being hired by a Native studies program for his research interest in the corollaries between Palestinian indigeneity and American Indian experience.

As Christopher Newfield alerts us in his chapter, the evaporation of public support for higher education has created an environment indifferent, even hostile, to humanistic scholarship and teaching, one where intellectual ferment is deemed a potential public-relations threat. No matter where a bad headline appears, it carries the possibility of further political opposition to higher education and can occasion a panicked administrative response. The substantial, carefully formulated concerns of thousands of faculty worldwide go unnoticed, while the grumblings of six-figure donors necessitate exceptional and insuperable action by those who style themselves the "campus leadership."

Yet how can we be surprised by such a turn of events? There is, to our minds, something of a dark inevitability to the Salaita affair. The pervasive corporatization of the university has led to this situation, which is not to say that donors have never before enjoyed such influence. The sorry fact here is how little influence humanities professors seem to have, how little consideration their concerns merit in such deliberations. Humanities department after department, along with several from the arts and social sciences, issued calls of no confidence to the chancellor, president, and trustees, all citing legitimate professional concerns: violations of shared governance and due process, a potential chilling effect on speech, as well as a compromised ability to recruit graduate students and faculty—particularly senior faculty. For weeks and weeks these administrative officers had no response, not even an anodyne public statement noticing the existence of the complaints. More lately, a subcommittee of the faculty senate has issued a detailed report on the chancellor's and trustees' abuses of due process. Plus, the university's engineers and scientists, with whom Dr. Wise is considerably more popular, have begun to recognize the overall impact of the Salaita affair and expressed their concern.[5] In the face of these pressures, the Board of Trustees has issued a statement declaring that its decision on the matter is final.

We say these events have unfolded ineluctably because the Salaita affair, whatever else it signifies, also captures a moment in the humanities' marginalization within the university. It reveals the bad faith of administrations—ours is only the one currently in the crosshairs—failing to credit the autonomy of programs that do not generate remunerative grants for research. Is it surprising that none of our university's upper-management echelons had any record of vigorously supporting the humanities, a condition that follows the one often invoked of running the university more like a business, more like the kind of operation whose protocols donors are used to?

Illinois's chancellor and trustees seem to be part of a national trend. Chancellor Nicholas Dirks of UC Berkeley also sparked considerable surprise and outrage in this same September, an academic year marking the fiftieth anniversary of the Free Speech Movement, with a message describing free speech and civility as two sides of the same coin.[6] Much more troubling is a fresh report from the American Council of Trustees and Alumni, *Governance for a New Era: A Blueprint for Higher Education Trustees*, which has "no doubt that leadership of higher education is out of balance. Trustees should take a more active role in reviewing and benchmarking the work of faculty and administrators and monitoring outcomes."[7] All of this, it seems, in the name of establishing campus bulwarks for reactionary ideas, typically coded as "intellectual diversity" and "institutional neutrality." Instead of "sticking up for the humanities," as Daniel Kleinman recommends in this volume, trustees are being exhorted into breaking them down. We would call this a new culture war, but, with Jeffrey Williams's insights in mind, we might more precisely diagnose it as an executive power-grab masquerading as a new culture war.

This push speaks a language of diversity and inclusivity, though certainly not the kind that Yolanda Moses describes in these pages. Instead, it is diversity turned upside down: placed in the service of the 1 percent rather than creating physical and intellectual infrastructures for broad, pluralistic participation in public institutions. It certainly does not make serious efforts along the lines that Kathleen Woodward here proposes: of bridging the gap between two-year colleges and flagship research universities as a means of expanding access. The new, even mendacious form of "inclusivity" on the lips of certain administrators has little truck with ideas of social justice rooted in historical consideration of institutionalized inequality. Which is also why it has no truck with the humanities, the branch of the university where those ideas are actively explored.

Let us be clear. When we advocate pursuing collaboration with professional and pre-professional programs, as well as nonacademic institutions—as John McGowan explores through the example of medical humanities and Bethany Nowviskie pursues in what has come to be known as alt-ac—it is in an equal partnership founded on the principle that the humanities style of thought has a salutary effect on all of life's pursuits. And we stress that any compelling vision of public higher education will have a place for the mass *Bildung* in which humanities education is fundamental. This project, as Sheldon Rothblatt shows and as Christopher Newfield affirms, has long been part of the public university in the United States. Given the increasingly polyglot nature of our society, and this century's sharp rise in global interaction, there must also be a recommitment to foreign languages, as Charlotte Melin recommends.

The challenges that public higher education will face in the coming decades are enormous, mounted especially by continued reductions in state support, the billions that the federal government and financial industry make on student loans, and alarming increases in the amount of federal student aid filling the coffers of for-profit diploma mills.[8] Distracting, donor-driven controversies begin to seem like a reckless indulgence, the bungling of a sacred public charge. We began this project emphasizing that breathing new life into the humanities must involve changes on campuses themselves. We close by iterating our call to advance an institutional culture committed to vibrant humanistic study. There was never a strong program in any discipline created by the politically motivated authoritarianism of chancellors and trustees. Strong programs arise when institutional structures allow energetic faculty and students to do their work. Administrators have a vital role to play in creating such structures, but the best of them will know the limits of that role. A year after we first articulated them, the core recommendations that we offer in our introduction seem now to be even more urgent: 1) stable funding for humanities programs; 2) self-generated means of evaluating outcomes and program viability; and 3) revising the institutional organization of knowledge, with an eye to strengthening those fields now housed in small, and therefore vulnerable, departments.

NOTES

1. See Scott Jaschik, "The Emails on Salaita," *Inside Higher Ed*, August 25, 2014, available at http://www.insidehighered.com.
2. For a debate on the issues surrounding the Salaita case, see Feisal G. Mohamed and Cary Nelson, "'A Growing Hunt for Heretics?': What's at Stake in the Salaita Affair," *Chronicle of Higher Education*, September 3, 2014, available at http://www.chronicle.com.
3. See "The Fight for Freedom of Speech and Expression in the 1960s," Student Life and Culture Archival Program, University of Illinois, available at http://archives.library.illinois.edu/slcold/researchguides/coldwar/freespeech/freespeech.php; and Katherine Franke, Michael C. Dorf et al., letter to Phyllis Wise, August 15, 2014, available at http://lawprofessors.typepad.com/files/faculty-letter-to-u-of-i.pdf.
4. See Colleen Flaherty, "A Second Chance?," *Inside Higher Ed*, November 10, 2014, available at https://www.insidehighered.com/news/2014/11/10/u-illinois-board-receives-report-recommending-reappointment-ex-convict; and Jodi S. Cohen and Michelle Manchir, "U. of I. Clears Way for Convicted Radical to Teach Again," *Chicago Tribune*, November 14, 2014, available at http://www.chicagotribune.com/news/ct-james-kilgore-decision-met-20141113-story.html#page=1.
5. See "Report on Investigation into the Matter of Steven Salaita," Committee on Academic Freedom and Tenure, Senate of the Urbana-Champaign Campus, University of Illinois (December 2014), available at http://www.senate.illinois.edu/aft_salaita_2014.pdf; and Dusty Rhodes, "UI Chancellor Responds to Salaita Report," WUIS 91.9, December 29, 2014, available at http://wuis.org/post/ui-chancellor-responds-salaita-report.
6. See Colleen Flaherty, "The Problem with Civility," *Inside Higher Ed*, September 9, 2014, available at http://www.insidehighered.com; and Scott Jaschik, "2015 Survey of Chief Academic Officers," *Inside Higher Ed*, January 22, 2015, available at http://www.insidehighered.com.
7. Benno C. Schmidt et al., *Governance for a New Era: A Blueprint for Higher Education Trustees*, American Council of Trustees and Alumni (August 2014), 2, 7, available at http://www.GoACTA.org.

8. On federal aid and for-profit colleges, see the College Board report *Trends in Student Financial Aid 2013*, available at http://trends.collegeboard.org/sites/default/files/student-aid-2013 -full-report.pdf, which notes that "as the share of undergraduate enrollment in the for-profit sector increased from 7% in fall 2003 to 9% in fall 2006, and to 12% in fall 2009, the share of Pell Grant funds going to students in this sector increased from 16% to 19% to 25%. By fall 2012, the for-profit share of FTE enrollments remained at 12% and the sector's share of Pell Grants had declined to 21%" (19). In 2012–13, for-profit colleges also received 37 percent of federal aid disbursed through the post-9/11 GI Bill (ibid.).

NOTES ON CONTRIBUTORS

ROGER L. GEIGER is Distinguished Professor of Higher Education at The Pennsylvania State University. His writings on higher education encompass historical and contemporary studies, most recently, *The History of American Higher Education: Learning and Culture from the Founding to World War II* (2015); and *The Land-Grant Colleges and the Reshaping of American Higher Education* (2013), coedited with Nathan M. Sorber. He has edited *Perspectives on the History of Higher Education* since 1993.

GORDON HUTNER, a professor of English, received his PhD from the University of Virginia and, since 1982, has taught American literature at the Universities of Wisconsin, Kentucky, and Illinois. He has also taught at Kenyon College, the University of Antwerp, and Cornell. He has written widely on US fiction, cultural criticism, and ethnic writing. Hutner is the founding editor of the journal *American Literary History*, which he continues to edit, now in its twenty-seventh year.

DANIEL LEE KLEINMAN is an associate dean in the Graduate School at the University of Wisconsin–Madison, where he is also a professor of community and environmental sociology. He is the author of *Impure Cultures: University Biology and the World of Commerce* (2003) and the coeditor of the *Routledge Handbook of Science, Technology, and Society* (2014).

JOHN MCGOWAN'S books include *Postmodernism and Its Critics* (1991); *American Liberalism: An Interpretation for Our Time* (2007); and *Pragmatist Politics: Making the Case for Liberal Democracy* (2012). McGowan is one of the editors of the *Norton Anthology of Theory and Criticism* (2010). His *Democracy's Children: Intellectuals and the Rise of Cultural Politics* (2002) collects essays on the shifting roles of the intellectual and of the university in our time. McGowan is a former director of the University of North Carolina's Institute for the Arts and Humanities.

CHARLOTTE MELIN is a professor in the Department of German, Scandinavian, and Dutch at the University of Minnesota. Her books include *Poetic Maneuvers: Hans Magnus Enzensberger and the Lyric Genre* (2003); *Notes from the Field: Toward a Model for Saving German Studies* (2010); and *With or Without: Reading Postwar German Women Poets* (2013). She served on the Modern Language Association's Committee on the Teaching of Language from 2007 to 2011.

FEISAL G. MOHAMED is the author of *In the Anteroom of Divinity: The Reformation of the Angels from Colet to Milton* (2008); and *Milton and the Post-Secular Present: Ethics, Politics, Terrorism* (2011). In addition to scholarly journals, his work has appeared in *Dissent Magazine*, the *Huffington Post*, the *New Republic*, and the *New York Times*. He was the 2014 president of the Milton Society of America, and professor of English at the University of Illinois. In September 2015 he joins the faculty of The Graduate Center, CUNY.

YOLANDA T. MOSES is professor of anthropology and associate vice chancellor for diversity, excellence, and equity, University of California, Riverside. Her books include *How Real Is Race: A Sourcebook on Race, Culture and Biology* (2007, 2013), coauthored with Carol Mukhopadhyay and Rosemary Henze; *Race: Are We So Different?* (2012), coauthored with Alan Goodman and Joseph Jones; and *Reaping the Benefits of Diversity: Leading Transformational Change in Higher Education* (forthcoming, 2015). She chairs the National Advisory Board of a public education project on RACE (see www.understandingrace.org).

CHRISTOPHER NEWFIELD is professor of literature and American studies at the University of California at Santa Barbara. His books include *Mapping Multiculturalism*, edited with Avery Gordon (1996); *The Emerson Effect: Individualism and Submission in America* (1996); *Ivy and Industry: Business and the Making of the American University, 1880–1980* (2003); *Unmaking the Public University: The Forty-Year Assault on the Middle Class* (2008); and a forthcoming book addressing the ongoing crisis in public higher education. He blogs on higher-education funding and policy at *Remaking the University*, the *Huffington Post*, and the *Chronicle of Higher Education*.

BETHANY NOWVISKIE is the director of Digital Research and Scholarship at the University of Virginia Library, where she also directs a digital humanities center called the Scholars' Lab and its program of graduate fellowships, and serves as special advisor to the UVa provost. She is a Distinguished Presidential Fellow at the Council on Library and Information Resources (CLIR), and is past president of the Association for Computers and the Humanities (ACH).

SHELDON ROTHBLATT is a professor of history emeritus at the University of California, Berkeley and sometime director of the Center for Studies in Higher Education. Awards include the Berkeley Citation for "distinguished achievement and for notable service to the University," an honorary doctorate from Gothenburg University, and a knighthood bestowed by the Swedish Crown. He is a fellow of the Royal Historical Society of Britain, a foreign member of the Royal Swedish Academy of Sciences, and a member of the National Academy of Education (USA). He writes on university history.

JEFFREY J. WILLIAMS'S most recent books include *How to Be an Intellectual: Criticism, Culture, and the University* (2014); and *Brave New University: Idea and Reality of American Higher Education* (forthcoming). He has also edited several books, such as *The Critical Pulse: Thirty-Six Credos by Contemporary Critics*, with Heather Steffen (2012), and he is an editor of the *Norton Anthology of Theory and Criticism*. He is currently a professor of English at Carnegie Mellon University.

KATHLEEN WOODWARD is Lockwood Professor in the Humanities and professor of English at the University of Washington. Since 2000, she has directed the Simpson Center for the Humanities. She is the author of *Statistical Panic: Cultural Politics and Poetics of Emotions* (2009); and *Aging and Its Discontents: Freud and Other Fictions* (1991); and editor of *The Myths of Information: Technology and Postindustrial Culture* (1980). Woodward is a member of the Steering Committee of HASTAC (Humanities, Arts, Sciences, and Technology Alliance and Collaboratory) and the Executive Board of the national organization of Phi Beta Kappa. From 1995 to 2001 she was president of the Consortium of Humanities Centers and Institutes. She holds a BA in economics from Smith College and a PhD in literature from the University of California at San Diego.

INDEX

CPSIA information can be obtained at www.ICGtesting.com
Printed in the USA
LVOW11s0123170816

500699LV00001B/123/P